The Hoof Book

A Horse Owner's Guide to Demystifying Hoof Care

Heather Beauchemin, CJF TE

DEDICATION

To the MWSFA
The best friends and mentors I could ask for,
And a special thanks to Mark,
Who knew I would write a book before I did.

CONTENTS

ACKNOWLEDGMENTS

Thank you to Travis Burns, Mike Miller, Paige Moritz, Matthew Ostergard, Vern Powell, Steve Sermersheim, and Amy Sierpien for photographs.
Thank you to Vern Powell for his time and effort reviewing this book for accuracy.
Thank you to my fantastic editor, Tanya Wilber.
Thank you to Dan, who never grudged the many, many hours that went into this project.
And thank you to all the teachers who brought me to this point.

INTRODUCTION

What do you need to know about your horse's feet? Picking out feet isn't the most glamorous activity. Chances are, you have a lot more pictures on your phone of your horse's face than of her feet. I'm guessing you didn't decide to buy a horse because you love cleaning manure out of the hooves of a one thousand pound animal. You probably chose to buy a horse because you enjoy riding, because you've been in love with horses since you were a child, or because you met that special horse that you just couldn't say no to. And all the things that you love doing with your horse, whether trail riding, competing, or just spending time enjoying each other's company, are based on the assumption that your horse is sound and happy.

If you've picked up this book, then I'm betting you guessed the connection -- your horse's soundness absolutely has to start with her feet.

Maybe you've had ongoing struggles with long term hoof lameness in the past. Maybe you have questions about why your horse's feet look the way they do. Or maybe you've been super lucky and had a horse with really healthy, low maintenance hooves, but you'd like to know more about how you can keep them that way. You could be a new horse owner who wants to get a good grip on the basics, or you might be a veteran horse owner looking for more in-depth knowledge about a specific issue. No matter what your reasons for picking this book, I hope you're excited to learn more about the amazing structure that is the equine hoof.

The hoof is truly remarkable, but it doesn't have to be a mystery! My goal in writing this book is to give you, the horse owner, the knowledge to make informed decisions when it comes to your horse's hoof care. As the old saying goes, knowledge is power, and in this case, it could be the power to keep your horse sound and healthy. When it comes to care and management, you are your horse's advocate, and luckily for your horse, you not only care about him, but you're hunting down resources to make yourself the most informed, educated advocate you can be.

No matter how much of a novice you are right now, I believe that you can turn yourself into an informed, well-educated, dare I say hoof expert. How do I know? Because when I was sixteen, the only thing I knew about horses was whatever I read in Marguerite Henry books and a few bits of vague (and in retrospect, sometimes incorrect) advice I had picked up from library books. No hands-on knowledge. I wasn't riding, I didn't grow up in Pony Club. I grew up cutting out pictures from kids' horse magazines and taping them on my bedroom wall, not studying equine anatomy. When I was in high school, I started volunteering at a therapeutic riding facility, mostly helping out with the riders rather than the horses, but slowly volunteering for more of the horse related tasks. The more experienced, horse savvy volunteers shared their knowledge, and I'm really thankful that they did, but I wasn't really learning a ton about hooves.

Enter the farrier. Seeing their shoer at work one day, I decided with all of my vast horse experience, that shoeing horses was the job for me. Something about it clicked with my brain and I set out on a mission to find out everything I could about horses' hooves. I enrolled in a farrier trade school, completed an apprenticeship and two internships, and started the certification process. My first week in farrier school, I didn't know a cannon bone from a coffin bone, but three years later I had become a Certified Farrier through the American Farrier's Association, and two years after that I became the first female Certified Journeyman Farrier in Illinois. Two years later, I received the Therapeutic Endorsement from the AFA, which at the time had only been achieved by fourteen other farriers. I had some great mentors and a lot of textbooks and scientific papers available to me, and I used them. I know all that sounds a little braggy, but what I'm trying to tell you isn't that I'm special. It's that anyone, even a horse crazy kid who's getting "facts" from Black Beauty can become knowledgeable about horses' hooves with a little study. That's what I hope this book gives you: the confidence to know what you're seeing and what to do about it when it comes to your horse's hooves.

As a professional farrier, I spend nearly every day working with horses from a wide range of breeds, ages, and disciplines. I also work with a wide variety of horse owners, some who have had multiple horses for twenty years or more, some who are enjoying their first family horse, and some who are avid competitors. Each horse is an individual and each situation is unique, but there are also a lot of common threads, questions that I hear from a lot of different people. Hearing some of the same questions and misunderstandings from horse owners all over the country made me realize that there must be some holes in the education of horse owners across the board: information that is just missing, no matter how you are trying to educate yourself. No book can provide the answer for every possible situation, but I hope this book will answer the common questions that are relevant and essential to horse owners everywhere.

One caveat before we dive in. I want to make sure that we're all on the same page that this book is not here to replace the advice of your equine professionals who have actually spent time with your horse and know all the details of her care, use, management, and soundness. I'm also not trying to teach you how to trim or shoe your own horse, although many excellent farriers have started by working on their own horse out of necessity. I'm basing this book on the assumption that you either have, or are looking for, a competent professional that you have hired specifically to trim or shoe your horse. Also, this book was written for your education and information, and I hope that it equips you to deal with issues you might face, but nothing in this book should be considered as a diagnosis or prescription for any medical condition, lameness, or pathology. Okay, now that we've got that out of the way…

Let's get started!

Part 1
Anatomy: What's Going On In There?

1 THE BASICS – FORCES AT PLAY

Anatomy - it's not just for vets and biologists. Although you might be having flashbacks to biology labs and frog dissections, hoof anatomy is pretty amazing. Not just because the equine hoof is an engineering marvel, but also because understanding hoof anatomy gives us a window into what is happening with our horses' hooves, and why.

What's so marvelous about your horse's foot? I'm glad you asked! I'm a hoof nerd and I get excited about these things.

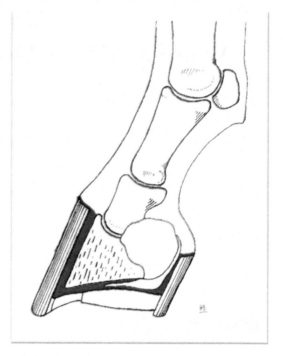

- Protection. First off, your horse's hooves are designed to provide remarkably versatile protection for the sensitive structures inside them. Wild horses throughout history have lived in some of the *least* hospitable places on the planet (think wild Arabians in the desert, Przewalski's horses in the Mongolian steppes, and feral Mustangs in the Rockies), which means they usually travel long distances every day in search of food and water.

Just how far do they travel? In 2010, researcher Brian Hampson of the Australian Brumby Research Unit fit lightweight GPS tracking collars to domestic horses and wild Australian Brumbies. He and his fellow researchers found that domestic horses in an 18'x18'

The hoof capsule protects many sensitive structures

paddock traveled an unsurprising 0.68 miles per day, while domestic horses in a generous ten-acre pasture traveled, on average, 3.7 miles. Compare that to the feral horses in the study. With unlimited space and sparse food and water, the Brumbies traveled an average 11.1 miles per day, more than *three times* the distance covered by their domestic cousins.[1]

If you're stuck hiking 11.1 miles every day across all kinds of rough terrain, you definitely want some good hiking boots. Horses' hooves function a lot like our hiking boots - they protect your feet from wear and tear, give you the ability to walk across rocks, give you traction, and insulate your feet against temperature extremes.

Your horse's feet were designed with long travel in mind, so every sensitive structure is covered, protected, and encapsulated. All the structures you see on the outside of the hoof below the hairline are made of keratin-based horn, and keratin is a fantastically wear resistant, force dissipating, elastic and dynamic material. In fact, keratin is considered one

---

[1] Hampson, B.A. and Pollitt, C.C. (November, 2011). *Improving the Foot Health of the Domestic Horse: The Relevance of the Feral Horse Foot Model.* Retrieved from http://horsefx.com.au/wp-content/uploads/2015/07/Pollitt-and-Hamson-Improving-health-of-domestic-horse-hoof.pdf

of the toughest biological materials in nature.[2]

- Remaining strong but light. For a substance that is extremely tough and abrasion resistant, hoof is also remarkably light, giving it a very high strength to weight ratio. Why is that important? Let's try a little experiment. Grab a can out of your kitchen cupboard.

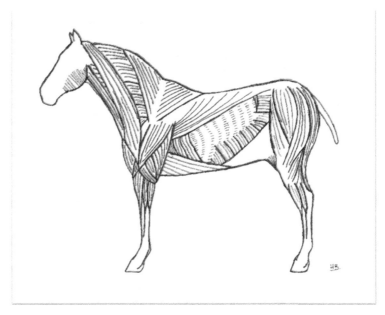

Muscle mass is centered on the torso while small muscles are found farther down the legs

Pretty light, right? It probably wouldn't bother you to carry that can around for most of the day. But now hold it out at arm's length. The weight hasn't changed, but by placing it farther away from your body you increase the lever arm. Increased lever arm equals more effort to hold it up. Decreasing the amount of weight at the end of the lever makes life easier, and it also explains why the horse only has light tendons and ligaments below the knee or the hock closer to the end of the lever instead of heavy muscle mass.

So let's say you're a horse, and you have long legs. If your hooves are too heavy, it's going to take you a lot of effort to move those feet at the end of those long legs. And if you're a wild horse and you have heavy hooves, and you have an 11-mile trek to get to water, you're going to be pretty tired by the time you get there if you're lucky; if you're not lucky, a predator catches up at mile 10 when you're already worn out. Clearly, having a super strong, super light material to protect your feet is a win-win.

- Shock absorption. Another really important aspect of hoof and leg anatomy is shock absorption. The average adult Thoroughbred weighs a little over 1000 pounds, while warmbloods and drafts can easily reach 2000 pounds or more. While there are many animals out there who are significantly heavier than horses (think rhinos and elephants) they are not designed to run fast for extended amounts of time. The only animals with sustained running speeds faster than the horse, cheetahs and pronghorn antelope, are designed to be light. In fact, a cheetah's average weight is around 170 pounds, and the average pronghorn antelope weighs in at less than 150 pounds. These guys are the racecars of the animal world: light and lightning fast. Meanwhile, the horse is almost ten times as heavy, and tops out at an insane 40-50 miles per hour. Sure, that's a short sprint, but the average galloping speed of a horse is still 25-30 mph, and that can be sustained for a decent distance. A well-conditioned horse can sustain a gallop for about 2-2.5 miles before

[2] Wegst, U.G.K. and Ashby, M.F. (2004). The mechanical efficiency of natural materials. Philos Mag 84, 2167-2181

becoming fatigued, but let's just take one mile for the purpose of discussion.

At a full gallop, the average Thoroughbred can cover about 20 feet in a stride. That means that over the course of a one-mile gallop, each hoof will hit the ground about 264 times, for an average of 1,056 total footfalls. If that sounds like a lot of concussion to you, add in the fact that with velocity included, the amount of force that moves through the hoof in each footfall is up to 2.5 times the horse's body weight[3]. This means that for the average-sized, 1000-pound horse, each footfall at the gallop results in 2,500 pounds of force in the hoof, one and a quarter tons, crashing down 1,056 times over the course of a mile. I don't even want to see the numbers for a draft horse!

All that force means that if your horse isn't going to shatter his bones, jar his vital organs, and smash every soft tissue in his body, we need some serious shock absorbing mechanisms. We will be coming back to this a lot as we talk about individual structures in the hoof because almost *every* structure contains some kind of shock absorbing feature.

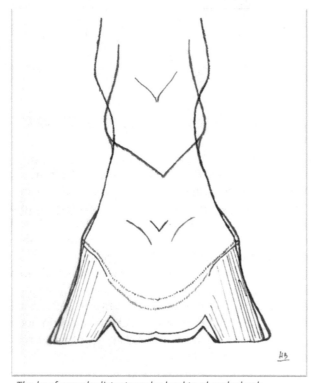

The hoof capsule distorts under load to absorb shock

Each structure doing its part to absorb shock is absolutely critical to the whole horse. You may have experienced this firsthand if you've ever ridden a horse with upright pastern angles and upright or clubby feet. Normally, the pasterns slope backwards to act as a sling and cushion some of the forces of each stride, but with upright pasterns, the whole stride takes on a much more up-and-down motion. Riders usually notice it as being a pretty choppy ride. And that's just a failure of *one* of the shock absorbing systems!

As we go ahead and start looking at each structure that makes up the hoof, we are going to come back to these three principles multiple times, because protection, being strong but light, and shock absorption are key to understanding the difference between healthy anatomy and broken anatomy. Ready to find out what farriers are looking at when we check out your horse's feet?

Quick Takeaways
- **Hooves are designed for maximum protection, since horses were designed to function in tough terrain.**

---

[3] Thomason, J.J., Peterson, M.L., (2008). Biomechanical and Mechanical Investigations of the Hoof-Track Interface in Racing Horses. *Veterinary Clinics of North America: Equine Practice, Volume 24, Issue 1*, Pages 53-77.

- Hooves are built as strong and light as possible, to reduce energy expenditure.
- Hooves are made to absorb as much shock as possible, since horses are heavy animals that travel at high speed.

2 THE COFFIN BONE

Coffin bone, pedal bone, third phalanx, P3 - any way you say it, the little bone at the end of your horse's leg is the piece that ties everything in the hoof together. A healthy coffin bone with good connections to the structures around it is the first step to a healthy hoof, and the coffin bone should dictate almost everything your farrier does when they pick up your horse's foot. Yet, the coffin bone is often smaller than the palm of your hand and weighs significantly less per cubic inch than most other bones.

So what is this small, fragile bone doing at the end of your horse's skeleton?

Since the coffin bone is the closest to the ground of any bone it your horse's body, by having motion-producing tendons attached directly to it, the horse puts leverage to work. Remember, action performed on the farthest end of the lever arm takes less energy than if you use a shorter lever. This is why if you have to shovel manure, you put one hand (probably your right if you are righty) near the end of the handle, and your other hand as close to the shovel head as you can. The hand near the end is doing the work and the hand near the shovel is creating a pivot point, so that you can use the handle length to your advantage. The horse's anatomy does the same thing. It puts the motion creating tendon attachment as near to the end of the limb as it can, so the leg length becomes an advantage, with each bone adding length to the lever. This is why both the deep flexor tendon and the main or common extensor tendon attach directly to the coffin bone.

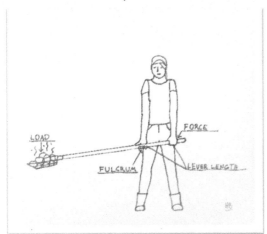 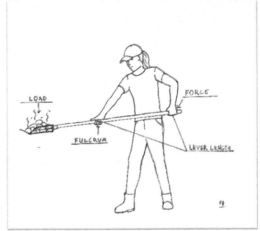

The back half of the coffin bone also serves as a solid attachment point for the collateral cartilages, a pair of hard, flexible cartilage plates in the back half of the hoof. The flexibility of these cartilages is what allows the back half of your horse's hoof to expand under load and then spring back when the load is taken away, which, you guessed it, is one of those shock absorbing systems I mentioned we were going to talk about. (It's also an important mechanism for moving blood out of the hoof.) The area between the collateral cartilages is also host to the digital cushion, a soft, springy, elastic structure that reduces shock and helps the blood pumping mechanism of the hoof. But as important as the digital cushion and collateral cartilages are, they would be completely useless without a solid attachment to something much more rigid. Enter the coffin bone.

If the collateral cartilages help pump blood out of the hoof when they open and close, where does that blood come from? If you think the coffin bone is probably involved, then you're catching on to just how important this little bone is! A large portion of the blood flow in the foot comes through arteries that are protected by the coffin bone. The lateral and medial digital arteries, which are the are major blood suppliers for the foot, actually run inside the coffin bone in a tunnel called the terminal arch, but many other arteries of the foot run through channels on the outside of the coffin bone. The coffin bone is also full of tiny tunnels known as vascular foramina, which allow blood vessels to radiate through the bone. But what does the coffin bone get in return for protecting all these blood vessels?

Well, most of these blood vessels are supplying the sensitive tissues that produce the hoof capsule, which in turn, protects the coffin bone. It sounds like the coffin bone and the blood vessels have a pretty good deal worked out. All those little tunnels actually make the coffin bone lighter as well, which is a benefit to the horse as a whole.

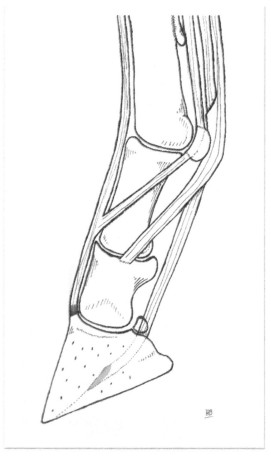

Blue indicates the main extensor tendon attachment and green indicates the deep flexor tendon attachment

The coffin bone has four distinct surfaces: the solar surface which faces down when the horse is standing, the parietal surface which makes up the majority of the sides of the bone, the flexor surface where the deep flexor tendon attaches and which faces backward, and the articular surface. The articular surface is the part of the bone that lies within the coffin joint... yep, that's the joint that most people talk about only when they have to inject it.

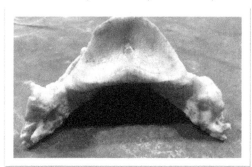

The articular surface of the coffin bone

There's a good reason a lot of people end up having to inject the coffin joint. Every time your horse isn't walking perfectly straight on a flat surface, the coffin joint gets tapped to compensate. It's mostly meant to flex forward and backward, but it can also open and close side to side. And every time that your horse steps in a divot, turns tightly, or stands half on and half off a concrete pad, the coffin joint compensates by opening side to side. Besides its side-to-side motion, the coffin joint also flexes and extends every time your horse takes a step. That's not so bad if she has pretty good conformation, but if she's got club feet or long, low feet, each step puts extra stress on the coffin joint. And that's not even considering horses whose feet are neglected and way out of balance.

Add to that stress the simple fact that literally the entire weight of the horse has to go through this one little joint to make it to the ground. As far as pounds per square inch, that's a pretty impressive number. Luckily the coffin bone gets a little help in the joint from the navicular bone. Sure, the navicular bone gets a bad rap, since you only hear about it when it causes trouble, but 90% of the time, it's just there, doing its job and getting ignored. What is its job in the coffin joint? It sits just behind the coffin bone in the joint, and thanks to some super strong ligaments, it fills in the back of the joint, increasing the joint surface area by almost a third. That means less pounds per square inch on the coffin bone's articular surface. See, I told you the navicular bone was there for something besides causing trouble. It also acts as a lever to give the deep flexor tendon more pulling power on the coffin bone. We'll talk about that more in Chapter 19 and Chapter 33.

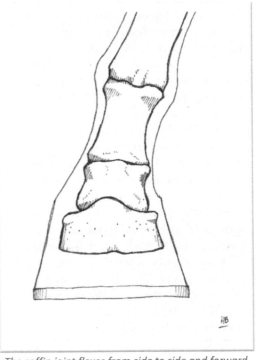

The coffin joint flexes from side to side and forward and backward

Speaking of all that weight, how is this tiny little bone that we already know has tons of little holes in it bearing so much weight without fracturing? Time to talk shock absorption again!

The secret to how your horse's coffin bone takes all this weight without crumbling into a hundred pieces is that it never actually bears that weight in the traditional sense. Most bones (in fact, all of the leg bones above the coffin bone) bear weight the same way. The weight comes down from the body, passes straight through the bone, and transfers that weight directly to the bone below it. Not the coffin bone! The coffin bone receives weight from the top, but rather than walking on the bottom of the bone and transferring the weight directly to the ground, the coffin bone is actually suspended within the hoof capsule, thanks to the lamina. The parietal surface of the coffin bone is covered with sensitive lamina, which looks like about 600 vertical pleats. Each of those

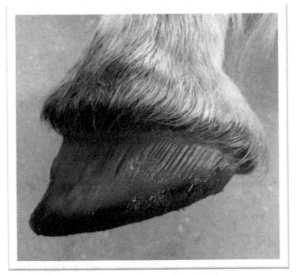

The coffin bone is covered by sensitive lamina

folds interlocks with a matching fold in the *insensitive* lamina, which is the innermost layer of the hoof wall (more on this in Chapter 3). This means that the coffin bone gets to just hop in a hammock and delegate all of the heavy lifting to the lamina, and through the lamina, to the hoof wall. The coffin bone is apparently a big believer in working smarter, not harder.

Remember when we talked about all the little blood vessels going through the coffin bone? A lot of them are there to feed the sensitive lamina[4]. The rest of them mostly go to the coriums of the hoof, which are the horn-producing structures of the foot. Producing horn is a tough process in which tiny, threadlike structures called papillae have to feed dividing protein cells (mostly keratin, the same thing our hair and nails are made of) which slowly harden and then are pushed down the assembly line so new cells can be made. It turns out that creating horn takes a lot of fuel, and that fuel comes from blood.

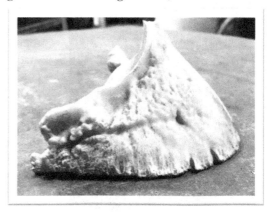

The coffin bone has many tiny channels for blood vessels.

The coffin bone plays host to a couple of areas of horn growth. Around the top of the coffin bone, a ring called the coronary corium, the area just above the hairline on your horse's foot, grows the hoof wall, including the insensitive lamina that helps suspend the coffin bone. In the same area, just at the hairline, lies the perioplic corium, which makes a soft rubbery horn called periople, which functions similarly to our cuticles. We'll talk more about this in Chapter 4.

A third corium grows on the solar surface of the coffin bone, and it creates the horn that makes up the sole. Hoof wall horn and sole horn are both made of the same type of horn, but with a slightly different arrangement, which allows it to function a little differently, but we'll discuss that in more detail later. The horn that makes up the frog has the highest moisture content of any of the insensitive structures of the hoof, and it comes from the frog corium.

The last type of corium that we see on the coffin bone is a pretty specialized structure. Around the bottom outer edge of the coffin bone, known as the solar margin, there is a small fringe of papillae which are there to create a soft, yellow, waxy horn. This horn fills in

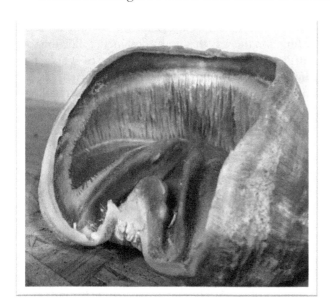

The insensitive lamina on the inside of the hoof capsule

[4] Mishra, P.C. and Leach, D.H. (1983). Electron microscopic study of the veins of the dermal lamellae of the equine hoof wall. *Equine Veterinary Journal, 15:* P. 14-21

between each of the vertical folds of the insensitive lamina, making up the structure we call the white line (another structure that, like the navicular bone, only gets talked about when

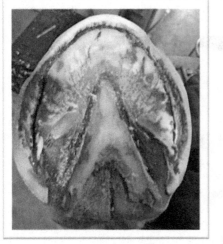

The white line marked on the bottom of the hoof

things go wrong!) Remember, the sensitive lamina grow off of the outside of the coffin bone and they perfectly interlock with the insensitive lamina, but once we go down the hoof past the coffin bone, there is no sensitive lamina. Without the horn made by those papillae on the bottom edge of the coffin bone, there would be an open gap between each fold of the insensitive lamina, creating a perfect spot for dirt, manure, and bacteria to get to the coffin bone. Luckily for your horse, there's that soft yellowish horn to save the day. It's also a fairly flexible horn, so it works well to fill in the gaps between the relatively hard sole and hoof wall, much like silicone caulking sealing a gap between two pieces of wood that might expand and contract.

The shape of the white line traced on plexiglass

Another super helpful thing about the white line, aside from the fact that it saves your horse from having constant foot infections, is that it gives us x-ray vision. If that sounds a little far fetched, think about the fact that it grows directly from the bottom outer edge of the coffin bone, and has a pretty short distance to travel to reach the ground, not much more than an inch, in most cases. Because of this, the inside edge of the white line gives us a perfect outline of the shape of the bottom edge of the coffin bone, and to anyone interested in allowing the horse's foot to function the way that it was designed, following the coffin bone shape is key. Even in cases where the white line has been stretched or distorted, as in laminitis or when a horse has really bad flares, the inner edge of the white line stays true to the coffin bone.

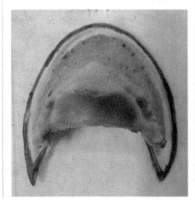

The coffin bone fits neatly inside the white line tracing. Photos courtesy of Steve Sermersheim

This is amazingly helpful for farriers who believe that nature knew what it was doing when it designed the horse. If we believe that the horse's hoof is an efficient and functionally designed piece of anatomy, then we should try to follow the shape of the coffin bone as closely as possible in both shaping the hoof in our trim and shaping any shoes that we may apply. That's not to say that there are *never* cases where we need to give anatomy a hand on a horse that doesn't have good conformation or has had an injury. But as a general rule, the coffin bone is shaped the way it is shaped for a reason.

Take the difference between front and hind coffin bones. There are a lot of differences between front and hind limbs in a horse, and that shows up in the coffin bone too. If you took radiographs of all four of your horse's feet right now, you would almost certainly find more rounded coffin bones in her front feet and pointed coffin bones in her hinds. Why? It goes back to the function of her front and hind legs. Her front legs are there for stability and steering, so they need a more rounded shape so they can go in any direction necessary, but her hind legs are her motor[5]. If you've ever watched her really get down and run, you can see that motor in action. All those massive muscles in her hind quarters are driving, pushing off the ground to propel her body forward. And those pointed coffin bones are there to help her dig in and really push off.

Imagine that you have to dig a hole. Do you choose a pointed spade or a square, flat bladed shovel? If you choose the flat shovel, you're going to be there a long time, working a lot harder than you need to. That pointed shovel will get the job done, because it bites into the ground, even if it's hard and dry. That's what your horses' hind feet are there for, digging in and driving forward. That's also why putting square toed shoes on every horse's hind end causes more problems than it solves. I'm not saying there is never an appropriate time for that square bladed shovel, but it's usually an inefficient choice that's going to make you work a lot harder and make your muscles a lot more sore than they need to be.

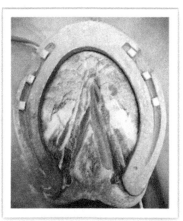

Classic hind shape

Luckily for us and for your horse we don't have to guess about the function and shape of his feet, since we get super x-ray vision with his white line. If you're interested in seeing the white line and coffin bone shape for yourself, you can easily see it when you pick out your horse's feet. Most of the time, it will be a darker line between your horse's sole and hoof wall, sometimes with a little dirt in it. If you want the easiest way to see it, check it out after your farrier has trimmed the hoof. In a trimmed hoof, it has a yellow color to it, and if you look closely, you may be able to see the insensitive lamina as tiny white striations radiating outward. You never know what you might see when you know where to look!

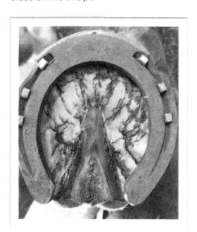

Classic front shape

Quick Takeaways
- **The coffin bone is an important attachment point for tendons, putting leverage to work for the horse.**
- **The coffin bone protects blood vessels in the hoof and supports the coriums**

[5] Crevier-Denoix, N., Camus, M., Pourcelot, P., Pauchard, M., Falala, S., Ravary-Plumioen, B., Denoix, J., Desquilbet, L. and Chateau, H. (2014). Effect of Speed on Stride Parameters and Limb Loading: Comparison between Forelimb and Hindlimb at Training Trot on a Firm Surface. *Equine Vet Journal, 46:* P. 38-38.

13

which produce horn.

- The coffin bone is suspended in the hoof capsule thanks to the lamina.
- The white line grows from the bottom edge of the coffin bone, so it shows us the shape of coffin bone.
- Front coffin bones are typically rounder while hind coffin bones are more triangular, and that's for a good reason.

3 THE HOOF WALL

What's the thing you probably spend the most time looking at on your horse's feet? If you're like most horse owners, and you don't have a weird thing for horse feet, you'd probably rather look at your horse's face than look at her feet, so you spend most of your time near her head. This means that if you look down at her feet, you're usually looking at the outside, top part of her hooves, which is mostly the hoof wall.

The hoof wall is the hard working, heavy lifting champ of the hoof structures. Everyone else helps out, but the hoof wall is definitely doing the lion's share of the group project. The hoof wall is considered a *primary* weight bearing structure in the hoof, and in the shod horse, it may be the only weight bearing structure, at least on hard ground. On a

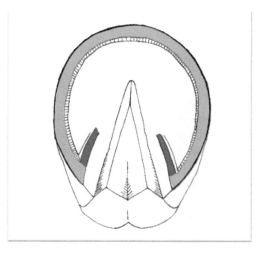

The hoof wall highlighted in green, with the bars highlighted in blue

barefoot horse, the frog should be helping out, and on soft ground, the sole is recruited too. Why should the hoof wall bear the majority of your horse's weight? Well, remember last chapter when we talked about the fragile coffin bone and how it lets the lamina hold it up instead of taking weight directly on the bottom of the bone? The lamina transfers the load outward to the hoof wall, and as we'll find out, the hoof wall is really well designed for that kind of responsibility.

But what happens if the sole becomes a primary weight bearing structure, for instance if the hoof wall gets broken off too short or in the case of certain aggressive trimming methods? Have you ever tried to hop in a hammock that's too close to the ground or getting worn out and saggy? If you have, I'm sorry about your bruised tailbone. The same thing happens if the lamina/hoof wall hammock gets taken out of commission by the sole

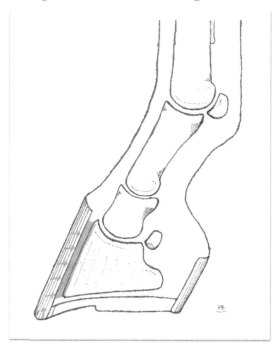

The hoof wall as a primary weight bearing structure

being a primary weight bearing structure. All of a sudden the hammock that the coffin bone is relaxing in is too close to the ground, and the coffin bone is going to know about it (and be pretty mad!)

So the hoof wall is an unquestionably important structure. Let's talk about what exactly makes it strong enough to do such a high pressure job.

The hoof wall is made up of two types of horn: tubular and intertubular horn. Recent research shows that these two types of horn are made of the same stuff, just arranged differently[6].

Tubular horn is the easiest to recognize by eye. Remember how we talked about horn being produced by papillae in the coriums? The papillae in the coronary corium make tiny hollow tubes that grow parallel to the angle of the hoof, from top to bottom. Just how small are we talking? Reports vary, but research suggests that it's between 16 and 10 tubules per square millimeter[7].

So what are all those tubules for? They function a lot like drinking straws. If you grab a straw (one that hasn't been kinked or bent) and push straight down on it, it takes a lot of pressure to bend or break it. Horn tubules work the same way, providing compressive strength. However, just like straws, they don't deal well with being bent, or worse yet, kinked.

Horn tubules are what give the hoof wall its toughness and rigidity, and because of that, the percentage of tubules in the hoof wall varies depending on the area of the hoof. The outside of the hoof wall has more tubules, so that it acts like a protective shell for the wall, while the innermost area of the wall has fewer tubules, making it softer and more

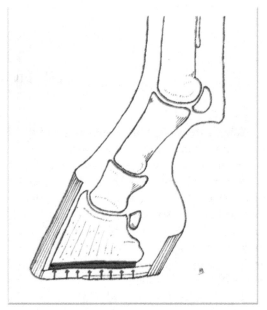

The sole as a primary weight bearing structure

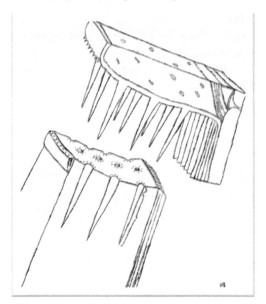

The papillae of the coronary band build the hoof wall

flexible since it's closer to the soft tissue structures inside the hoof. This is the reason hooves can run into trouble if the outer layer is rasped or worn through, because that protective shell is gone.

---

[6] Curtis, S., (2018). *The Hoof of the Horse.* 59, The Street, Icklingham, Bury St. Edmunds, IP28 6PL, UK, NFC

[7] Reilly, J.D., Collins, S.N., Cope, B.C., Hopegood, L. and Latham, R.J. (1998). Tubule density of the *stratum medium* of horse hoof. *Equine Veterinary Journal, 30*: P. 4-9.

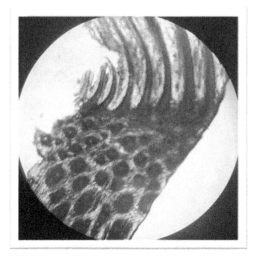

The dark circles are tubular horn, and the white area is intertubular horn. The long stripes are insensitive lamina.

Going back to keeping the hoof light … horn tubules being hollow means that they are lighter than a filled-in cylinder, and almost as strong. But if you've opened a package of drinking straws and let them go everywhere, you know that if you want them to have any strength as a structure, you need to stick them together, and that's where intertubular horn comes in. Intertubular horn is the glue that holds all those separate tubes together. It's made up of the same stuff as the tubular horn, but it comes from all the areas in between the papillae, and instead of being laid down in tubes, they fill in all the gaps and connect each tubule to the next one. Intertubular horn is what gives the horn it's flexibility and a fighting chance to resist cracking.

Both the tubular and intertubular horn grow from the coronary band downward. As you've probably noticed if your horse has ever blown out an abscess at the coronary band, it takes a *long* time for new cells at the coronary band to grow all the way down. According to research on the Lipizzaners at the Spanish Riding School in Austria, it took 11 months for complete hoof renewal, and that is in working horses who probably had pretty good circulation[8]. It may take longer in horses living a more sedentary lifestyle. If you are curious about the growth rate in your own horse, keep track if he blows an abscess out the coronary band. You will see a horizontal crack which slowly moves down the hoof wall. If you write down the date that first appears and the day that it is finally completely gone, you will know what your horse's hoof renewal rate is. Just don't tell him if he's not as good at growing hoof as a Lipizzaner.

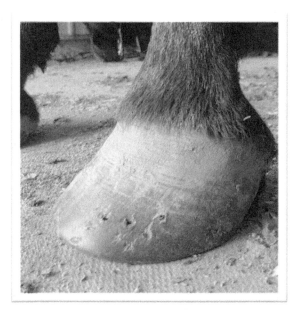

Even growth rings

For the most part, your horse's hooves probably grow down pretty evenly and without too much drama. There are a few times that you might see some noticeable differences though, including if your horse has club feet, laminitis, or has experienced major changes in nutrition or blood flow. Changes in nutrition or blood flow, such as when your horse goes from eating dry hay to fresh spring grass or if

---

[8] Josseck H., Zenker W., Geyer H. Hoof horn abnormalities in Lipizzaner horses and the effect of dietary biotin on macroscopic aspects of hoof horn quality. (1995). *Equine Vet J. May;27(3)*: P. 175-82.

your horse has a fever or other inflammatory event, can cause what is known as a growth ring or fever ring. Usually if these rings are evenly spaced between the toe and heel, there's not much to worry about. You can think of it as a snapshot of a moment in time when your horse had a little extra fuel getting to her hooves. On the other hand, growth rings that are spaced wider in the heels and narrowing at the toe let you know that she isn't getting even blood flow to the whole coronary band. Classically, this can be a sign that your horse could have experienced some coffin bone rotation, though it can also indicate that your horse has a naturally occurring club foot. Again, growth rings show you purely what is happening; they don't have any negative affect on their own.

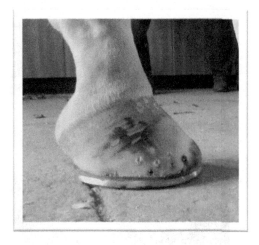

Uneven growth rings from laminitis

Along with spotting growth rings, one thing you may have heard repeated about your horses' hooves is that his white feet will be weaker than black feet, or conversely if he has black feet, people might be jealous. This one is a really common idea, but luckily for all the white footed horses out there, it falls squarely in the "old wives' tale" category. Several studies have been performed where researchers tested hoof samples for strength and elasticity and found no difference between black and white hoof samples[9].

So why is this one so persistent? Probably because it's a lot easier to see defects in white feet than in black feet. Bruises and superficial cracks are so obvious on white feet that it only takes a passing glance to see them, but black feet hide a lot. Plus, chances are if you've been around enough horses, you've seen a horse with really bad white feet, so that comes to mind when you hear someone say that white feet are weaker. You've seen bad black feet too, but no one came up with an old wives' tale about that, so we don't really think about it.

Now that you know you can ignore hoof color the next time you're looking at a horse, what should you be checking out?

Hoof angle and flares for sure. This goes back to coffin bones and those kinked straws. Remember that the

Severe flaring

[9] Douglas J.E., Mittal C., Thomason J.J., Jofriet J.C. (1996) The modulus of elasticity of equine hoof wall: implications for the mechanical function of the hoof. *J Exp Biol. Aug;199(Pt 8):* P. 1829-36.

coronary corium (where the hoof wall grows) is near the top of the coffin bone, and that the hoof wall in a healthy horse is firmly attached to the outer surface of the coffin bone via the lamina. It stands to reason from those facts that the hoof wall should be at the same angle as the outer surface of the coffin bone if it's going to keep a tight connection through the lamina. But what happens if there's a lot of leverage on the bottom of the hoof wall, like when a hoof gets really long?

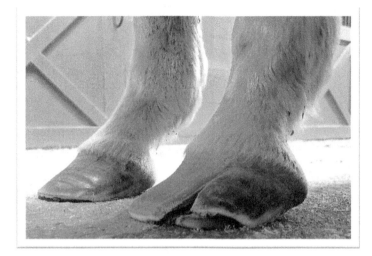

Flare happens, and when the hoof wall flares, each of those tiny tubules is bent outward. Like a drinking straw, once the tubules are kinked, that spot isn't going to unkink, it will have to grow out and be replaced by fresh horn. The problem is that if the leverage isn't taken away, it's just going to kink the new tubule that grows down.

So is flare a deal breaker? Not necessarily. Some flare is in response to poor

Flared hoof wall

management, inadequate nutrition, super wet conditions, or neglect. In those cases, the feet might improve drastically once those things are under control.

On the other hand, sometimes flare indicates a bigger problem. If the hoof is flared more on one side than the other, it could be telling you to look at the horse's conformation. Crooked legs lead to uneven stress on the feet, which can show up as a flare on one side of the hoof. Flares can also indicate genetically poor feet, which doesn't necessarily have to be a deal breaker. It does mean that you'd better be ready to deal with hoof problems for the rest of that horse's life though, and that you'll really have to stay on top of managing his feet.

How can you tell the difference between manageable flare and flare that's warning you of a bigger problem? Obviously if the horse is suffering from neglect or malnutrition, you can guess that could be affecting the feet. Likewise, if the horse has obviously crooked conformation, you know that isn't going to change and you'll be dealing with that for the foreseeable future. This is where it can be helpful to include your farrier in a prepurchase, even if you aren't having a formal vet

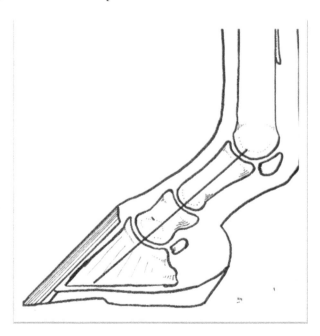

A low angled foot with bones evenly aligned

prepurchase. Your farrier can probably give you a pretty good idea of whether they think the flares are something they can correct or something you're better off avoiding. Part of that just comes from experience and seeing a lot of horses' feet.

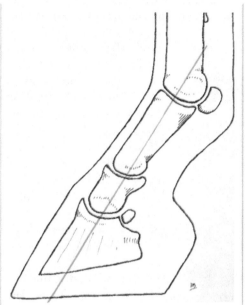

A normal hoof angle with straight bone alignment

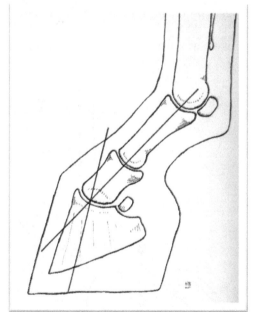

An upright foot with uneven bone alignment

So if there's no flare on a hoof, and the hoof wall follows the angle of the coffin bone and continues at that angle all the way to the ground, why are some feet low angled and flat and other feet upright? For one, the coffin bone can be at a higher or lower angle, depending on other factors like deep flexor tendon tension and digital cushion health (the digital cushion is a fibro-fatty pad in the back half of your horse's foot. You can feel it for yourself if you push your finger just above the heel bulbs).

There's no perfect angle that every hoof needs to match, and nowadays, most farriers trim based on lining up the bones of the digit correctly, rather than shooting for an arbitrary textbook angle. Typically we will try to match the angle of the front of the hoof wall and the angle of the pastern bones, because this means that the coffin joint should be lined up evenly. For some horses, this angle will be different between a pair of feet, which you may have heard of as high/low feet.

High/low conformation means that one hoof has a more upright angle while the other is lower angled. Both can be healthy feet if they are maintained, but they do function differently and each comes with different risks. Although we usually worry more about low angled feet, a recent study of superficial flexor tendon injuries showed that if the horse had high/low feet, it was more likely to have a superficial flexor tendon injury in the high foot than the low foot[10].

High and low feet also absorb shock differently. If your horse's foot is really low and flat, it can lose out on the opening and closing of the back half of the foot, simply because the hoof wall in the heels is too crushed and run forward to spring back easily. On the other hand, if you have an upright foot that goes into the territory of being a club foot, sometimes the frog is so far off the ground that it can't help

---

[10] Hill, S., (2017) The Relationship Between Superficial Digital Flexor Tendon Lesions and Asymmetric Feet in Equine Forelimbs.

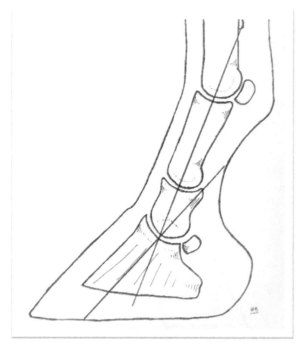

A low foot with very upright pastern

the foot expand and contract either. Sometimes the bones are stacked up directly above the hoof so that the force comes straight down, rather than having some angulation in the pasterns that can absorb shock. Obviously, the ideal is somewhere in the middle.

Now that we've covered the hoof wall, let's talk about something that covers the hoof wall. If you've ever asked yourself what in the heck that thing is on your horse's wall, chances are you'll be interested in the next chapter.

Quick Takeaways

- **The hoof wall is the primary weight bearing structure of the hoof.**
- **The hoof wall is made up of tubular horn and intertubular horn.**
- **Flare is a sign of an overloaded hoof wall.**
- **The hoof wall angle should match the pastern angle, showing that the coffin bone is lined up with the bones above it.**

4 THE PERIOPLE

If you're anything like me, the first time you read the word periople, your first thought is something along the lines of, "How the heck do I pronounce that?" If that's the case for you, let's clear that up- it's pronounced per-ē-ˌō-pəl, or pair-ee-opal for those of us (me) that have trouble reading pronunciation symbols.

The periople is technically the outermost layer of the hoof wall, but it functions a lot more like our cuticles. It grows from a corium called the perioplic corium, right below the hairline, and it's softer and more rubbery than the rest of the horn. Extra high fat and moisture content is what keeps it so flexible.

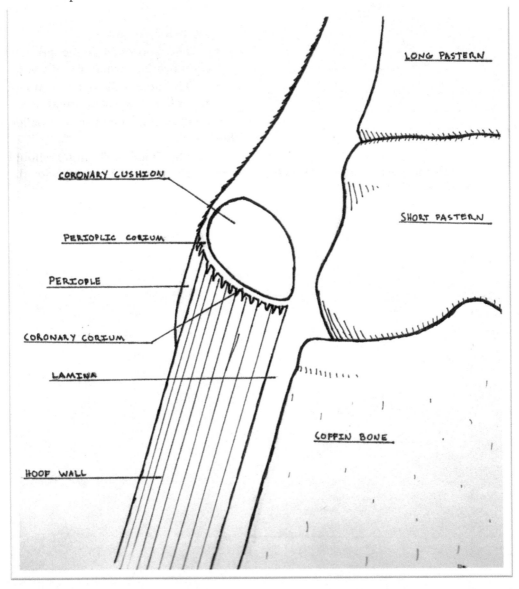

Being soft and rubbery is really important, because the periople covers the seam between the relatively rigid hoof wall and the soft, deformable skin above the coronary band. Any time that you are joining two different types of material, it pays to be flexible, especially when one has a lot more movement than the other.

Aside from covering and protecting the seam at the top of the hoof wall, the periople also is thought to help the hoof wall regulate moisture content by forming a moisture barrier on the top third or so of the hoof wall. Why is the top third of the wall more susceptible to

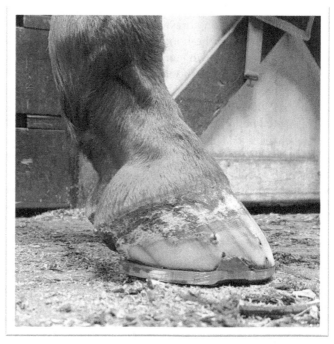

A strong periople

variations in moisture? If we go back to how the hoof wall is formed, the top part of the hoof wall has tiny papillae and corium which is creating brand new horn cells, and those new cells aren't exactly ready to go out into the world on their

Dry periople

own yet. The top three-quarters of an inch or so of the hoof wall contain newly formed cells, some of which are not yet keratinized (the hardening process in which the horn cells die off). Coincidentally, this is exactly the area most thickly covered by the periople[11].

Most of the time, the periople gets worn off about a third of the way down the hoof wall, especially if your horse is working in a sand arena or has turnout in deep,

---

[11] Stewart, J., (2013). Understanding the Horse's Feet. The Stable Block, Crowood Lane, Ramsbury, Wiltshire, SN8 2HR. Crowood Press.

abrasive footing. If your horse is stall bound for a while or only worked and turned out on hard ground or very non-abrasive footing, her periople might not wear off, and you could be able to see it covering the hoof wall from top to bottom. How can you recognize it? When dry, the periople is a brown, tan, or white scaly looking layer. If you scrape it with a hoof pick or wire brush, the scratch should look whiteish. There's nothing wrong with leaving it on the hoof, and if anything, it might add a little moisture protection, though your farrier may have to rasp some of it off if they have to tidy up any flares while trimming.

This useful periople is also responsible for the occasional panic attack due to the fact that it totally changes its' appearance when it gets water saturated. If you've ever pulled your horse in from a muddy field, hosed his legs, and wondered what that gummy white stuff on his hoof wall is, you've probably had a small periople-induced panic attack yourself! When it's exposed to moisture for several hours, such as if your horse is turned out in very wet conditions, if you've had to soak a foot for a while, or, if you're unlucky enough to live in an area where you

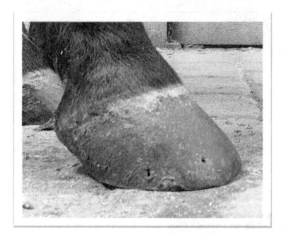

The periople may appear white in color

deal with frequent snow, the periople becomes saturated and swells up. It also turns a very pale, whitish color and becomes soft enough to scrape off with your fingernail.

Just because you can scrape it off, doesn't mean you should. Some horse owners mistake a wet periople for a fungus and scrape it all off. Remember, once it dries out, the periople will return to normal and it will continue to do its important job of protecting the coronary band and new hoof growth. If it really freaks you out to look at it, dry your horse's hooves as much as you can with a clean towel, throw her in a clean stall with plenty of dry shavings, and wait it out. When it's had a chance to dry out, you'll see normal, healthy looking perioples again. Your horse worked hard to grow those things, so don't throw them out just because they got wet.

Quick Takeaways
- **The periople covers and protects the seam between the hoof wall and the skin.**
- **It also may help regulate moisture for the new hoof wall.**

5 THE FROG

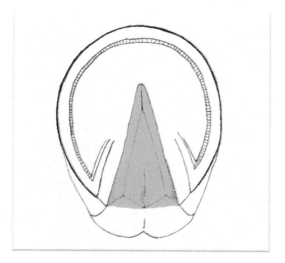

In what must surely be one of the strangest episodes of anatomical naming, someone decided to call that big wedge-shaped chunk of tissue in between your horse's heels "the frog." Why, you may ask, would this structure be named after another animal? The most common answer that I've been told, and I'm not making this up, is, "It looks like a frog, crouching to hop!" I question if these people have ever seen the amphibian in question. Another theory is that it looks like a part of a sword belt, also called the frog. The most intelligent argument I've heard is that it comes from the German word for the frog, *frosch*. Another decent theory is that early railroad men may have thought the frog looked like the junction of two railroad lines, also called a frog. The true answer, though, might be lost to history at this point.

The more relevant, though less colorful, question that we have to ask is what is the function of the frog and how can we keep it doing its job?

The frog is another insensitive structure made of horn; but aside from the periople, it has the highest moisture content of any horn in the hoof. This helps it stay soft and flexible -- at least inside. (In dry weather, the outside of the frog hardens and dries out.) And staying flexible is a major part of the frog's job.

If you think about all the surfaces your horse walks on every day, it's probably a wide variety. In turnout, he might be walking on soft, divoted turf, slogging through mud, or stomping flies on dry dirt and rocks. If it's winter and you live above the Mason-Dixon line, your horse might be playing in deep snow or carefully picking his way across frozen, churned up mud. Working, he might be in sand, synthetic footing, or on a trail or even a paved road. And then if he spends the night in a stall, he might stand on rubber mats, deep shavings, or uneven, hard packed dirt. But through all of it, his hooves have to compensate for every step on uneven ground, or half-on-half-off a mat or concrete pad, or every time his foot hits the ground not quite evenly. Thanks to the frog,

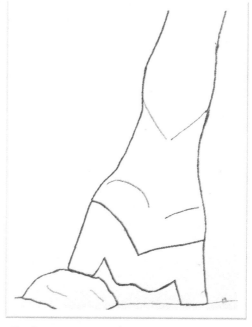

The frog compensates for uneven footing

most of the time all of that compensation goes off without a hitch.

How does the frog manage all that work? Well, with a fairly rigid hoof wall and sole, the frog gives the back half of the hoof the ability to flex and recoil, both up and down and side to side. If you think of your horse standing in gravel, if the hoof capsule was completely rigid, she might have one side of the hoof on a rock and the other side completely floating in the air, which means the side on the ground is doing all the work. But if one heel has the ability to sink toward the ground a little while she's bearing weight, and then spring back up into its normal position once the hoof is on flat ground, then the hoof can share stress much easier.

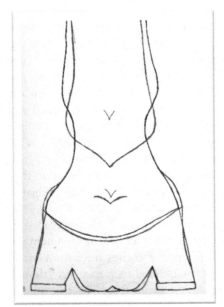

Weight bearing with the frog contacting the ground

You may have also heard the frog referred to as the "heart of the hoof" or heard someone say that the frog pumps blood up the leg. This is a little misleading since, as you've probably realized, the frog is made of horn which is going to make a really inefficient blood pumping organ! There is still a lot of truth to that statement, but it just works a little differently than we imagined.

Above the frog, between the collateral cartilages in the heel bulb area, is a structure called the digital cushion. We've already briefly touched on it when we talked about shock absorption, but it wears another hat too, and this one is the blood pumping hat. The digital cushion gets compressed every time that the fetlock drops under load, and that compressed cushion has to go somewhere. If it can, it pushes the collateral cartilages outward, which creates a vacuum that sucks blood out of the foot and starts it on the journey back up the leg. So what does the frog have to do with it? If the frog is not in contact with the ground, there's no resistance for the digital cushion. Instead of pushing the collateral cartilages outward, the digital cushion will collapse downward toward the frog. The frog provides important support to make that blood pump work, plus the frog and digital cushion helps absorb a lot of shock.

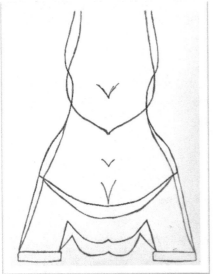

Weight bearing without the frog contacting the ground

That doesn't mean that your horse's frog is non-functional just because it's not touching the ground when he stands on hard ground. If he does a lot of work or has turnout in soft ground, there's a good chance that when his foot settles into that dirt, the gap between the frog and the ground fills in with dirt. Also, according to two studies that looked at frog contact and heel expansion, there was always some heel expansion occurring even if the frog didn't touch the ground at all, so there are still some back-up systems if the frog isn't helping.[12]

But what if your horse has a really small, narrow frog that is stuck way up in between really high heels? In that case, there is a good chance her overall hoof health might be suffering since the frog isn't doing its part. It often becomes a self-fulfilling cycle. A small, atrophied frog doesn't help your horse out by pumping blood, so there's less blood being moved through the corium, and that means less blood to grow more frog horn. And since the atrophied frog has less flexion and movement, it typically doesn't "self-clean" the dirt and manure that she inevitably steps in. All that dirt and manure carries the bacteria that causes thrush, which then degrades the frog more.

If that sounds familiar, what can you do about it? Some of it comes down to genetics, so it may not be possible to give your horse the ideal frog. But there are definitely some things you can do that will make a difference.

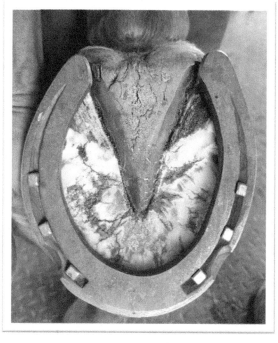

A strong, healthy frog helps in shock absorption and circulation

The single biggest thing you can do to help your horse's frogs is to keep them as hygienic as possible. Yep, you guessed it, picking feet is the magic step to helping your horse. Atrophied frogs are extremely susceptible to thrush, and every time he gets thrush, he temporarily looses important frog mass and strength. The good news is, this is super preventable. A good, thorough cleaning of the frog each time you see your horse will make a noticeable difference in frog health. When you pick out feet is almost as important as how often you do it; if you're picking your horses hooves and then immediately sticking him out in a muddy paddock, you're probably not getting all the benefit of your hard work. Pick them out when he comes in so that they have a chance to dry out and be exposed to oxygen before he heads back outside. If you've already got a good case of thrush going, you might need to treat it topically, but we'll talk about that more in Chapter 26. We're also going to talk about other reasons that regular

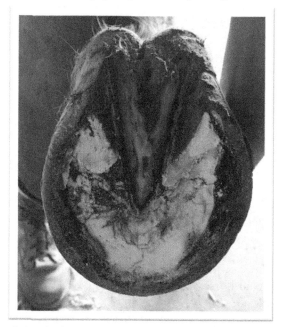

A thrushy frog

[12] Colles, C.M. (1989). The relationship of frog pressure to heel expansion. *Equine Veterinary Journal, 21:* P. 13-16

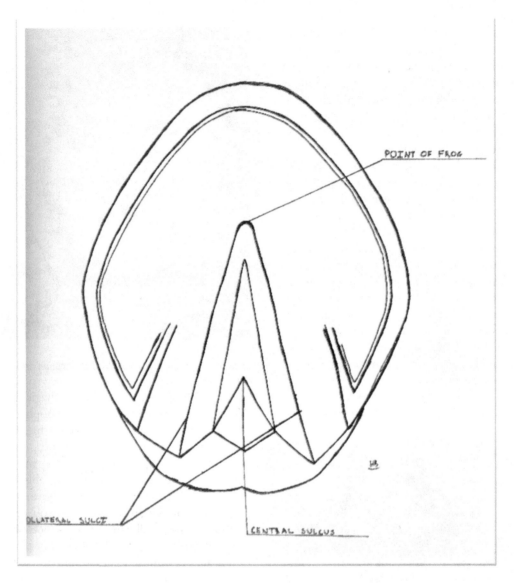

POINT OF FROG

COLLATERAL SULCI

CENTRAL SULCUS

hoof picking is super important in Chapter 25, if you need a little motivation. Feel free to skip ahead if you want -- you're not going to hurt my feelings.

Want to know a common myth that is huge culprit for lack of frog care? You've probably heard this one, and maybe you've even said it yourself. Here it is: *The frog is really sensitive so you can't/shouldn't pick too deep/ pick in the central sulcus.* Let's call in the mythbusters because it's time for this one to die.

The insensitive frog horn has no nerve endings or blood vessels. Remember, your farrier trims it with a sharp knife every time they see your horse. Any time that you pick out a frog and the horse winces, or worse yet, you see blood, *there is something wrong.* A healthy frog is supposed to be a nice, thick covering for those sensitive structures underneath it, so if you are *seeing* sensitive structures, the insensitive, protective frog has been severely damaged (usually by thrush). If that's the case, the very last thing you want to do is to leave it be and not clean it out. Think of a sensitive frog as a wound. You wouldn't leave a wound packed full of manure and not treat it just because the wound is painful. You have to get it cleaned up so that healing can take place.

Obviously, you don't want to cause the horse more pain, so you will have to be careful while you clean out the frog; but you really, *really* need to do it, and you need to pick it out thoroughly and often. If you can't tell, this is my authoritative, don't-talk-back voice, because it really bothers me when I see a horse suffering unnecessarily because someone thought it was okay to skimp on hoof cleaning, and I know you're not interested in putting your horse through pain either. Now that we're clear on that, I'll hop back off my soap box.

How can you clean out a frog that's got a lot of deep thrush? Start by picking out any easy-to-get-at dirt, then slowly and carefully explore any deep cracks or flaps. Usually, manure and dirt gets

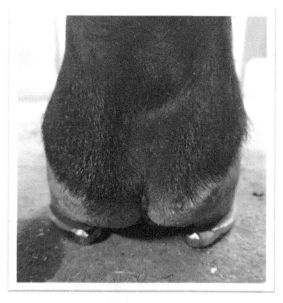

A deep split in the central sulcus

wedged way up in there, along with bedding and sand (ouch). Once it's been in there a while, the bacteria starts to go crazy and turn that good clean dirt into a black, gooey, smelly mess. So when you're picking, if you start getting thick black crud, you're on the right track. You need to keep on gently picking until you stop getting any more of that stuff. Otherwise, the bacteria is still in there eating away at the frog. Once you can't get any more gooey stuff out, you can treat it with a topical thrush remedy.

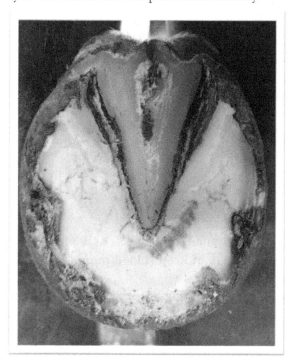

A healthy, strong frog can do its share of the work

If your horse's frog has a really deep, narrow crack down the middle of the frog and into the heel bulbs, you're going to have to get a little more creative. You can start by cleaning as far as you can reach with your hoof pick. Sometimes turning the pick sideways can help if the crack is really narrow. Then, you can grab some gauze, disposable shop towels, or cotton, and "floss" in the crack. You'll be surprised at how much nasty black goo and gritty sand comes out. If that still doesn't get to the bottom, or you aren't able to get it all the way clean, get a plastic syringe with a long plastic tip, not a needle, and start flushing the crack. Stick that syringe (carefully) into the crack as far as it will go and then pump in the fluid until it runs clear. You can use clean water or add some betadine or a little iodine if you want some extra bacteria killing power, but we're going to talk a lot more about treating and preventing thrush in Chapter 26.

You might be reading this right now and thinking, *none of that sounds like my horse. I'm pretty sure my horse's frog is so big that it comes down below his heels.* A lot of lower angled, flatter footed horses have very prominent frogs (I'm looking at you, Thoroughbred people!) This can really be a blessing for horses with collapsed, weak heels, because the frog can help take some of the weight and give those heels a break. The great thing is, those low, flat feet usually shed dirt and manure pretty easily since they don't have too many deep crevices for them to pack into.

The frog sometimes exfoliates in layers.

Even if you have the world's healthiest frogs, and you always take care of them, and you never get thrush, you might still have the extremely disconcerting experience of picking up your horse's hoof and finding out that her frog looks like it is peeling off. Underneath is a smooth, smaller frog that looks pretty fragile, and warning bells start going off in your mind. Good news - this is actually how frogs self-trim. Because of how rubbery they are, they don't tend to wear away the same way that the hoof wall does, but luckily, frog horn is laid down in discreet layers. When the frog gets too long, or when there is a big environmental change (in my area, this usually means a wet spring), the frog will peel off a layer or two and start over with the nice fresh frog underneath. It's called sluffing, or sloughing if you're British, and it's a little like skin cells exfoliating after a new layer of skin is built underneath. It is a totally healthy and normal process, and it results in an amazing chew toy if you have a dog with a strong stomach.

So what's next on the anatomy list? Let's talk about the frog's next-door neighbor and partner in shock absorption and protection: The sole.

Quick Takeaways

- **The frog is flexible so that it can allow movement in the heels of the hoof.**
- **Allowing flexibility in the back half of the hoof keeps blood pumping out of the hoof.**
- **Frequent and thorough hoof picking will keep a frog healthy and functioning.**

6 THE SOLE

Another multi-tasking hero of the hoof, the sole, not only protects about 75% of the bottom of the hoof, it also acts as a major shock absorber and even gives your horse more traction. If that's not enough to make you a little curious as to how it manages to get all that done, you might be a multi-tasking genius yourself.

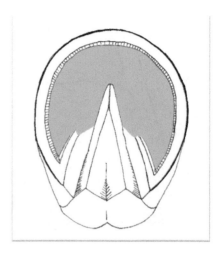

The sole is a hard covering which protects the coffin bone, and just as importantly, the blood vessels and corium on the bottom of the coffin bone. It's a little self-serving, because a large portion of that blood flow goes to the solar corium, the structure that grows the insensitive sole. Okay, the sole isn't a completely selfless hero, but it still gets the job done. Nobody wants sharp rocks poking those sensitive structures, or bacteria finding its way to the coffin bone, and a nice thick sole takes care of that.

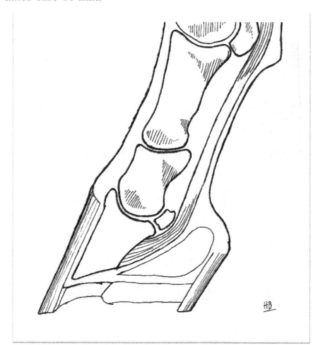

The sole should be about 3/8 inch thick to protect the sensitive structures inside the hoof capsule

The ideal, textbook sole thickness is about three eighths of an inch (or one centimeter of our friends on the metric), but actual sole thickness varies quite a bit. In a 2014 study that examined 50 cadaver feet with radiographs and MRIs, researchers found that the average sole thickness measured in around 11.5-13.2 millimeters, with a standard deviation of a few millimeters either way[13]. That measurement comes in slightly above the three eighths measurement we talked about, but you should also take into account that we don't know how recently the hooves in the study were trimmed. A sole that isn't trimmed for six months might be thicker than one that was trimmed yesterday.

[13] Grundmann, I.N., Drost, W.T., Zekas, L.J., Belknap, J.K., Garabed, R.B., Weisbrode, S.E., Parks, A.H., Knopp, M.V., Maierl, J. (2015) Quantitative assessment of the equine hoof using digital radiography and magnetic resonance imaging. *Equine Vet J. Sep;47(5):* P. 542-7.

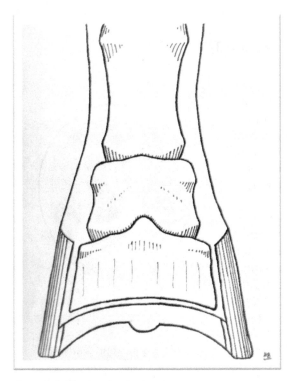

A cupped sole absorbs shock

One important distinction when you're looking at x-rays of your horses' hooves with your vet is that sole *thickness* is not the same as sole *depth*. Sole thickness is the amount of sole measured from the bottom edge of the coffin bone to where the sole ends. On modern digital radiographs, it's pretty easy to see where horn structures are, but sometimes vets will use barium paste to mark the hoof to make sure. Sole thickness is literally how much sole the horse has. Sole *depth* measures from the bottom edge of the coffin bone all the way to the ground. It measures the entire amount of clearance the coffin bone has from the ground, and it should be a bigger number than your sole thickness measurement. It might sound like semantics, but it can have very serious consequences if the two are confused!

In a sole depth measurement, we're also measuring the air gap in between the sole and the ground, and we see an air gap because the sole is slightly cupped, concaved away from the ground. That's a great shock absorbing mechanism for the foot because the sole is slightly flexible, so that when the hoof loads, the cup of the sole can flatten slightly and then spring back into shape. It's a big improvement over landing flat on the sole with all that force going straight into the coffin bone.

If you don't quite get how the cupped sole helps the foot, put your hand on the table next to you, palm down. Now bend your fingers a little so that there is about an inch of air in between your palm and the table and smack the top of your hand with your other hand. Now put your palm flat on the table and try again.

In the first experiment, your hand has a chance to flatten slightly and absorb some of the blow without your palm coming in to contact with the hard table. In the second experiment, you hit your hand with the same amount of force, but that force had nowhere to go, except your

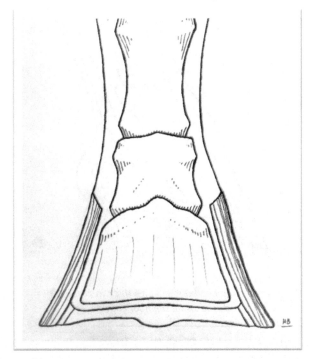

A flat sole increases concussion

hand! It's the same principle with your horse's sole. If it's nicely cupped, she has more ground clearance and she can comfortably cover a lot more miles because she's feeling less force with every footfall. If she has flat soles that don't have much ground clearance, she's probably going to feel sore sooner, and her coffin bone will have a greater risk of becoming inflamed.

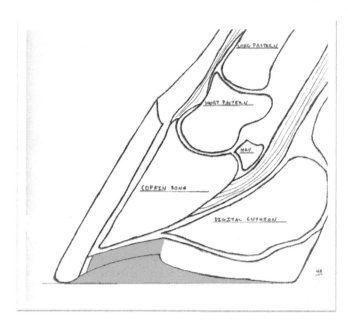

Sole depth

We've talked about the difference between sole thickness and sole depth, but what were the dire consequences I warned you could happen if you mix them up? Well, luckily there's only one situation where this could go wrong, and that's when you look at x-rays with your vet and you're telling your farrier what you saw. If the vet saw a scant quarter inch of sole thickness and an inch of sole depth, remember that means that three quarters of that sole depth measurement is cup. So if you were to tell your farrier that the vet said your horse had an inch of sole *thickness*, instead of an inch of depth and a quarter inch of thickness, the farrier is going to start trimming your horse's hoof with a very incorrect map in their head.

Good thing you know the difference now, right?

Speaking of sole cup, that's also how the sole gives your horse more traction. If you've ever watched a video of horses galloping in slow motion (or you have a quick eye) you've seen pucks of dirt fly out of the hind feet when they flick backwards. This is because the sole cup digs into the ground, and as the horse drives off of those hooves, they carry a clod of dirt which usually gets launched as the leg extends backward. A narrow rim of hoof hitting the ground digs in a lot better than a flat surface.

All that cup flexing also plays an important role in sole shedding. The sole, like the frog, doesn't really wear away much, but as it gets older and more crumbly, the flexion of the sole pops out sections that are ready to shed. You might see this as crumbly, gray or whiteish horn that scrapes away when you are picking out your horse's hoof, or in

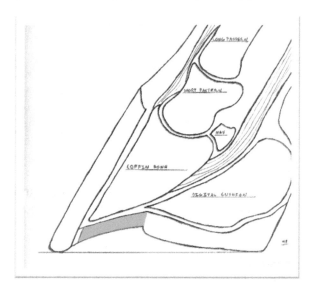

Sole thickness

extremely wet environments, you may even see a whole layer of sole trying to peel off. Again, as unsettling as this can be the first time, it is a totally natural process and there should be a nice thick layer of sole underneath it.

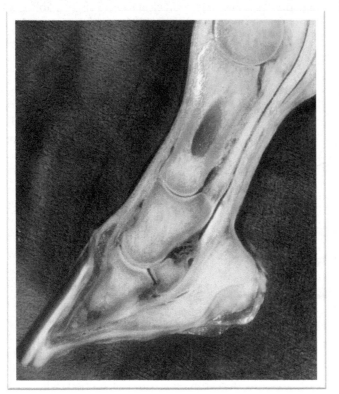

A freeze dried hoof showing very little sole thickness on a flat foot

Just how flexible is the sole? With about 30% moisture content, it is more flexible than the hoof wall, but when we talk about it flexing, it's important to remember that it is flexing under a load of a thousand pounds or more[14]. Unless you're the hulk, you shouldn't be able to flex your horse's soles with your thumbs. If you can, there's probably not enough protection there to keep your horse comfortable, especially if he has to walk across rocks.

What can you do if your horse has super thin soles? Unless your horse has damaged blood flow to the sole, he *is* probably growing sole, but he's also probably shedding it faster than he's growing it. Keeping him off of rocks or other uneven, hard footing is a good start, because, of course, preventing lameness is priority number one. You might also find it helpful to keep your horse in as dry an environment as you can, since wet horn is softer and more likely to shed than dry horn. If your horse is barefoot, it may be time to talk to your farrier about shoes, and if he already has shoes, you may need to add some kind of flat pad for protection until his sole growth can catch up. Both of these options are good things to consult your farrier about. You can also consider adding a hoof supplement if it seems like his overall hoof quality isn't that good, but you can read more about how nutrition affects hooves in Chapter 24.

With all the flexing the sole is doing, what's sealing the edges so that a gap doesn't open up when the sole springs back into shape? In the next chapter we'll talk about the little hoof structure with a big job and bigger insight into hoof health: the white line.

Quick Takeaways
- **The healthy, thick sole protects the bottom of the coffin bone.**
- **A concave, flexible sole helps absorb shock.**

---

[14] Curtis, S., (2018). *The Hoof of the Horse.* 59, The Street, Icklingham, Bury St. Edmunds, IP28 6PL, UK, NFC

7 THE WHITE LINE

If you remember the coffin bone chapter (Chapter 2), you might recall we talked about the white line growing from the fringe of papillae on the bottom edge of the coffin bone. The soft, yellowish horn produced by those papillae (the terminal papillae, if you want the exact name), is only half of the structure we call the white line. The other half is made up of the insensitive lamina on the inside of the hoof wall. Remember that the lamina looks like small mushroom gills or vertical pleats, and the sensitive lamina on the coffin bone fit into the insensitive lamina on the hoof wall and lock together. But once the hoof wall grows past the coffin bone, there is no sensitive lamina to match the insensitive lamina. So the yellowish horn that grows from the terminal papillae is there to fill in the gaps.

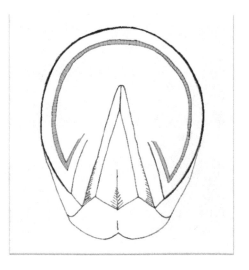

That's really important, because your horse's hooves are constantly exposed to dirt, sand, manure, and tons of bacteria. If there were gaps in her feet that let all that junk find its way to the coffin bone and the other sensitive structures inside the hoof, you'd be dealing with constant infections. Luckily the white line is there to protect all those sensitive structures.

And let's not forget, since the white line grows directly off of the bottom edge of the coffin bone, it gives us a great x-ray view of the shape of the coffin bone, which we talked about earlier in Chapter 2.

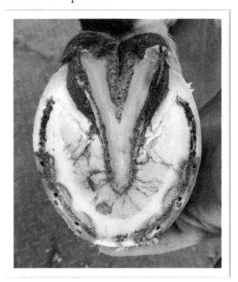

The white line should be consistent in thickness

Since the horn of the white line is soft and flexible (and we'll talk about why that is necessary in a second) it can still get sand and small rocks wedged into it occasionally. If you have a barefoot horse that is kept in a limestone paddock, you've probably noticed this when you pick out his feet. As long as it's near the surface, this doesn't cause any pain. But if you don't clean it out and it continues to pack more and more grit into the white line, it will eventually wedge the insensitive lamina outward and make it to the sensitive structures that the hoof is supposed to be protecting. If your horse is really prone to this, it might be necessary to add shoes to protect that vulnerable seam.

If the soft, flexible nature of the white line is so unhelpful when your horse is in sand or limestone, why wouldn't it be made from something harder, more wear resistant and less flexible?

Flexibility is key to the function of the white line because its other primary purpose is to

A stretched white line

join the sole and the hoof wall, and both of those structures are relatively hard, and both flex in different ways under load. A rigid joint between the two of them would split almost immediately, so the body had to make a soft, flexible joint that is able to take stretching and compression and spring back. Enter the white line!

In a freshly trimmed healthy hoof, the white line should be about 2 millimeters in width.[15] If you've taken a peek at your horse's white line and that doesn't sound right at all, there's a couple things that could be at play.

One, if you're looking at your horse's white line a few weeks after they've been trimmed, you could be seeing some distortion, especially if your horse's hooves commonly flare. If that's the case, leverage could be stretching the white line or causing a separation in it, usually noticeable because they're packed full of dirt. On the other hand, even if there's no distortion, you could be seeing more of the white line if her hoof wall has done some growing and some sole has shed out. Remember, that insensitive lamina grows out as far as the hoof wall does, so if there's no sole on the inside of the wall, you are essentially seeing a cross section of the insensitive lamina. Either of these scenarios is not super concerning.

On the other hand, you could be seeing a wider white line because it is actually stretched. This would be the case if you are looking at a freshly trimmed hoof and seeing a wide white line.

What does it mean if you see a stretched white line? Essentially, it

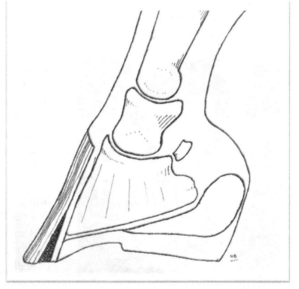

Debris in the white line

[15] Curtis, S., (2018). *The Hoof of the Horse.* 59, The Street, Icklingham, Bury St. Edmunds, IP28 6PL, UK, NFC

means that something is adapting to stress, and you're seeing the results. For instance, it's common to see stretched white lines in horses who have had very long hooves (think neglected horses that have been rescued) because all that extra length has translated into a lot of leverage. If a structure is under a lot of leverage, you know it's the softest structures that show it first. Imagine about trees on a windy day. The most obvious reaction is always in the smallest, most flexible branches. However, that's not as big a disadvantage as it might seem; because of their flexibility, they have a chance to bend and spring back, where the larger, tougher branches don't

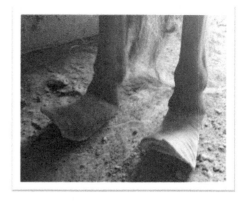

Neglected feet will have stretched white lines

show the force of the wind as easily, but are more likely to completely snap off when their strength is exceeded.

A more concerning reason for a widened white line is a case of laminitis. This is usually what happened if the white line is significantly widened through the toe. Especially if the coffin bone has rotated, you often see a really wide white line, known as a *laminar wedge*.

So ... should you panic now? Not necessarily. Especially if there is no blood or bruising in the white line, you are probably looking at the effects of laminitis that happened a while ago rather than an active case especially if your horse is sound. Even if your horse has never had an apparent case of laminitis, the white line can get wider if he struggles with metabolic issues (think Cushing's disease or insulin dysregulation) thanks to changes in growth. If your horse has a widened white line but no lameness, and as far as you know he's never had any laminitis, this is a great opportunity to nip a problem in the bud before it becomes an issue. Laminitis is never a good thing, and

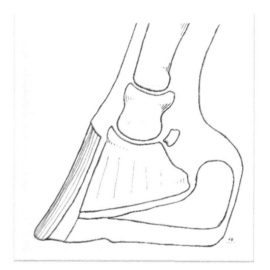

White lines may become stretched from laminitis

prevention is much more effective than trying to cure it once it has started.

Being overweight is both a huge predisposing factor for laminitis and a big trigger for insulin dysregulation. If you see a stretched white line and your horse is overweight, now is a great time to talk to your vet about weight loss ideas for your horse. Even if she's not that overweight, if you see a stretched white line, it can be a good idea to get your vet to pull bloodwork to make sure that she is processing sugars in a healthy way and creating the right amount of insulin. If you can find out about these factors before they cause trouble for your horse, you can manage them and possibly save your horse from a world of hurt later on. We're going to talk a lot more about laminitis in Chapter 34, so feel free to hop over there to learn more.

I told you the white line was important and a good source of information about your horse's health, but that might be understating it. If you catch a potential laminitis episode before it happens, the white line throwing a red flag (and you paying attention to it) could save your horse's life.

Quick Takeaways

- The flexible white line seals the junction between the sole and the hoof wall.
- A wide white line could be a warning sign of laminitis.

9 FOALS AND DONKEYS AND DRAFTS, OH MY!

What we've talked about so far is basic anatomy that relates to all equines, but what if you have a donkey? What about draft horses? Is it all the same if you have a newborn foal or an old campaigner who is nearing thirty?

The majority of what we've gone over is true of most situations, but we're going to take a look at some of the specifics that you might need to know if your horse doesn't quite fit into that elusive category of "average." Ready to dig in?

Foals - If you have a foal, first of all, congratulations! You are the proud owner of an adorable, fuzzy little, long-legged ball of energy and curiosity and fun. Not only is this a super exciting part of your life, it's also an incredibly important time in his life, mentally and physically. It's up to you and whatever professionals you bring on board, like trainers, vets, and farriers, to set your foal up for success. The formative experiences he has now will influence him for the rest of his life, and now is the only time in his life when you can actually improve his conformation. What that means is that you have an amazing opportunity to change his entire life for the better, and all it takes is some time invested right now.

Tom Roberts wrote: *If you are fond of a horse and wish to do him a real favor - train him well. Teach him good manners, good habits, both in the stable and under the saddle. You need never worry about the future of such a horse if for any reason you may have to part with him. You assure him of friends wherever he goes. Perhaps the greatest kindness you can do any horse is to educate him well,* and that is definitely the case when it comes to foals. If you want to give your foal the gift of feeling comfortable and happy to have his feet handled instead of experiencing fear at every farrier appointment for his entire life, training him as a foal can do that. If you want to give him the best chance of getting the most skilled hoof care he can get, helping him know how to politely interact with people can do that. And if you want to make sure that if he gets a hoof issue or injury later in life that he can get the treatment he needs, make sure that he is good for the farrier right now.

A horse that understands how to stand politely when someone asks for their feet and knows how to wait patiently while their feet are trimmed or doctored will always experience less stress and fear during trimming and shoeing, will receive more accurate hoof care, and have much greater chances of survival if they develop a severe hoof issue. Even if your farrier is trying to do the best work they can, if your horse is scared and pulling their legs away or rearing, there's no way your farrier can do a great job.

Now, while your foal is small and easily impressionable, you can instill good habits that will last a lifetime. If you bred the foal and have access to it immediately after birth, make picking up her hooves part of imprinting, the formative first interaction that you have with her. Then, continue picking up her hooves whenever you see her. It does take time, but a little effort now is much easier than trying to break bad habits later. The great part is, you can work this training into your regular playtime with your foal. While you're petting her cute little puffy mane, practice touching her legs too, and gently asking for her feet. To start with, just pick up each foot and then let her have it back right away. You can do this a couple times during a session, but you know her attention span is short, so a quick lesson is better than doing it until she doesn't want to be there anymore. Aim for at least once each time you see her -- pick up each foot and pick it out so she gets used to it.

Once she's confidant letting you pick up her feet, practice holding onto it a little longer. This is also a great time to introduce her to stretching her legs forward. When she's a little older, her farrier will be bringing her feet forward for trimming and shoeing, so if you can practice now, she'll be a lot more comfortable when a stranger asks her to do it later!

You also want to teach her to pick her feet up in any order that you ask. If you always pick up her feet in the same order, she learns to pick up her feet, but she also might be confused if someone asks her for her feet in "the wrong" order. You want to make sure that she is comfortable going through the hoof picking routine in any order, at any time. It's also important to practice in different locations. Remember that at her age, she is trying to put together patterns and figure life out, but she might jump to the wrong conclusions sometimes. If you always pick her feet in her stall, she knows that she should pick up her feet for you, but she might also think it's *only* safe to pick up her feet in the stall. It's okay to start there since that's probably her safe space, but you will want to expand to picking up her feet in the barn aisle, outside, in a trailer, in the field, anywhere you can think of. Remember, the more variations you teach her, the less likely she is to find herself in a scary situation later on that

she doesn't understand. If you start picking up her feet right away and making it a good thing with plenty of pets and affection, she won't ever have to wonder if picking up her feet is scary.

Since your foal is super curious and learning constantly right now, make sure that when you pick up his feet, he doesn't pull it away and put it down until you decide to give it back. This might mean that you are only holding his foot up for a second at first, but if you consistently hold up his foot until he pulls it away, you're actually teaching him that he can take his foot back whenever he wants. So if he does pull it away, make sure you don't end the training session on that note. Take the time to pick it back up until he holds it up long enough for you to give it back. This reiterates to him that he not only needs to pick his foot up when you

The small crease visible in this 6 month old foal foot divides the horn that was grown in utero (below and the horn that was grown after birth (above)

ask, but he also needs to wait until *you* are ready to put it down. That attitude will make it much easier for your farrier to work on his feet, as well as making it easier and safer to treat any hoof problems that might happen later in his life.

So you've been picking up and playing with her feet since she was born. When should you schedule her first farrier appointment? It might seem unnecessary at first because she probably doesn't have a lot of hoof to trim. But trust me when I say, you should schedule that first appointment as soon as possible. Assuming your farrier is coming out to provide hoof care for her mother, you'll want to make sure that she gets to meet the farrier. Of course, you should let your farrier know as soon as the new foal arrives, and ask

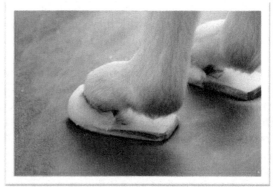

Foals with conformation issues may need corrective shoes

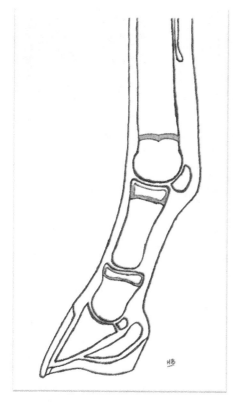

Growth plates (marked in green) on a newborn foal

that they take a look when they are scheduled to come out.

This is important for two reasons. First, it's really good for a curious young foal to meet the farrier and start developing what will hopefully be a great lifetime relationship. Make sure that it's a good, pleasant first interaction. You want to make sure both you and your farrier have time to spend a few minutes with your foal so it doesn't have to be a rushed, business-like visit. Remember, this is your foal's first time ever meeting this strange person who is asking to see their feet, and it takes a lot of trust for a flight animal to let a potential predator handle their feet!

Second, this is your chance to get an extra set of eyes on your foal's conformation, and it's important to do that *before* your foal's bones are done growing. Most of the bones in your foal's legs grow in length via cartilage growth plates, and if you need to change the direction a foal's legs go, you need to do it before the growth plates start closing. The first growth plates typical are fully ossified by 3 months, so that's why your farrier (and hopefully your vet) should take a look at your foal as soon as possible.

It's not uncommon for foals, and later adult horses, to have slightly different hooves from left to right. In a study performed on 106 thoroughbred horses, they were found to have "handedness" just like humans. Although some horses appeared to be ambidextrous, the majority preferred to use one front hoof more than the other[16]. And just like humans, the more they use one hoof over the other, the stronger that leg gets. This could mean that some differences in hoof size and shape between a pair of front feet might be due to the foal's handedness. According to *The Hoof of the Horse*, 75% of steeper hooves are on the right front foot instead of the left.

When your farrier first takes a look at your foal, they'll be checking out how your foal's legs are put together, because crooked legs mean uneven weight bearing on the hoof. It's important to remember that at this young age, if part of the

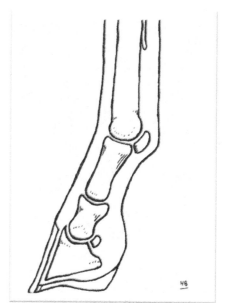

Foal feet are normally upright

[16] McGreevy, P. & Rogers, L. (2005). Motor and sensory laterality in Thoroughbred horses. *Applied Animal Behaviour Science - APPL ANIM BEHAV SCI. 92.* P. 337-352.

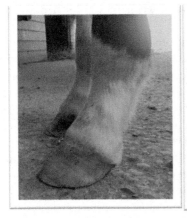

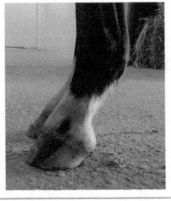

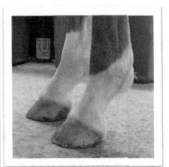

Front hooves on an 18 month old

Front hooves on a 6 month old

Front hooves on a one year old

hoof capsule is damaged because of excessive weight bearing, the bottom of the hoof becomes uneven. If the hoof is uneven, the leg tries to compensate, and the problem becomes more severe, and eventually permanent. However, if you and your vet-farrier team catch the issue at a young age, you can make a plan to get your foal back on track for healthy legs and hooves. Sometimes this involves special glue on foal shoes or surgery, but often it just means some frequent corrective trimming, managing exercise, and keeping a careful eye on your foal's progress.

You might be looking at your foal's foot and wondering, *His hoof looks really upright and tight. It's way more upright than his mom or dad, does he have a club foot?* You don't need to worry if your foal has upright hoof angles. Most foals, even Thoroughbreds (who are known for having lower angles later in life) have average hoof angles of around 59.5 °, but as the foal gets heavier, the hoof will slowly drop to about 56° at six months and all the way down to an average of 52° by one year.

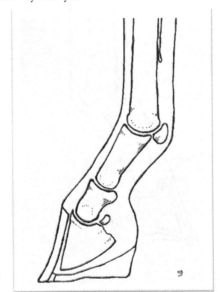

A club foot is more upright than a normal foal foot

When should you worry? If one foot looks a lot more upright than the other, if the front of the hoof wall has a big flare on the tip of the toe, or if your foal's heels don't touch the ground while the leg is loaded. These are all indicators that your foal needs some intervention to help correct the issue. Again, it is important to bring this to the attention of your vet and farrier as soon as you notice it. It may not be something that needs immediate action, but they will want to keep an eye on it and make sure that it is improving, not getting worse.

Speaking of things that look pretty weird, did you notice the weird, soft covering on your foal's hooves when she was born? It looks like whitish, waxy floppy fingers, and it usually falls off or is worn off within a day or two. So what is that stuff for if it only lasts a few days? If you've given birth to a baby yourself, you might already have a fair idea, but for those of us who haven't, remember how hard and pointy your little foal's hooves are? If they didn't have a protective covering while the foal was in utero, she could easily injure mom, and that's not even taking the birthing process into account. That whole process is difficult enough without pointy little hooves jabbing everywhere. Once the foal has safely exited mom, the hoof covering can shed off, giving it the descriptive name *deciduous hoof*. It's also known as the eponychium in scientific settings.

One final difference between foal feet and adult horse feet is that since foals are growing ridiculously fast, they will go through a stage when the top of their hoof at the hairline is actually wider than the hoof at the ground level. Her coffin bone is growing, her hoof is widening, and the angle is lowering to a normal angle. You will be able to watch her hoof go from a narrow cylinder shape to a tapering cylinder with a wider top and narrow bottom, and then finally it will go to the normal wider at the bottom and narrower at the top shape that we see in adults.

If you have a foal in your care, it is a great time in both of your lives, and a time for you to bond and learn and teach each other. And the best part is, you have the chance to set that adorable little foal up for a healthy, happy life through your patient work and careful observation.

Quick Takeaways
- **Beginning training a foal to have good manners for the farrier at a very young age is extremely important.**
- **Early intervention is important with leg or hoof deformities.**

The Geriatric Horse - If your horse is at the been-there, done-that stage, if you have done it all together, you've definitely developed a long-term friendship and you're going to do everything you can to keep him sound and enjoying his golden years. It doesn't matter if he's still taking you on easy rides or if you spend more time enjoying time together in his retirement. Either way, there's a few changes that you might see. (If he has any opinions about changes he's seen in you over the years, he's smart enough to keep his mouth shut!)

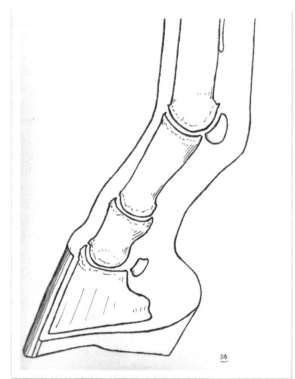

Arthritis can develop in any joint

The first battle that older horses face is dealing with any lameness or breakdowns that they may have received during their working career. Most horses aren't retired if they have *no* issues. It is much more likely that you noticed your faithful buddy slowing down, starting to limp a little, or not seeming quite so happy about heading out to work. Even if he was totally sound when you retired him, sometimes as horses age, injuries that seemed completely resolved can come back to haunt them, like a college volleyball injury making your knee sore when you're in your fifties. It's not a new injury, but over time, the weakened structure keeps taking wear and tear and it gets to the point where you notice it again. Since a large proportion of horses are now living well into their twenties and even their thirties, there's a lot of time for horses to start feeling those old injuries again.

Plus, of course, you're dealing with fun new things like arthritis. Just like in humans, arthritis in horses can start with a little inflammation and extra fluid in a joint, but it can progress to the point where a joint becomes completely immobilized. If the amount of movement in your horse's joints becomes reduced, sometimes the horse will compensate by moving her feet in an uneven pattern instead of moving straight. This will show up as uneven wear on the hooves, especially if she drags her feet a little.

Remember when we talked about how foals have really upright feet and that they lower slowly over time? That process usually continues throughout the lifespan of the horse, just at a slower rate than it does when they are young. However, you might notice your horse sporting slightly lower hoof angles than he did when he was young. It's probably not that your farrier decided to lower his angles. More than likely, it's just the natural relaxing or even slight breakdowns of his tendon and ligament fibers.

You also have to keep an eye on nutrition and overall body condition. Of course, this affects your horse's health in every aspect, but if she's not getting enough nutrition, or not correctly processing the nutrition she gets, she doesn't have enough extra energy to build strong, healthy hooves. Sometimes this is a matter of upping feed, changing feed to something more digestible, or even getting more frequent dental care. As always, if you notice major changes in weight or body condition, talk to your vet to make sure that there aren't any underlying conditions causing these fluctuations.

Soft tissue injury and breakdown can change the way your horse looks and stands

One last change you might see? Why do older humans decide to move out of New York and Michigan and head to Florida and Arizona? Maybe it's because a human can only shovel so much snow in their lifetime, but maybe it also has to do with decreased circulation making them feel colder. Horses are the same way, with blood circulation decreasing slightly, especially in the extremities (read hooves). Though we don't know if it affects the way they deal with cold, it does affect the amount of nutrients getting to the coriums that make their hooves. That means slower hoof growth, and the potential that they could wear away more hoof than they grow. Good thing they have you as a friend, and you can talk to your farrier about ways to reduce hoof wear so their growth can keep up. Hint: this usually involves either a change in activity (less work) a change in environment (turnout in less abrasive footing) or adding protection (shoes or hoof boots).

You've probably already discovered that although your senior horse still has the same good heart and mind, her body isn't quite as strong and energetic as it was even five or ten years ago. She might still love doing the same fun things together, but you might have to modify it a little to keep her comfortable. If your 85 year old grandma has always loved dancing, she might still like to take a spin around a dance floor, but you might not want to enter her in a dance marathon! If your horse is still excited to head out on a trail, that's a great thing to do together, but you might only cover a few miles and you probably want to limit her to slower gaits. If she gets tired, you can turn around sooner next time. There is no one-size-fits-all answer for how much you should expect of your older horse, but she will probably let you know if you listen to the clues she's giving you. Remember all of those times that she took care of you and rocked what you asked her to do? Now's the time to show her how much you appreciate all those years of good times and take good care of her through her well-earned retirement.

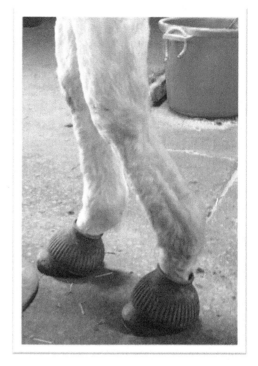

Soft tissue damage may affect mobility

Quick Takeaways
- **Older horses can struggle with the impact of years of wear and tear.**
- **Maintaining healthy body condition will help produce strong hooves.**
- **Geriatric horses might have reduced circulation over the years.**

Donkeys - If you have a donkey in your care, there are a few things you will want to be aware of if you are going to provide a good life for them. Though donkeys are typically smart, stubborn, and deeply entertaining creatures, they have a few other predispositions that set them apart from the majority of horses.

To have an informed discussion about donkey hooves, we need to know what kind of environment and conditions they evolved for, and what kind of traits they have been bred for over the 6000 or so years we've lived together.

The first records we have of domesticated donkeys comes from burial sites in Egypt. They were thought to have been first tamed by nomadic tribes, where they quickly replaced the ox as the pack animal of choice. Since oxen and other bovines need time to chew their cud for good digestion, they were slower moving than the new, quick eating donkey models. Donkeys seem to have spread quickly in popularity. In fact, ceremonially buried donkeys have been found in the tombs of some of the earliest pharaohs, showing that they were very important to even the wealthiest Egyptians of the time.

North Africa geographically looks a lot different than most of North America. The average yearly rainfall in Alexandria, historically the wettest part of Egypt, ranges from 7.87 inches to a measly 0.79 inches in dry years. Cairo is even drier, with the average yearly rainfall ranging from almost zero to 0.97 inches at most. This low rainfall, combined with almost constant winds in some areas and seasonal sandstorms where temperatures can easily reach 114°F mean that there isn't much vegetation growing for donkeys to chow down on.

If you're breeding an animal that has to work every day in a harsh, arid environment like that, and you don't have time or money to find or buy special forage, you need to breed an animal that can survive on a bare-bones diet, and that's what those early adopters found waiting for them in the hardy donkey. Donkeys managed to carry tons of weight for their size while not only *surviving* on the minimal vegetation available, but actually thriving! If you were looking for an animal to give you the best bang for your buck, the donkey took all the awards in ancient Egypt.

Now fast forward five or six thousand years to your pet donkey. Just like us, he certainly doesn't have to work as hard as his early ancestors, and if he's like most domesticated donkeys in North America, he earns his keep by being a companion for another horse or by entertaining us humans. He doesn't have to ensure his survival through backbreaking and calorie-burning labor.

But he also lives in a vastly different environment. If he lives in the very driest state in America, Nevada, there is an average of 9.5 inches of rainfall yearly, already a few inches more than Egypt's *wettest* region. The overall average rainfall for the continental US? 30.21 inches. That's a lot more grass to eat than Egypt was offering. And if that lucky donkey lives in the wettest state in the US, Hawaii? *63.7 inches of rain every year!* If you are a donkey and you like grazing, that's the jackpot. In fact, it's eight times the rainfall in the wettest area of Egypt in the wettest year.

So if you have a metabolism that is designed to give you plenty of energy for a hard job on a tiny bit of dry forage, and you find yourself in a place where you don't have to work hard, with about eight times as much food, what do you do? Your instincts tell you to eat all that great food, because you might not have the opportunity tomorrow, and you need to build up fat reserves for the lean times … Except that if you're a domestic donkey in the US, those lean times probably ain't coming. It's just more lush grass as far as you can see.

Similar to taking a two-week cruise and spending all your time at the buffet, that kind of diet-to-exercise ratio shows some pretty quick results if you hop on the scale. Since those extra calories aren't expended, they are stored away like your hoarding great aunt keeps magazines from the seventies. *We might need these someday!* And like those magazines arriving every month, those extra calories just keep coming, and your thrifty little donkey keeps squirreling them away in the form of fat, just in case. And slowly, you notice your donkey going from a trim, energetic little jenny, to a sleepy girl weighed down with fat pockets and constantly expanding saddlebags.

The average donkey in North America struggles with obesity. I said it, and I'm not taking it back. If you're reading this, and you have a donkey, and you don't live in the desert, your donkey is probably overweight. If you've put some serious effort and thought into your management and kept your donkey at a healthy body weight, I apologize. Keep up the good work. For the rest of you that are wondering why your donkey is starting to have a square tabletop on their back, this is for you. *Your donkey needs to lose weight.*

They might look cute being chubby, but imagine carrying around a hundred pounds in a backpack all day, every day. You would be sore. Your feet would hurt, your knees would hurt, and your back would hurt. You wouldn't want to move around much. That's what your donkey is dealing with every day. Plus, being overweight contributes to arthritis and laminitis, both of which can do irreversible damage to your donkey's health.

If your donkey is overweight, remember the environment that he was bred for. If you

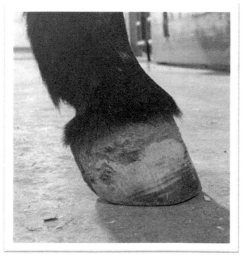

A healthy donkey hoof is relatively upright

have a dry lot that he can be turned out it, that's great. Talk to your vet about diet, but a little stemmy hay probably has more than enough calories for him. High calorie grain choices aren't even on the table. If he must go out in pasture, make sure he wears a grazing muzzle. And if you have the opportunity to increase his exercise, do it. If he's good at leading, you can hand walk him or even pony him off of a horse. You might also be able to increase his exercise by turning him out with a more active buddy who will keep him moving. Get creative; some people have even trained their donkeys to go on runs with them!

Because donkeys tend to be overweight, they are at a very high risk for laminitis. Obesity and insulin dysregulation often go hand in hand, and you can read more about it in Chapter 34. We'll also talk about body condition scoring in Chapter 35, which is a great way to keep an eye on your donkey's weight.

Donkeys share all the same basic anatomical hoof structures as horses, but in slightly different forms. The hoof wall tends to be more upright, and the hoof is more U-shaped instead of the rounder shapes usually seen in horses. The frog also tends to be quite prominent and extends behind the heels of the hoof. One less obvious adaptation is that the inner part of the hoof wall, which is not as tubule-dense, tends to be proportionately larger, and the wall in general has fewer and larger tubules. Since tubules are the part of the horn that gives the hoof rigidity, this means that the donkey has a more flexible hoof wall[17].

Why would this make sense for a donkey? When horn dries out, as it would in

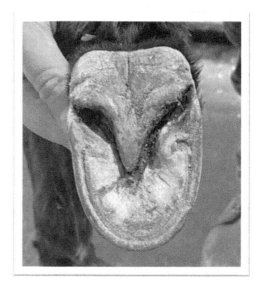

Donkey hooves often have a U shape

an extremely dry, often hot environment, it becomes less flexible, harder, and more rigid. Since some flexibility is important in the hoof to enable shock absorption and redistribution of stress, it makes sense that if you were breeding the perfect hoof for a dry environment, you would start out with something extra flexible. When it is exposed to that dry weather, it will become less flexible which would probably make it right about normal.

Only now, those extra flexible feet are being exposed to a lot more water than what

---

[17] Stewart, J., (2013) Understanding the Horse's Feet. The Stable Block, Crowood Lane, Ramsbury, Wiltshire, SN8 2HR. Crowood Press.

they were designed for. Since they are less tubule-dense, they are more prone to attack from bacteria or fungus, or even dirt and gravel. This may explain why donkeys are notoriously prone to White Line Disease, a mixed fungal and bacterial infection that attacks the inner part of the hoof wall. We'll talk about it in depth in Chapter 28.

To compound the fact that they are more prone to infection and laminitis, donkeys often get overlooked when it comes to routine hoof care. Just because they are smaller and not used for performance doesn't mean that they don't deserve regular maintenance. Make sure to pick your donkey's hooves out and keep

Sadly, donkeys are frequent victims of neglect

your donkey on a regular appointment schedule with your farrier, just like any other horses in your care. The last thing you want is to miss something preventable, just because the hooves didn't look too bad and so you skipped an appointment.

Donkeys were bred to be the super low maintenance, heavy lifting work vehicle of ancient times, and they still do that job in many undeveloped nations. They have changed civilizations and worked alongside many families to help ensure their survival in desperate times. Today, in North America, the donkey's luck has changed and they get to sample the finer things in life. It's up to you to help keep them healthy so they can enjoy it.

Quick Takeaways
- **Donkeys developed in extremely harsh environments, so they have very small caloric requirements and develop obesity very easily.**
- **Donkeys are prone to laminitis and White Line Disease.**

Miniature Horses and Small Ponies - For the purposes of the hoof, we're going to lump together all of the little ones - true Miniature Horses, Shetland Ponies, Falabelas, Section A Welsh ponies, and any other very small pony breed. I know, I know, they are not all the same, but when we're talking hooves, there are a lot of similarities. There are also a few issues that we see more in one breed than the others, so we will call out specific breeds too.

The first thing to know, if you own any size pony, is that these suckers are energy efficient foraging machines. As you are aware if you have tried to keep your pony with full sized horse, ponies will hold their own when it comes to eating. Often they finish their own food and then head over to "help" the slower eating horses finish up. Although they may not come from environments as harsh as where donkeys were developed, any time you see a pony, it usually was developed out of necessity. If you need an animal to use for transportation or agriculture, the most efficient choice is the smallest, easiest keeping one that can get the job done. Not enough forage for the high metabolism of a Thoroughbred? Breed a pony. Don't have enough land to keep a draft horse? How about his tiny but hard-working cousin, the pony? Heck, they even sent ponies into coal mines so that they didn't have to use big horses. Ponies have done it all, and they have done it without requiring too much in the way of feed. Take the Shetland Islands, where the famous Shetland ponies originate. They are rocky, windy islands which are considered sub-arctic, but Shetland ponies are, pound for pound, the strongest horse breed out there.

So what does all that metabolic efficiency mean? It means they fall squarely into the easy keeper category, which you may know as the gets-fat-on-air category. There are definitely some ponies who are working hard in athletic fields, and weight management might be a little easier for them. Let's be honest though, if you have a mini, she probably thinks she's in early retirement. No work, tasty pasture, maybe some treats… sounds good!

What she doesn't know

Ponies and minis often struggle with weight management

(but you do, because you aren't thinking with your stomach) is that eating your weight in sugary grass and plopping your butt on the proverbial couch all day is more likely to get you featured on *My 600 Pound Life* than give you the 6-pack abs of your dreams. Your pony is programmed to eat food while the eating is good - as much and as fast as she can. Remember those wild Brumbies we talked about in Australia, way back in Chapter 1? The Brumbies that were in dry areas traveled 34 miles per day just to get food and water. They definitely are not letting any food they see go uneaten. Inside your fuzzy little pony's brain, there is still a little bit of that wild horse instinct that says, *hey, this might be the last food for 34 miles! I should eat all of it that I can so I have enough energy to make it to the next food source without getting eaten by a lion!* Unfortunately, the fact that your pony has never known a day of hunger in her life doesn't factor in when that voice starts talking.

When a pony has a tiny caloric expenditure and a massive food intake, you know where that's heading. They put on weight faster than a pregnant woman in a sitcom. Unfortunately, obesity has a number of health concerns attached to it. For one, the mere fact that your pony is packing around all that extra weight means extra wear and tear on *everything*. Joints, hooves, tendons, you name it. Everything has to work harder and gets worn down faster. Since a lot of minis and ponies have really impressive life spans, it's important that he doesn't wear out his body unnecessarily.

Second, obesity is a huge risk factor for developing laminitis[18]. There's a common saying among farriers that there are two types of ponies: those who *have* had laminitis and those that *will* have laminitis. That's really just reflective of the fact that about 90% of ponies that we see are either overweight or obese, and that puts them at risk. Insulin dysregulation often goes along with obesity (and usually goes away when the weight problem is resolved, if you needed some good news.[19]) so getting blood work done on your overweight pony and managing any insulin/blood sugar imbalances is really important.

[18] Carter, R.A., Treiber, K.H., Geor, R.J., Douglass, L. and Harris, P.A. (2009). Prediction of incipient pasture-associated laminitis from hyperinsulinaemia, hyperleptinaemia and generalised and localised obesity in a cohort of ponies. *Equine Veterinary Journal, 41:* P. 171-178
[19] Freestone, J.F., Beadle, R., Shoemaker, K., Bessin, R.T., Wolfsheimer, K.J. and Church, C. (1992). Improved insulin sensitivity in hyperinsulinaemic ponies through physical conditioning and controlled feed intake. *Equine Veterinary Journal, 24:* 187-190

A laminitic mini hoof

Third, obesity puts the entire body into a constant state of inflammation, which is literally damaging to every tissue in the body[20].

So if obesity is so unhealthy for your pony, but the wild horse in his head won't let him stop eating, what's a pony to do? Rely on you to be his conscience for him! He doesn't know when he's eaten enough, but with a little research, you can figure it out for him. If you need to enact a weight loss plan, you should talk to your vet to make sure that you're considering the whole picture and not missing any pieces to the weight loss puzzle. A lot of the work will go into limiting food quantity, like keeping your pony in a dry lot or wearing a grazing muzzle, but some of it will also be a matter of choosing low sugar, low starch food options. There's a big difference between eating a pound of cucumber slices or a pound of butter, calorie wise. Likewise, your pony can eat a lot more stemmy hay than he can grain. In fact, unless he needs a ration balancer, he almost certainly doesn't need any grain at all. And increasing exercise can help burn off some of those calories, whether that means turnout with an energetic friend who will encourage him to play, playing active games with you, or pulling a cart or working with a small rider. Any calorie burned is one that's not contributing to health problems, so get to work!

Miniature horses, like many animals who have been bred over a long period of time for a specific look, have developed some health problems. A lot of these will show up at birth, and there's a few to be aware of when it comes to hooves.

Some minis suffer from Angular Limb Deformities, which is just a fancy way of saying that her legs are crooked. Depending on genetics and how well the deformity was managed when she was young, this could be mild to pretty severe, and its effect on the hoof will be correspondingly more or less drastic. If there is a noticeable deviation, oftentimes the hoof will grow higher on one side than the other, and it might flare. Usually this can be managed through consistent trimming, but in severe cases your farrier might need to use a shoe of some kind to prevent uneven wearing and rebalance the hoof. In an adult, you cannot correct conformation, but you can limit some of the hoof distortion. If the mini is young and their bones haven't fully ossified yet, now is the time to make a plan with your vet and farrier to see if it is something that can or should be corrected.

The good news is, if you keep your pony at a good, trim weight, and on a regular trimming schedule, they often have really good, healthy feet. Most non-working minis and ponies don't need any hoof care besides regular trimming, and even many working ponies manage to stay comfortable barefoot. Of course, if they have delt with some laminitis in the past, they may need a little extra hoof help.

A quick word of advice - just because your pony is small doesn't mean she shouldn't

[20] Vick M.M., Adams A.A., Murphy B.A., Sessions D.R., Horohov D.W., Cook R.F., Shelton B.J., Fitzgerald B.P. (2007). Relationships among inflammatory cytokines, obesity, and insulin sensitivity in the horse. *J Anim Sci. May;85(5):* P. 1144-55.

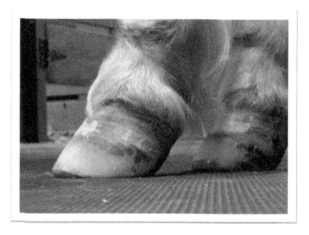

Regular trims are an important aspect of health care for your pony

have good, regularly scheduled hoof care. As Dr. Suess wisely pointed out, a person's a person, no matter how small! Just because she doesn't have an athletic career doesn't mean that she will suffer less if her hooves are neglected. Don't forget to help her practice her farrier manners either. Just because your farrier *can* wrestle with her, doesn't mean they want to. Your pony will get better quality work with less stress for her, and you and the farrier, if she can stand politely to be trimmed.

And now, for something completely different…

Quick Takeaways

- **Minis are extremely prone to obesity, and therefore laminitis.**
- **Minis may struggle with conformation issues.**
- **Even though they are small, they should still be kept on a regular trimming cycle.**

Drafts - The last type we're going to talk about is draft horses. Once the Mack trucks of historic transportation, the tanks of mediaeval warfare, and the super powered tractors of family farming, draft horses were literally the engines that powered the world before. Nowadays, they usually have it a little easier, but they are still revered for their awesome size and strength, and oftentimes have kind and gentle hearts to boot.

If one of these giants has found its way into your barn (and heart) you already know that everything is a little different when you double the size, and hooves are no exception. Although their hooves increase proportionally in size, they are still bearing a terrific amount of weight. Going back to the fact that at a gallop, 2.5 times the horses weight passes through the hoof, we're talking big numbers now. With weight ranges from a light 1700 pounds for a small Clydesdale or Percheron up to 2700 pounds for the larger Shires, you could be looking at 6,750 pounds of force per hoof if your draft gets to galloping. That's about the same amount of weight as a Chevy Tahoe.

So what happens to your draft horse's hoof when you drop a Tahoe on it? All those shock dissipating structures go into overdrive, and sometimes they go past their critical limit. When the hoof wall has to absorb more shock than what it can take, you start developing flares, which is super common among draft horses.

Another heavy-weight breakdown that you might see in your draft is in the collateral cartilages, those flexible, springy cartilage plates in the back half of her hoof that you can feel near the heel bulbs. When the collateral cartilages are asked to flex more than what they can compensate for, the body tries to compensate by making them stronger and more rigid. In this case, that means converting cartilage into bone, a process called ossification. If you see or feel a very hard, inflexible bump above the hairline in the heel bulb region on your draft, she may have gone through this process. It's called sidebone, and we'll discuss it in more detail in Chapter 31, but the important thing to know right now is that it is a symptom of a lot of concussion, but in and of itself it isn't painful or damaging to your horse.

A lot of draft breeds sport some pretty cool feathering, or long hair in the fetlock and pastern region, sometimes completely covering the hoof. Typically the more feathered breeds were originally bred primarily as war horses, while non-feathered draft breeds were more frequently farm horses. As you know if you have a draft with feather, it can be really hard to keep clean if your horse is in the mud (say, plowing a field) so farmers may have avoided feather for that reason. It is thought to provide some protection from water running down the legs (standing out in the rain for instance) something that was

Even regularly trimmed draft feet can experience bruising, flaring, and cracks

probably considered when breeding a war horse that had to perform in any weather.

One downside to all that cool feather is that if it gets wet, it does hold moisture against the skin and allow bacteria and fungus to multiply. The most common infection that we see is scratches, or pastern dermatitis, an itchy, scabby, sometimes painful disease that can cause some serious inflammation. According to Purdue University, scratches can be a mix of bacteria, fungus, and even parasites, so if you've been treating unsuccessfully, your vet may be able to take a look and design a more targeted approach based on the exact mix you're dealing with[21].

Since moisture is a big risk factor when it comes to scratches, keeping your draft horse in a clean, dry environment can really help. This might mean changing turnout, especially if he goes out in a muddy area, or even waiting until the dew dries off the grass before turning him out. It also could mean bedding with more absorptive shavings, or stripping his bedding more frequently if he likes to make a mess in his stall.

You can also use topical antibacterial or antifungal shampoos and creams to get scratches under control. In order to get it down to the affected skin

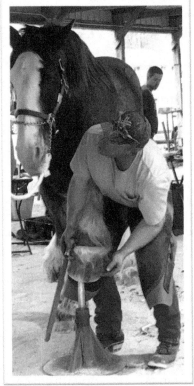

Feathers can be a challenge when it comes to hoof care

[21] College of Veterinary Medicine, Perdue University. *Understanding and Treating Scratches in Horses*. Retrieved from https://vet.purdue.edu/vth/large-animal/equine-health-tip-understanding-and-treating-scratches-in-horses.php

instead of just the hair, you may need to temporarily clip the affected area. I know it's going to kill you to see all that beautiful feather on the floor, but trust me, get him healthy first and the feather will come back. Clipping will also help his infected skin to dry quicker, so that's another bonus.

Also, if you've noticed that he's sensitive in the infected area, make sure you warn your vet and farrier before they try to pick up his legs. Not only will they try to keep him comfortable, but it will also help them stay safe since nobody needs to accidently poke a sensitive spot on a creature as big and strong as your draft horse!

One last word to the wise if you have a draft horse in your care: please, please, *please* teach him how to stand politely to be trimmed. If you've ever had to look for a farrier for your draft, you might have noticed that a lot of your phone calls weren't returned, and those you had conversations with got a little less interested when you mentioned your draft horse. That's nothing personal, but as a working farrier, I can tell you that I have higher behavior standards for a draft horse on my books than I do for a pony or even a small saddle horse.

Yes, I would like every horse that I get under to be cooperative and help me to do the best job I can for them, but when a pony or small horse tries to pull a leg away, I've got a pretty good chance of hanging on and getting done. When a 2000-pound draft pulls her leg? I'm flying across the aisle and hoping I land on my feet. I certainly can't guarantee quality work under those circumstances and for my own safety, I usually have to say no to draft horses that don't stand appropriately for trimming. I'm not trying to be rude, but my risk of injury goes up a lot when the size of the horse doubles. It's not that draft horses are mean, or trying to hurt people, it's just that they are way, way bigger than us and sometimes they forget that.

What can you do to make sure that your draft horse is on your farrier's "good list"? As with any horse, practice picking up her feet often and make sure that she's not putting them down until you give her the okay. Especially if you have a draft foal in your care, practice this as often as possible. If she has this one skill, it's going to hugely improve the quality of hoof care that she gets, and her overall hoof health throughout her life. You know she's a sweetheart who would never purposely hurt anyone, so all you have to do is put in a little training time to make sure she doesn't *accidently* hurt anyone.

How can this help you when you're trying to find a farrier? As soon as you say *draft horse* they are starting to wonder, *is this a good draft horse or a draft horse that is going to launch me into a lunar orbit?* So follow up that information with some facts to allay their concern. For instance, you can say: *I have a draft horse that I am looking to get trimmed. I practice picking up hooves with her every time I'm out at the barn and she is usually very good for it.* Or, *I have a draft*

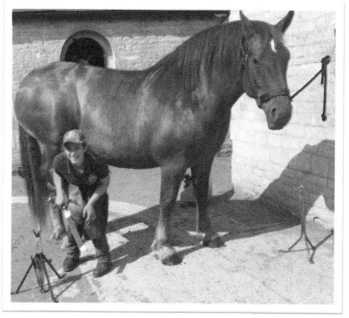

The sheer size of draft horses means that being well-behaved is very important

horse who used to be really bad with his feet. He liked to try to pull them away, but we've been working on it and he usually holds them up for a minute or so now. This gives the farrier some information they can work with and lets them decide if that sounds like something they can work with. It is really important to be honest in this stage, even if you think they won't like what you have to say, because you never know what health issues that farrier might be dealing with. If the farrier you are talking to has a slipped disc in her back, she may not want to take on a draft horse that likes to lean, but she might also be able to refer you to a healthier farrier.

So to recap - practice picking up hooves with your draft, and then be honest and considerate when talking to a potential farrier. Remember, just because the farrier might have their doubts about taking on a draft, doesn't mean you can't win them over, especially if your draft is well behaved. You already love your draft horse. It's up to you to convince the potential farrier that they will love your draft too!

Quick Takeaways

- **Draft horses' hooves take a terrific amount of stress, so they can be prone to flaring and arthritis.**
- **Good behavior for trimming or shoeing is extremely important in draft horses.**

9 PUTTING IT ALL TOGETHER

You've read all about the structures that make up the hoof and what their functions are, and hopefully you learned something new and gained an appreciation for what an amazing and specialized structure your horse is walking around on. And honestly, the more in depth you go in equine anatomy, the more fascinating and remarkable it gets, down to the molecular level.

However, I'm guessing that you are less interested in molecular biology and more interested in applying this knowledge to improve your horse's life. So in this last anatomy chapter, we're going to talk about what makes up a healthy foot, go through a visual good foot checklist that you can use to assess your horse's hooves, and I'm going to tell you why it's worthwhile to get input from your farrier before purchasing a horse.

First up: what is a good foot? Is it some kind of arbitrary textbook ideal? Any assessment of the quality of a hoof should be based on whether or not the hoof is strong enough to function the way it should to keep your horse sound and happy. That's the whole point anyway, isn't it? Unless you're planning a career for your horse in hoof modeling, the most important questions to ask are more about function than some aesthetic goal. A good hoof does the following things:

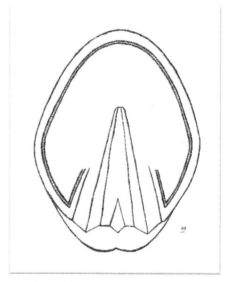

Classic front shape

Classic hind shape

- Protects the sensitive internal structures of the foot from the outside environment, including rocks, mud, and bacteria. This means that your horse *doesn't* frequently experience painful hoof bruising and abscesses and is able to walk comfortably across any footing she's usually exposed to.

- Absorbs shock appropriately so that impact doesn't cause damage to the internal structures or other parts of your horse's body. This also means that absorbing shock doesn't cause damage to the hoof structures such as hoof cracks or flares, since these both show an overloaded structure.

- Is a balanced, useful structure for movement. In other words, there are no imbalances

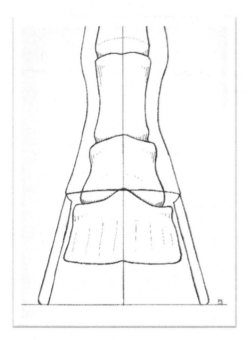

Hoof walls should be straight and even

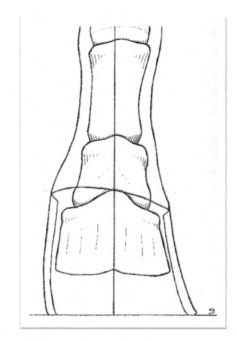

Flared hoof walls are not as strong

that cause unnecessary leverage that will damage the muscles and tendons involved in movement.

Essentially, a good hoof allows your horse to lead an active life without causing either immediate or long-term damage. If there's anything you take away from all this anatomy, I hope that it's a greater respect for each structure and how important it is for your horse that they all function well and work together. Hooves aren't just lifeless blocks of horn at the end of your horse's legs.

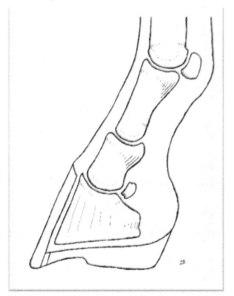

From the side, the toe should be a straight line

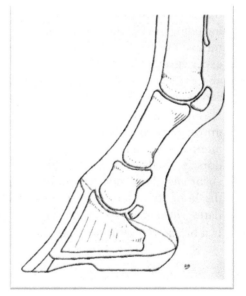

A dished toe adds extra stress to the lamina

Now let's get into the specifics of physical signs you can look for that will tell you if your horse's hoof is doing those jobs, and if they have a good chance of doing it long term. I'm calling this the Good Foot Checklist, and I'll tell you what we're looking for in each category, how to find it, and why it makes a difference. Now, this checklist is not pass or fail. Your horse might tick a lot of boxes but have one or two things that don't look so good. That doesn't mean you should fire your horse and look for a different one who is Practically Perfect in Every Way. It just means that those are areas that might need some extra maintenance, either from you or your farrier, or both. So grab your hoof pick and pen and let's get started!

Structure	Where you'll see it	Good structure	Weak structure	Why it's important
Hoof wall	From in front of your horse, at hoof level	Straight walls continue at the same angle from the coronary band to the ground, wider at the bottom and narrower at the top, coronary band appears straight. Horn quality is smooth and shiny.	Walls are flared and bent, horn is cracked or split, coronary band is higher on one side than the other. Horn appears rough, ridged, or dull.	Essential for protection of the coffin bone, even weight bearing, and shock absorption.
	From the side, hoof level	Straight walls continue at the same angle from the coronary band down, toe angle matches pastern angle, coronary band is only	Toe is dished or flared, heel changes angle, toe angle is higher or lower than the pastern angle, hooves have splits or cracks, coronary band has severe arch, growth rings are wider	Essential for protection of the coffin bone, even weight bearing, shock absorption.

		slightly curved, heels are at a similar angle to toe, any growth rings are even from toe to heel.	in heel than toe.	
	With the hoof picked up	Wall has good thickness all the way around, even in the quarters. Wall has a relatively symmetrical shape, heels are roughly at the highest, widest point of the frog. Wall extends past the sole.	Wall is very thin, broken off, or ragged. Wall is flared, heels are crushed forward, sole is contacting the ground before hoof wall.	Protection, shock absorption, traction
White Line	With the hoof picked up	White line is narrow, tight, and even. There are no gaps or stretched areas.	White line is stretched, wide, or wider in some areas than others. White line shows blood or bruising. White line has wide gaps.	Protection of internal structures, allowing flexion of sole and hoof wall while sealing the seam between them.
Sole	With the hoof picked	Sole is arched away from	Sole is flat against the ground. Sole is	Protection, shock absorption,

	up	the ground. Sole is thick enough that you cannot flex it at any point.	prolapsed near the toe. Sole is thin enough to flex with your thumbs.	traction
Frog	With the hoof picked up	Frog appears smooth, wedge shaped, and fills in most of the space between the heels. Frog either contacts the ground when weight bearing or is close to contacting the ground.	Frog is ragged, narrow, flat, and doesn't contact the ground under any circumstances. Frog has deep central sulcus. Frog has pockets of black, foul-smelling material. Frog is sensitive to picking	Protection, shock absorption, blood pumping
Hoof shape	With the hoof picked up	Front feet are basically round or oval in shape, hinds are rounded diamond shapes or narrow ovals	Feet are square in shape, fronts are excessively pointed, hinds are excessively rounded.	Pointed hinds are necessary for propulsion, Fronts are rounded to give freedom to break in any direction necessary.
Hoof pairs	From the front and side, looking at both hooves	Both front feet or both hind feet are roughly the same size and have roughly the	One foot is excessively larger or smaller than its mate, one foot is much more upright or lower	Excessive differences in size might indicate a long-term injury. Extreme

	together	same angles.	angled than the other	angle differences between pairs puts each foot under different stresses and makes it harder for a horse to move evenly and efficiently.

How'd you do? If your horse got all A's , good for you and your very well built horse. If you discovered a few places where your horse seems to be lacking, ask your farrier next time you see them if they feel that it falls within the range of normal or if there's something you should do to try to help your horse out. Sometimes just being aware of a potential problem before it occurs means you can change up something with management or shoeing and never have an issue.

You can also use this checklist if you are looking at a new horse that you're thinking about purchasing. Again, just because they fail on a few points doesn't mean you have to rule them out, but you might want to talk to your vet

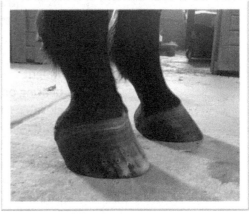

Feet with drastically different angles will require skilled management

and farrier about it.

Speaking of which, let's talk about an underutilized resource that you have when you're looking at a new horse: The farrier. If you already have a farrier that you work with, by all means show them the horse you are considering! With today's good quality cellphone cameras, it is

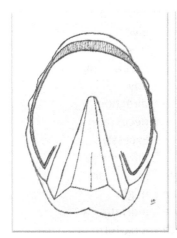

The white line should not be stretched, nor should the hoof wall be missing in any area

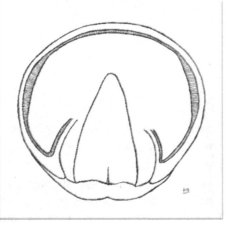

The white line should not be stretched in the quarters

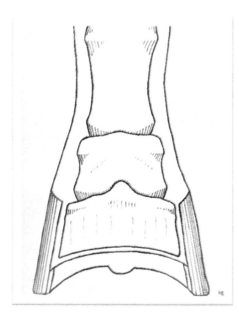

A cupped sole absorbs shock

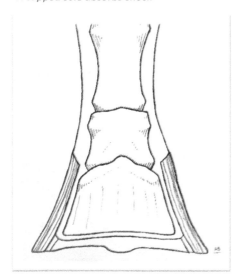

A flat sole is less functional

really easy to take a few quick hoof shots and send them on to your farrier. Whenever you are taking hoof photos for your farrier, take the photos with your phone at ground level. This gives a good, undistorted image so they can see the hoof clearly. Side views, front views, and solar views (a shot of the bottom of the hoof) will all give your farrier valuable information. Just make sure the horse isn't standing in grass, sand or deep bedding when you take your pictures.

Better yet, see if your farrier has time to come with you to the pre-purchase exam, or to come see the horse in person.

Although you've learned a lot of pointers for looking at horse's hooves, your farrier has probably spent quite a few years looking at and working on hooves, so they have developed an eye for what type of problems are fixable and which ones would require a magic wand or a full hoof transplant (sadly, neither is available for purchase just yet). This is more about experience than anything. Plus, they probably won't be as emotionally invested in your potential horse yet, so they aren't wearing rose-colored glasses.

The other side of the coin is that the horse's current farrier can be a valuable source of information too. Ask the seller if you could get their farrier's contact info so your farrier can talk to them

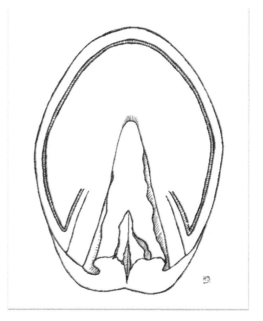

The frog should not be ragged or have deep crevices

about any special needs the horse might have. Don't expect their farrier to start dishing dirt on the horse, but they will often let you know if there's anything out of the ordinary so you can be prepared. They can also provide a history if your farrier has any questions about what they are seeing or why a specific shoe was chosen.

The more you know about your horse (or your potential horse) the better you can keep tabs on their hoof health and keep everything running smoothly. After all, buyers, sellers, horse owners, vets, and farriers, all of us should have the same goal of keeping horses sound, healthy, happy, and in a good situation for their individual needs.

Quick Takeaways

- **A good hoof is one that protects the internal structures of the foot, one that efficiently absorbs shock, and one that is balanced.**
- **Assessing the hoof can be broken down structure by structure, allowing us to accurately grade a hoof's long term chances of soundness.**
- **Use your farrier as a resource of hoof knowledge.**

Part 2

Questions About Farriers: All The Things You Wish You Knew But Don't Want To Ask.

10 HELP, I NEED A FARRIER!

One of the worst feelings is when you lose a professional that you really liked and trusted, and now you're adrift, with no leads and no clue who to call or how to know if they know what they're doing. It's enough to make anyone take up a nail-biting habit. But for right now, don't think about that. Think about how much better you'll feel when you have a step-by-step plan of action that lands you a great new farrier. They're skilled, polite, and smoking hot … Okay, I can't actually guarantee that part. I *can* help you figure out what to do next and get you out of the purgatory of trying to find a farrier. I'm going to use the word farrier for this discussion, but I realize you might be looking for a barefoot trimmer as well. All the same steps apply, but it's easier to write farrier than "hoof care professional" every time.

There are any number of reasons why you might find yourself farrier-less, like either you or your farrier moving, your farrier retiring or cutting back, or either one of you decided to end the professional relationship because it wasn't working out. Each scenario comes with its own challenges, but there are still a lot of things that hold true for everyone.

And you do need to find somebody pronto to take care of your horse's hooves. According to a study performed in 2016, horses' hooves had already showed noticeable angle changes at the end of a 4-6 week shoeing cycle, leading researchers to suggest that a cycle longer than 6 weeks might increase the risk of long-term injuries through cumulative, excessive loading[22]. Putting off hoof care isn't an option.

So your plan, of course, is to find the absolute best farrier available for your horse. Notice I didn't say the most expensive or the most popular. There are some people who charge a fortune that are better salesman than they are farriers, and there are some extremely skilled farriers who might be charging a lot less. The only red flag I would watch for in price is if you find someone *significantly* below the going rate for your area. If they don't have the confidence that they can keep clientele if they charge a fair price for their work, they are saying that they don't think their skills are up to snuff (and I would take them at their word on that one). Remember, quality farriers keep clients through their work, not through their pricing. That said, a little higher or lower than the going rate? Probably not a big deal.

There are also some farriers who may not qualify as the most popular, but might be doing the best job. For instance, if you are in a sport that has a big Florida circuit, you might be tempted to think that a shoer who doesn't do the circuit probably isn't that good. There's also a chance that they do great work, but they don't want to put up with the hassle of travel, enjoy having a little slower winter, or don't want to be away from their family for that long.

You may also find that some farriers don't have the best bedside manner but consistently keep their horses sound. If you can put up with blunt conversation, then they could be the best choice. If you tend to let things like that bother you, you might be better off with someone a little more diplomatic.

I think we can all agree that a good farrier is one who keeps your horse sound, interacts safely with your horse, and is reliable and professional to deal with. So how do you actually find someone who checks these boxes?

The most useful tool available to you is word of mouth. If you keep your horse at a boarding facility, take a look at the other horses there. Do their feet look well cared for and are they typically sound? If so, ask the owner who their farrier is, but don't just ask if they like their

---

[22] Leśniak K., Williams J., Kuznik K., Douglas P. (2017). Does a 4-6 Week Shoeing Interval Promote Optimal Foot Balance in the Working Equine? *Animals (Basel). Mar 29;7(4):* P. 29

farrier. It's a little like getting set up on a blind date. You don't just ask if they think he's a nice guy, you want specifics. So ask questions like these:

- Does your farrier explain things to you if you have a question?
- Is your farrier compassionate with lame or old horses?
- How is your farrier at keeping appointments?
- Does your farrier listen to you if you have a concern?
- Is your farrier taking on clients?

Don't start by asking about price. They could charge $5 and still be a really bad deal if they lame up your horse. Find out about their relevant skill sets first, and *then* find out how much they charge if you decide they sound like a good fit.

The type of questions listed above will give you some good clues about whether they respect the horses and clients they work for. If they don't, they are not a good fit. End of story. Obviously there are some negotiables. Maybe they don't like to work on babies but you don't have one and don't plan to get one. That's a non-issue for you, but it would be a deal breaker if you had a stud farm.

If the person you're talking to likes their farrier, see if you can get them to put in a good word for you. Even if a farrier's books are pretty full, they will often make an effort to take on new people who have been recommended by a client they trust.

What if you keep your horse at your house and there aren't any other horse owners around? You can ask your vet who they would recommend in the area. Vets work closely and frequently with a lot of farriers, so if they know you, they will probably have a pretty good idea of what local farriers you might get along with.

If you are looking for a new farrier because your old farrier retired, use them as a resource. If the retiring farrier is willing to recommend you to another farrier, that's the golden ticket. Not only will they be recommending a farrier that they trust, who they believe will take good care of your horse, they have also put their stamp of approval on you and your horse, and that gives you a big boost in your odds of having the new farrier take you on.

Even if they aren't able to set you up with a new farrier, ask them for a list of farriers in your area that they think do a good job. At least that narrows down your choices and increases your odds of getting someone with the skills to take good care of your horse.

What if you move from another area and you don't know *anybody* here yet? Don't worry, you still have options.

Ask your farrier before you move if they know of anyone in your new area. If your farrier is involved in local or national farrier associations or attends farrier competitions (yep, that's a thing!) there's a good chance they've got connections somewhere near where you are moving. At the very least, they can put you in contact with someone who knows the farriers in the area. At best, they might be able to recommend you to a trusted farrier friend.

If they can't help you, you're still not to the point where you have to start google searching. Look up your state farrier association and take a look at which members are near your area. You can also go on the American Farrier's Association website, americanfarriers.org, and use their Find a Farrier tool to search for farriers in your area. Being a member of an association doesn't guarantee that they are a great farrier, but these associations were formed by and for farriers who want to improve themselves, so members are at least likely to be involved in continuing education of some kind. Websites like these also usually list certifications that each farrier has earned. We'll talk more about why that's important in Chapter 11.

Okay, hopefully at this point you've got a couple names from sources you trust. That's the toughest part, so give yourself a pat on the back and grab your phone for step two.

What do you say on the phone? Be prepared to leave a message because most farriers are pretty busy people and they probably aren't picking up every unknown number that calls their phone (okay, I guess that's pretty much everybody nowadays). But regardless, there are a few things that you should include whether you are leaving a message or having a conversation. Want another bullet point list? You got it.

- Your name, obviously.
- Where you got their info. This is especially helpful if one of their clients or a farrier or vet told you to call them, because this acts as a reference for you.
- How many horses do you have and what type? You don't have to go into great detail here, but you could say something like *I have one thoroughbred in four shoes that I use for eventing and one retired warmblood that's barefoot*. This is also the time to tell them if you have a horse that needs special therapeutic care, though again, keep it basic: *I have a 25-year-old walk-trot pony who has had a lot of laminitis in the past*. Info like this lets them know what type of work you need and gives them an estimate of what kind of time slot you might require (which is important if their books are pretty full). I know you don't want to hear this, but now is when you come clean about any behavioral issues. *I have a four-year-old OTTB and he's pretty nervous for shoeing*. Then you immediately follow with the good news: what you are doing to help with the situation. *I've been practicing holding up his feet and I will always be there to hold him for shoeing*. Or, *we have sedation available if you feel that it is necessary*. Let them know that you're not expecting them to get beat up arm wrestling your thousand-pound baby!
- Where are your horses located? This one is really important and a lot of people forget to mention it. Unfortunately, every farrier has a limited range that they can cover with their business, so if you tell them what town your horses are located in, they know immediately if that's within their range or not. Some farriers might be negotiable on this point, adding a trip charge if you are outside of their range. Even if they don't cover your area, that's not the end of the line; ask them who they would recommend in your area.

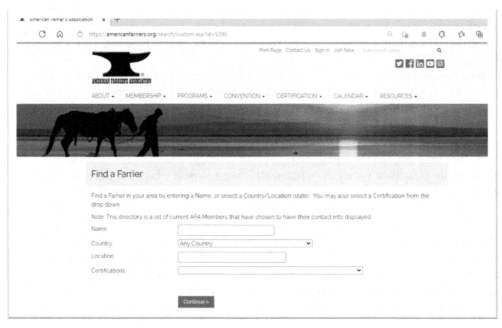

The AFA's Find-a-farrier page

- When are your horses due? If you know ahead of time that you are losing your farrier, I would highly recommend starting the process of finding a new farrier *right away*. We all like to procrastinate on unpleasant experiences, but trust me, you will have way better luck finding a farrier if you need an appointment in six weeks than if you need an appointment in the next few days. Remember, good farriers are likely to be booked out for weeks, so get in early.
- End with a repeat of your name and your best contact number, and something like *I look forward to hearing from you*. Like any interaction, a little bit of good manners goes a long way to making people feel good about working with you.

Again, don't lead off your phone call with the question *how much do you charge?* This is a pet peeve for a lot of farriers, and with good reason. Although farriers understand that most people aren't working with unlimited funds, when that's the first, or only, question you ask, the farrier is likely to feel that you are more concerned with cost than quality. Understandably, you might want to get a ballpark number so that you can confirm that it fits your budget, but wait to ask this question until later in the conversation so that the farrier understands that your first priority is getting high quality care for your horse.

Awesome, you've given them all the basic info they need to know if you might be a good fit for their business! Hopefully at this point you will have at least one farrier from your list who can come out for your horse. When they actually are there in front of your horse, don't forget to share any history you have on the horse. A past lameness, even if it is totally resolved, might give them some ideas about what they need to keep an eye on for your horse.

There is one tough circumstance that some horse owners run into. What if you only have one horse and you can't get a farrier to come out for her? It's not nearly as efficient for a farrier business to have a bunch of one-horse stops, since they have fuel and drive time invested between each stop. You still have a couple of options though. If it's within your budget, ask the prospective farrier if they would be willing to come out for a higher fee. They may offer you a number, and you can decide if that sounds worthwhile or not. You may also be able to trailer your horse to a facility that they already work at. If you already trailer to a barn for lessons, this can especially be a good option. Or, if they already go to another barn in your area, see if they would allow you to bring your horse there to be shod. Lastly, if you have nearby friend or neighbor with a horse, maybe you can get on a farrier schedule together.

You've done your research, made your call, and you're scheduled for your first appointment with a new farrier. Let's say you see some letters written after their name. If you've paid attention, you may have noticed a variety of different abbreviations on farriers business cards or on websites. What does all that mean and which ones are the best? Let's find out about certification and qualifications in the farrier trade.

Quick Takeaways

- **Use your past farrier, vet, or a knowledgably horse friend as resources for farrier recommendations.**
- **Ask questions to make sure you're getting a good fit for your horse.**

11 FARRIER QUALIFICATIONS – DOES THIS PERSON KNOW WHAT THEY'RE DOING?

If you read the title of this chapter and thought, *"Of course they do. They don't just let anyone be a farrier, you have to be trained and take a test to shoe horses, right?"* you may be in for a surprise.

Want to hear something scary? In the United States, there is no legal qualification to be a practicing farrier. There are no educational requirements or certifications necessary. In fact, if you decided today to go out and start shoeing other people's horses, no one would be able to stop you.

If you were a hairdresser in the US, you would have to go to school, pass a certification test, and clock continuing education hours every year, in order to cut and color people's hair. What happens if you mess up? Someone gets an ugly haircut or maybe, worst case, you give someone a reaction by incorrectly using a hair dye.

If you're a farrier in the US, none of those things apply to you. You don't need to educate yourself. You don't need to go to school or pass any kind of basic skills test. You don't need to let anyone know if you are continuing your education or not. What happens if you mess up? Maybe you hot nail a horse and it's lame for a few weeks, or maybe you miss a vital warning sign and cripple a horse for the rest of its life. It's no laughing matter.

So what can you do to make sure that the farrier you choose is educated and knowledgeable? Fortunately, there are several farrier associations in the US that exist to further education in the trade. If you see a farrier who has letters printed after their name, they most likely got it by participating in voluntary certifications through one of these associations.

What are these associations and what credentials do they offer?

The two largest certifying bodies in the US are the American Farrier's Association and the American Association of Professional Farriers. There are also a few smaller organizations which, as of 2021, each have less than 200 active members, including the Brotherhood of Working Farriers and the Equine Lameness Prevention Organization.

The American Farrier's Association is primarily interested in farrier education, certification, and research. Their certification program is the only one recognized internationally, and they offer three levels of certification and three specialty endorsements.

The American Association of Professional Farriers is based on the tracking of continuing education, and they offer a slightly different system. They have two levels of accreditation which represent the amount of time you have been a member, and two credential levels that are task-based assessments. How about another handy dandy chart to explain?

Association	Initials	Full name	Requirements
American Farrier's Association (AFA)	CF	Certified Farrier	CFs must shoe a pair of feet with pre-made shoes in one hour, submit a shoe display of common modifications, perform a modification on site in 30 minutes, and pass a written exam.
AFA	CTF	Certified Tradesman	CTFs must shoe four feet with premade

		Farrier	shoes within two hours, forge a handmade shoe to a pattern in 30 minutes, and pass a written exam
AFA	CJF	Certified Journeyman Farrier	CJFs must shoe four feet with handmade shoes within two hours, forge a handmade bar shoe to a pattern in 35 minutes, and pass a written exam.
AFA	TE	Therapeutic Endorsement	TEs must present and defend two case studies to a panel, submit a shoe board with a selection of therapeutic shoes, forge a handmade therapeutic shoe on site to a pattern, and pass a written and an oral exam.
AFA	FE	Forging Endorsement	FEs must write an instructional article explaining the process of forging a specific shoe, submit a shoe display made up of handmade shoes, and forge a specified handmade shoe on site.
AFA	EE	Educators Endorsement	EEs must submit a paper on education to the panel, write an educational article, deliver a lecture at the AFA national convention, and perform a hands-on demonstration.
AAPF	AF	Accredited	AFs must have

		Farrier	between 2 and 5 years of experience and maintain at least 24 hours of continuing education (CE) credits per year
AAPF	APF	Accredited Professional Farrier	APFs must have 5 or more years of experience and maintain at least 24 hours of CE credits per year
AAPF	AF-1 or APF-1	Accredited Farrier or Accredited Professional Farrier with Foundation Credential	AF-1s or APF-1s must complete a 395-question multiple choice open book test within 1 year.

As you can see, each organization takes a different approach. AFA certification tests are far more rigorous, but they don't require CE credits. AAPF credentialing is more of a study resource than a test per se, but they do require yearly CE credits. Letters from either association do prove that the farrier in question makes an effort to improve themselves professionally, and that's what you're looking for.

North American farriers can also earn certification through the Worshipful Company of Farriers, which is the certifying body for the United Kingdom. Certification through the WCF is the gold standard throughout the world, so a small number of very motivated farriers from other countries choose to pursue it. The levels available are the Diploma of the Worshipful Company of Farriers (DipWCF), the Associate of the Worshipful Company of Farriers (AWCF), and the Fellow of the Worshipful Company of

A shoe display showcases the farrier's forging skills

Farriers (FWCF). These are all extremely rigorous tests, and farriers who have these initials have put an immense amount of time, money, and sweat into their craft.

Most new farriers start out in the trade by either attending a trade school, doing an apprenticeship, or both. Trade schools are a great way to get a foundation in both the book work side of the business and the hands-on aspects of the trade. The quality of an apprenticeship depends on the skill of the farrier they are learning from, but an apprenticeship with a quality professional gives a new farrier indispensable knowledge and experience in a one-on-one learning

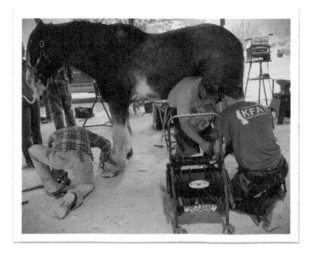

When farriers work together, everyone benefits

environment.

As an aside, if your farrier has an apprentice, don't get nervous every time they touch your horse. Although apprentices may not have the experience and skill that your farrier brings to the table, remember that your farrier has put their stamp of approval on this student. Responsible farriers only allow apprentices to do the tasks that they can safely and correctly complete. If you trust your farrier, trust their assessment of their apprentices' skills. Most farriers are going to err on the side of caution when it comes to assigning new tasks to apprentices for safety's sake. In time, you'll find that the apprentice will bring plenty to the table too.

Completing school or an apprenticeship doesn't mean you know it all though. It should be only the beginning of the educational journey. Experience is also a great teacher, provided you're open minded enough to learn from it. There are some people who have one year of experience repeated 20 times and learn nothing, and other people who learn from every experience they have.

Even if your farrier doesn't have any letters behind their name, you can ask them what kind of continuing education they are involved in. There are a *ton* of educational resources out there for farriers, and all of them will develop different skill sets and make your farrier more well-rounded.

Farrier competitions are a big way that farriers can get together and push themselves. In most competitions, farriers can sign up ahead of time to get a list of the shoes and tasks that they will have to do in each section of the competition. They may not be familiar with some of the types of shoes, but that's just a good opportunity to practice something new and it'll come in handy if they ever run into a horse that needs it. On the

Farrier competitions are a great learning resource

day of the competition, all the competitors will get together and each person will do the best work that they can under the time limit. The judge, usually a well respected farrier, will look at each job and often give pointers or feedback to the individual competitors. This can be a really good way for farriers to get out of their comfort zones, improve their skills, and get advice from skilled farriers from around the country. Some competitions have even added a theory section, where the competitors have to write a paper explaining what they would do for a specific case.

There are also multiple national conferences and conventions available to farriers in the US and internationally. These are awesome opportunities for networking, lectures by skilled farriers and vets, and a chance to peruse the latest products available. There are also multiple small, local clinics available with lectures and demonstrations.

Even if a farrier can't get away for a weekend, there are also trade magazines available which cover a huge range of topics, farrier podcasts, and even online lectures and classes available. In our

Farrier clinics are offered around the country

modern time, there is really no excuse for a farrier not to be educating themselves.

If they're already a professional farrier, what's the need for continuing ed, you might be asking, if you're not in a field that requires it. Aside from the fact that nobody knows everything about their field, there have been some amazing jumps in diagnostic technology in the last few years, and that means our knowledge of what is actually going on inside the hoof is growing by leaps and bounds. If you haven't learned anything new about hooves in the last fifteen years, you're way behind, and that makes this a really exciting time to be involved in continuing education in the farrier trade.

Quick Takeaways
- **Farrier training and certification is completely voluntary in America.**
- **Farrier certifications vary hugely in requirements.**
- **A farrier who takes part in continuing education is a good choice because they are pushing themselves to constantly improve.**

12 HOW TO KEEP A GOOD FARRIER

If you don't know why your farrier seems grumpy, don't worry, you've come to the right place.

Drop yourself into this scenario: You show up right on time for your farrier appointment and run out to catch your horse from the field. By the time you come back in with your horse, your farrier has his stuff set up, but you're picking up some grumpy vibes. You throw your horse in her stall to pee and move some stuff out of the shoeing area.

"Is that enough space?" you ask your farrier, eyeing the heavy hay bales that you'd really rather not have to move.

"Sure," comes the terse reply. You shrug it off, wondering if he got up on the wrong side of the bed today.

You grab your horse and put her in the crossties, then grab a wheelbarrow to start cleaning her stall while she's in the aisle. Might as well multi-task, and she doesn't usually need supervision for shoeing. It's a little tight in the aisle but you can squeeze the wheelbarrow past your horse. You get the stall cleaned, squeeze the wheelbarrow by without even making your farrier get out from under the horse, and then run out to get your checkbook from the car. Crap… it's not in your purse. Where did you leave it? Oh yeah, you took it out to pay the gas bill last night and it's still on the counter. You go back inside to find your farrier putting your mare back in her stall. He still looks grumpy.

"Was she okay?" you ask, trying to figure out if she did something to make him so frustrated.

"She was fine," he answers and starts packing up his tools.

"Hey, I forgot my checkbook today. Is it okay if I mail it?" you ask, wishing you didn't have to when he's already not happy. "I promise I'll get it sent today."

"Okay," he says, and scribbles you a bill. Next thing you know, he's halfway down the driveway, leaving you confused and a little irritated yourself. Why are farriers so crabby sometimes?

Maybe that sounded familiar to you. You know something's wrong but your farrier gives you no clue what it is, so you're left guessing. Maybe his back hurts today? Let's look at that story again, but through the farrier's perspective. Most farriers have been in this scenario many times and, unfortunately, we usually have handled it about as well as the farrier in the story. Here we go.

It's been a busy day in your farrier business. You had an emergency abscess to deal with earlier that you had to squeeze in, even though you didn't have the time. Luckily, you managed to get back on schedule by eating lunch in the truck on your way to the next stop instead of stopping to eat. You manage to show up right on time for the next appointment, so you're feeling good. Back on schedule!

When you hop out of the truck, you see your client walking into the barn. She waves "hi" and heads…out to the field. Crap. You know it will be a couple minutes for her to catch the horse. No worries, you get all your equipment unpacked, roll your box and hoof stand to the shoeing area and put on your chaps. Still no horse. You go back to the truck and sharpen your hoof knives, even though they aren't dull yet. Finally, after five minutes of waiting, you hear hooves coming up to the barn. Your client is back with the horse you need -- covered in mud.

She throws the mare in a stall and starts clearing things out of the shoeing area. *Why wouldn't you come early and get this stuff out of the way?* you think.

"Is that enough space?" She asks. You look over. There's still hay bales in the back of the shoeing area that are going to crowd you a little, but by now you're tired of waiting and you know the horse is pretty well behaved.

"Sure," you say, even though you're not super happy about the set up. You don't want to be too demanding anyway.

Your client pulls her horse out and clips the crossties on, and you assess the mud situation. It's slimy, and it's obviously fetlock deep out there. You silently curse mud season and start trying to scrape and squeeze mud off the legs and hooves. You know that no matter how much you try to clean it up your hands and legs are going to be wet and muddy by the time you're done, and your tools will be dulled and gummed up with mud too. Yuck. Ten minutes after your appointment was supposed to start, you're finally getting under the horse.

As you're wrestling to keep the slippery, muddy leg from moving while you trim it, your client squeezes past you with a wheelbarrow that just barely fits between the wall and the horse. The mare tries to lean away from the wheelbarrow to make more room, but her leg slips out of your grip and you have to pick it up and start over.

You pick up a hind hoof and find out that those hay bales are definitely in your way, but you contort yourself a little and get it done.

When you're done with the horse, you don't see your client anywhere, so you put the mare back in the stall. Just then the client reappears.

"Was she okay?" your client asks.

"She was fine," you say, trying to hide your annoyance with the fact that you're probably going to be late to your next appointment because you had to wait around and clean up muddy legs. You start packing up your tools when you hear one of your least favorite phrases.

"Hey, I forgot my checkbook today. Is it okay if I mail it?" your client asks, and then seems to notice your frustration. "I promise I'll get it sent today." Dang, you were really hoping to get some checks deposited today so you could get the mortgage payment sent out.

"Okay," you answer, since there's no other option. You look at the dashboard clock as you fire up your truck. Already late. You can tell your client seems unhappy about something, but you have a lot more horses to take care of today and you're going to get grumpy texts in a minute if you don't get to the next barn ASAP.

So whose fault is this scenario? Both you and the farrier are responsible. You probably should have made sure you grabbed your checkbook this morning, and if you knew it was muddy, it would make sense to get there early to get your horse cleaned up. But the farrier also never explained to you why they weren't happy with the situation because they assumed you already knew, because they didn't want to be too demanding, or because they were already behind schedule and didn't want to take the time for the conversation. But they were still upset about it. What is the number one lesson to learn from this scenario? Ask your farrier if there's anything you can change to help them out.

Most farriers don't want to be called divas or dismissed as being crabby for no reason, so they will keep things to themselves. If you ask them what you can improve, this gives them the opportunity to politely share what might be bugging them.

What can you do to prevent this kind of scenario from happening at all? Luckily, it's not a mystery. I'm going to let you in on a little secret: there are a number of closed Facebook groups just for farriers, where we can discuss shoeing problems, pathologies, tools, victories, and frustrations. And let me tell you, the same frustrations show up over and over. The bad thing is, we all agree about these things in our closed groups, but we rarely share them with horse owners, who could actually do something about it! So, want to hear the things that horse owners do that bug farriers the most? They fall into a couple different categories.

- First, not being respectful of the farrier's safety. This includes things like not managing unsafe behavior from your horse, not communicating that your horse has a dangerous habit like kicking or biting, not providing a safe work space, allowing other horses to bite or harass the horse they are working on, and allowing dogs or children to spook the horses.

- The second category covers not respecting the farrier's time. This means canceling appointments last minute (unless you have a legitimate emergency, of course), not communicating ahead of time if you must cancel, being late to appointments, not following their payment protocol which may vary between farriers, calling or texting late at night or early in the morning (again, unless it's a real emergency), and bringing muddy or wet horses to your farrier. It also means recognizing that your farrier is human and does need days off and time to spend with their family, so they may not be able to accommodate a request for an evening or weekend appointment.

- Third is not respecting your farrier's knowledge. You hired an experienced professional to shoe your horse, so when you question them based on the opinion of your uncle's second cousin who used to ride a little, it's pretty frustrating. Likewise with Facebook opinions from people who have no credentials to be offering that advice. This does *not* mean you can never ask for an explanation about something or ask why your farrier is changing something. It's also fine to share what your vet has said about the hooves or concerns your trainer might have had. We're just talking about unqualified opinions here, not concerns from you or from other qualified professionals. Cool?

Now let's be honest, a lot of these things carry through no matter what your job is. You wouldn't want your boss telling you that you had to work through the weekend, so don't expect your farrier to be thrilled about it either. You definitely wouldn't be cool with it if your boss said your paycheck was going to be a week or four late, so make sure that you have payment ready for your farrier when they request it. And no matter what your job is, you don't want to be putting your life at risk when you clock in, so make sure that you take your farrier's personal safety seriously.

Ok, let's talk safety. Not the most exciting, but very important.

What constitutes a safe work environment? The specifics will change depending on region and budget, but the basics stay the same. You don't need a million-dollar barn to have a good work space where your farrier can safely shoe.

The biggest requirement is a flat, clear area to work in. This should be large enough that the farrier can move around the horse in any direction without running the risk of getting squished into a wall or tripping over an obstacle. This should also include a clear escape route so that if an emergency should happen, they won't be trapped behind a scared or upset horse.

A firm surface is best, whether that is a concrete aisle, rubber mat, or packed dirt. This makes it much easier for your farrier to assess the hoof when it's on the ground. One caveat about concrete though - you don't want the super slick smooth concrete that is often used in garages. When it gets wet, it can be really hard for your horse to keep his footing. If that is what you have, rubber mats can solve the problem.

A cluttered, dark work environment poses multiple safety hazards

It's also important to have trip hazards like hoses and electrical cords out of the area. It's fine if they run along the edge, but you don't need your farrier tripping and spooking the horse. Plus, both of those things can get damaged if a horse steps on them.

You'll want to provide some shelter from the elements, which is going to look different depending on your region. If you live in an area that gets cold, snowy winters, you'll want an indoor setup to protect from snow and cold winds. If you're in a hot area where there's not a lot of precipitation to worry about, you'll probably be better off with something that casts a shadow so your farrier can work out of the sun but still have some airflow.

Lighting is another important factor. You don't want your farrier trying to shoe by brail! If they can see the hooves clearly, you will be getting much

A clean, flat, well-lit work environment with horses safely spaced out

more accurate work. And if you don't have good lighting wired in, you can always buy a construction light from your local hardware store. Your farrier will appreciate it.

If you are having your horse shod rather than just trimmed, you will probably also need to provide water and electricity. Most farriers today do use some electric tools in the process of preparing your horse's shoes, and if they hot shoe or use a grinder, they will need some water to cool the shoes off.

Lastly, you will need to manage other animals, and possibly people, who have access to the shoeing area. Of course, you don't want other horses wandering loose and harassing the horse being shod, but you also will want to pay attention to horses stalled or penned close enough to reach your horse. On the flip side, if your horse is a little herd bound, she might stand a lot more quietly if you bring her best friend in and keep her nearby (but out of reach!). Sometimes other animals can also wreak havoc on a shoeing too. Dogs who try to sneak up and snatch hoof trimmings, or worse, try to nip at your horse's heels while she's being shod pose a danger to themselves and to the horse and farrier. If your horse tries to kick at the dog in question, the dog could be injured, the farrier can get jerked or thrown, and the horse may hurt herself if she runs into other objects in the area.

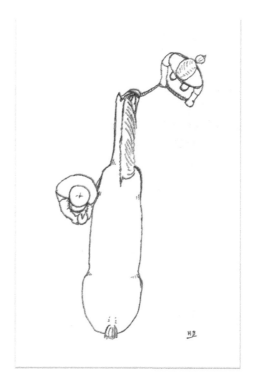

When the farrier is under a front leg, you should be on the opposite side

Other people in the barn can also cause hazards if they aren't paying attention or aren't very horse savvy. Many well-meaning people in barns start feeding other horses treats in front of the horse that's getting worked on, without realizing that your horse is going to be very distracted by this. Keep an eye out for people about to do silly things like trying to sneak a horse past your horse in the aisle while the farrier is underneath it. When a horse needs to come past in the aisle, the farrier should always be warned first so they can get out of the way.

Also, I know this is going to hurt some peoples' feelings but keep an eye on any kids in the shoeing area. If your horse is well behaved and your kid wants to watch, that is fantastic! Most farriers will have no problem with this scenario. Make sure your kids are in a safe spot to watch and that they're using their indoor voices. It can also be an issue if your kid gets bored and wanders off, only to come running into the barn later on yelling excitedly, spooking the horse. If you have a kid who likes horses and wants to be at the barn with you, make sure that you instill

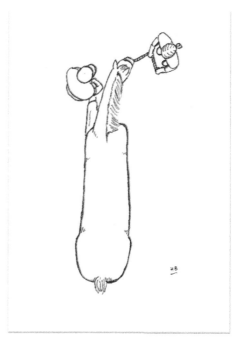

basic horse safety in them and remind them to be careful around horses. Of course, if your horse has behavioral problems like kicking, biting, or trying to run backwards during shoeing, keep your kids safe by keeping them out of range of your horse.

You'll also want to make sure that if you're holding your horse for the farrier, you are in the right place at the right time. This ensures that you are out of the farriers' workspace, but close enough to manage any disruptive behaviors from your horse.

While your farrier is working underneath your horse's front legs, you should be standing in front of your horse on the opposite side. Remember, it is always easier to pull your horse's head toward you than to push it away. If you are on the opposite side than your farrier and your horse tries to swing his head around to nip your farrier, it is easy to pull his head toward you, away from your farrier. Likewise, if your horse decides to jump around, you can pull him away from your farrier, keeping them safe.

When your farrier brings your horse's front feet forward, you will have to move a little, but the principle is the same; be in a position where you can pull your horse away from your farrier if something goes wrong, but staying to the side so that your farrier has room to work.

On the hind feet, the concept changes a little. This time, you want to be on the same side as your farrier, because when you pull your horse's head toward you, his hind end moves away from you. So if something goes wrong and your horse spooks while your farrier is on the hind feet, you want to be able to pull his head toward you so that his hind end pivots away from your farrier, allowing them to safely get out of the way.

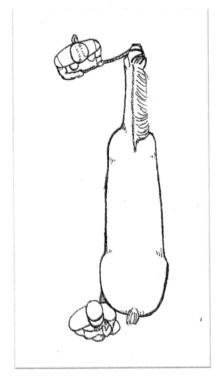

When the farrier is under a hind leg, you should be on the same side

Okay, so you've got a nice safe environment for your farrier to work in. Now for the very biggest make-or-break element in your professional relationship -- safe horse behavior. A good horse in a not-quite-perfect environment is much safer to shoe than a poorly behaved horse in a perfect, ideal setting.

A lot of people take it personally if someone suggests their horse isn't absolutely perfect in every way. But remember, no horse is born knowing how to be the ideal shoeing patient. Your horse wasn't born knowing how to carry a person around on his back either, but through consistent teaching and practice, he probably got pretty good at that, and he can get good at being trimmed or shod too. If any of this stuff sounds like something your horse does, don't take it personally, just take it as a pointer to work on. There are very, very few horses who can't learn good manners for hoof care; it just takes work on your part.

So what is the ideal behavior for a horse being shod?

- They stand still, in one place.
- They are quiet, both physically and mentally, and they don't feel the need to scream for other horses the whole time.
- They pick up feet when asked and hold them up until the farrier lets them go.

- They have enough patience to maintain that behavior throughout the entire time it takes to shoe them.

What behaviors don't fit into that picture? The horse that is be moving the whole time, the horse who paws constantly or tries to pull his hooves away while the farrier is working, heavy leaning, not lifting feet when requested, and trying to walk around while the farrier has a foot held up all make it a lot harder. Obviously, horses who show aggressive behaviors like biting, kicking, rearing, or striking definitely don't make the good horse list! Fearful reactions like trying to run away or breaking crossties don't make it easy to do a good job either. Even playful, curious nips can be very painful, so those behaviors should be avoided too.

If your horse fits into the first category, congratulations and keep up the good work. If the second category sounds more like your horse, you might be feeling a little uncomfortable. Let that feeling be the motivation to improve your horse's behavior. Imagine how much better you'll feel when your farrier says: "Your horse was so much better today. What are you doing differently?"

You might be saying to yourself, *Hey wait a minute, my horse has been trimmed or shod every six weeks since she was a foal. It's not like she's never done this before. So how come she acts up?* I'm going to answer that with a slightly embarrassing story from my childhood.

When I was about eight, I started learning to play piano. My mom was a really good pianist, and when she played it sounded great. So I started learning. My mom showed me how to play scales and simple tunes ("Mary Had a Little Lamb," anyone?) but I didn't really like those because they didn't sound that great. It was hard work and the reward didn't seem worth it, so I avoided practicing like the plague. Oh sure, every so often I would practice, but I didn't do it nearly enough to get the results I wanted, and when I did, it sounded like crap, so I got more frustrated and eventually stopped practicing altogether. Now, if you put me in front of a piano today and asked me to play "Mary Had a Little Lamb," I could maybe stumble through a really

You can help your horse practice the motions of shoeing by holding up feet and stretching legs forward

rough version of it, but I definitely couldn't play anything that sounds like what my mom plays. Why not? Because I never practiced enough to really learn, and she has practiced a lot.

What I'm trying to say is, practicing every six weeks isn't going to teach your horse much, and if she makes mistakes and it's not an enjoyable experience, she starts not wanting to be there. Rather than getting better at standing for a shoeing, she either practices bad habits or tries to avoid it more and more. Asking her to stand for an hour or more to be shod when she hasn't practiced for the last six weeks? She probably gets the same feeling in her gut as I would if you told me that I was going be in a piano recital.

It's up to you to change that cycle. Help her to enjoy practicing, do it more frequently, and be prepared when it's recital time so she can do a great job and you can be there like the proud parent, clapping in the front row.

How much practice you need will really depend on how far behind your horse is. If he has a few small bad habits, you'll probably be able to tackle them on your own in a short amount of time. However, if he does things that are a danger to himself, the farrier, or you, like full blown panic attacks or aggressive behaviors, then it might be a good time to get help from a trainer or an experienced horse handler.

If you're not sure where to start, ask your farrier if there are specific things your horse struggles with, particular parts of the shoeing process that upset him, or things your farrier would like to see improve. They might have a specific behavior pinpointed, which will save you time and energy. You can then focus directly on the issue.

Let's say your horse is just generally impatient during the process, and that exhibits in different ways throughout the shoeing. Maybe she's pawing as soon as she's in the crossties, trying to pull her legs away while your farrier is shoeing her front feet and trying to walk away while your farrier is under the hinds. In order to work on this, you're going to want to recreate this situation frequently in the six weeks between shoeing appointments. Start putting her in the shoeing area to groom her before riding instead of doing it in the stall. Every time you see her, put her on the crossties and pick up each of her feet, taking your time to pick them out. Practice putting her front hooves between your legs like your farrier does, and don't give it back until *you* are ready. If she pulls it away, you need to pick it up again, or else she is learning that she doesn't have to hold them up if she doesn't want to. Then stretch her legs forward like the farrier does. Bonus: A lot of horses also enjoy a good stretch before going to work! Do the same with her hind legs, placing them in your lap to pick them out. Remember, she's not done until you tell her she is. As far as the pawing issue goes, remember to *never* give a horse treats or attention while she is pawing. You might think you're distracting her, but she sees it as a reward for the bad behavior, so she will continue to paw (and probably more frequently). After you're done riding, go through the routine again. You want it to become an ingrained routine that she doesn't have to worry about; she just knows that it has to be done. You want her to be able to do it as automatically as my mom can play piano scales. Then, when the big recital comes around, she isn't nervous. She knows what she's supposed to do. She's not afraid of messing up, the farrier is happy because she's letting him do his job, and they can get along together just fine. And you're happy because your farrier can do their best work to keep your horse sound and comfortable.

If you have a horse that is dangerous to shoe, such as one who panics and tries to get away, or one who rears up or strikes, get a professional on board. You could be dealing with some serious past mental scarring that will take a lot of work to get over. In the meantime, if it is safe to do so, go through the same steps with him we talked about above. Remember, you are probably the person he trusts the most, so help him understand that it is safe to let people pick up his feet. Do it often, and reward him when he does it well. Until he is safe for your farrier to work on, you may need to have a vet present to sedate him for shoeing. There are a wide variety of sedatives and dosages available, and your vet and farrier can help you decide what will be the most beneficial. Some horses just need a little something to help them calm down, and others need to be pretty checked out to not panic. Remember, your horse does need hoof care, and if he has severe problems with being trimmed or shod, sedation is usually the safest for everyone involved. Then, once you've helped him get those behaviors under control, you can start backing off the sedation until he's able to be shod with no chemical help. That is the day when you should pop that bottle of nice champagne and toast yourself and all your hard work.

Quick Takeaways

- Make sure to provide a safe working environment, as well as a horse who is safe for your farrier to work on.
- Respecting your farrier's time and their knowledge shows respect for them as a professional, and increases their job satisfaction.
- When it comes to your horse's manners for trimming or shoeing, practice makes perfect.
- Listen to your farrier if they voice concerns about your horse's behavior.

13 HOW TO GET INTO THE GOOD CLIENT HALL OF FAME

While there's no actual Hall of Fame for good clients, most farriers do have an informal mental list of their favorite clients. Let's say you're an overachiever and you want to know how to make it? Don't worry, I gotcha.

In Chapter 12 we talked about how to get yourself off the $*#! list. (Just kidding, you probably weren't on it. Probably.) In this chapter we're going to talk about how to be the client that your farrier brags about. Don't worry, it's not *all* bribery.

First, obviously, you've still got do all the stuff in the last chapter. No one makes the Good Client Hall of Fame with a horse that tries to kick the farriers head off, but I'm guessing you already knew that. Now that we have that out of the way, let's get to the fun part: How to win friends and influence farriers:

- Try to be there for your horse's appointments, or at least stop in. Take a minute to chat and ask how they are doing, or how their day is going. Ask about their kids sports or how their oldest is doing in college. Farriers, being human, like talking about things that they enjoy, like their hobbies or their kids. This is part of developing a human relationship with your farrier, which research has shown leads to higher job satisfaction[23]. And folks, job satisfaction is what keeps someone coming back to shoe your horse for the next twenty years.

- If it's a blazing hot day, and you're sweating by the time you walk to the barn, grab a bottle of water or a sports drink for the farrier. In summer it can be really hard to stay hydrated, and trying to work dehydrated is never healthy! A cool water bottle can make a huge difference when you're feeling overheated and exhausted. If you bring an ice cream sandwich, you're a goddess.

- In winter, grab your farrier a coffee or hot tea on your way to the barn. Not only will it help them stay warm, your consideration might make your farrier's day.

- Have your horse ready in the crossties or wherever your farrier works when they arrive. They will appreciate not having to go find you or your horse.

- Have her hooves picked out and her legs clean and dry, which includes not bathing your horse before her appointment.

- If you have an appointment near the holidays, consider giving your farrier a card or a small gift. Tips are always appreciated, but homemade cookies or other goodies will be remembered. You might be the person who makes the awesome cookies, and *you can't get rid of the client that makes awesome cookies.* If cooking isn't your thing, a small gift card to their favorite coffee place or lunch spot is a solid choice too.

- Keep your farrier up to date on your horse. Farriers like to know what their horses are up to and take a personal pride when they do well. Even if your horse is an old retired

---

[23] Wahyuni, S., Widodo, S.E., Retnowati, R. (2016). The Relationship of Interpersonal Communication, Working Motivation and Transformational Leadership to Teachers' Job Satisfaction *Post Graduate Program, Universitas Pakuan Bogor, Indonesia International Journal of Managerial Studies and Research (IJMSR) Volume 4, Issue 8, August* P. 89-93

guy, your farrier would probably like to hear that he's got a new pasture buddy that he likes and he always comes trotting up when he hears your voice. Call us suckers, but most farriers got into the profession because we like horses.

- If it's the dead of summer, and your farrier rolls up to see that you have a fan set up in the aisle, you're automatically bumped up at least five Good Client points. Likewise, if you have your horse fly-sprayed for them. Good job, you considerate horse owner!

- If your horse just got shod and she's doing great, text your farrier and let them know. Most of the time, your farrier only hears from clients when something is wrong (horse is lame, horse pulled a shoe, etc.) Chances are, after a long week your farrier dreads seeing their phone light up. *What's wrong now?* They wonder, opening the text. Oh wait, it's you, their favorite client, telling them that your girl is going great and you appreciate their work. Trust me, this kind of text is like a unicorn sighting and makes your farrier feel super, super good. If you don't do anything else on this list, try this one. It will probably make your farrier's day.

Quick Takeaways
- **Use the Golden Rule and try to put yourself in your farrier's shoes.**
- **Build a personal relationship with your farrier.**

Part 3
All About Shoes

14 DOES MY HORSE NEED SHOES?

What's up with horse shoes? Obviously wild mustangs aren't trotting by to see the farrier every six weeks, and they seem to be getting along just fine. Did something change with the domestic horse? Why do horses need shoes anyway?

Contrary to popular belief, it isn't just to make farriers money. In fact, when you consider that it takes much longer to shoe a horse than to trim it, plus the overhead from extra tools and supplies needed to shoe a horse, most farriers actually have a higher profit margin on their trims.

And you're totally right, mustangs and other feral horses don't wear shoes and never have. We've been told quite a few times that natural means healthy when it comes to horses' feet and that we should try to trim them to be as close to the natural model as possible.

If we're going to find out if that's true, we have to talk to the expert, and that's Brian Hampson, a researcher who has spent 14 years studying Australian Brumbies and earned his PhD in feral hoof studies. He has done studies tracking Brumbies, watching how different terrains effect their hooves, and even done dissections on the hooves of Brumbies that had to be culled from the herd. So did he find healthy hooves or unhealthy ones?

It turns out that the hooves of the wild horses in his studies had a *ton* of abnormalities, which were classified in this study as anything from flare to evidence of laminitis. Looking at the left front hooves from 100 Brumbies, the research team found over *300* different abnormalities present, and only saw 3 hooves that didn't have any kind of abnormality.

These weren't all minor issues like a little flare or a hoof crack here and there. Although horses that were in hard, rocky desert areas tended to have the classic "Mustang roll" wild horse foot and less superficial abnormalities, a whopping 67% of them showed signs of chronic laminitis. In areas where Brumbies traveled moderate distances, 70% of the examined feet had sidebone, while horses that traveled shorter distances on softer ground showed extreme lateral flaring (85%), toe flaring (90%) and long toe conformation (35%). Plus, 45% showed signs of chronic laminitis and 75% showed remodeled coffin bones[24].

So obviously, those rates of pathologies aren't what we're shooting for. How are those horses getting along? (Because who cares if their feet don't look great if they are living long and happy lives).

The feral horses on the Outer Banks of North Carolina live in a relatively kind environment, where they are rarely exposed to extreme temperatures and don't have to worry about predators. According to the Cape Lookout National Seashore's annual wild horse survey, the average lifespan of their horses is a short 11 years, and that number has been consistent since 1999[25].

---

[24]Hampson, B.A. and Pollitt, C.C. (November, 2011). *Improving the Foot Health of the Domestic Horse: The Relevance of the Feral Horse Foot Model.* Retrieved from http://horsefx.com.au/wp-content/uploads/2015/07/Pollitt-and-Hamson-Improving-health-of-domestic-horse-hoof.pdf
[25] National Park Service, (2018). *Cape Lookout National Seashore Shackleford Banks Horses 2018 Annual Report.* Retrieved from https://home.nps.gov/calo/learn/management/upload/Annual-Horse-Findings-Report-2018-final.pdf

A short hoof may need protection

Brumbies, some of whom live in far more extreme conditions, show annual death rates of 20% in each herd[26]. Sounds pretty grim to me.

Now it would be a fairly big leap to say that those death statistics are *purely* because of lack of hoof care. Wild horses also don't have any parasite control, and have no protection against starvations or drought, which was cited as one of the largest contributing factors for Brumby deaths. In some areas, they also have predators who are actively trying to eat them for lunch (poor zebra!) Regardless, I think it's fair to say that nature is pretty cruel to wild horses, and we don't necessarily want our domestic horse management to copy it to a T.

So should every horse be rocking out in a set of four shoes? Do they fix every issue we've said wild horses have? Unfortunately, lucky as they may be, horse shoes aren't a magic fix, plus many horses are perfectly sound and happy without them, and don't die at age 11.

When is the right time to put shoes on? There are really only a couple circumstances when it makes sense.

- Protection: First, and most commonly, you should add shoes if your barefoot horse is wearing away more hoof than they can grow. Since you know there are sensitive structures inside that hoof, you can guess that if he wears away enough of that outer covering, there's not going to be enough protection left to keep his coffin bones safe and sound. Sometimes you see this when he is reluctant to walk across rocks (not enough sole depth) or acts a little "pinchy" or short when he's walking. You might also be able to physically see a really heavy or uneven wear pattern, often in his toe.

  Luckily, this is usually an easy fix. Just about any type of shoe will help, because the rim of the shoe is replacing the rim of foot that he would like to have, but can't quite manage to grow. If he's really sore, a full pad can also help since it protects his sole, too. Steel is also more wear-resistant than hoof, so he'll have a little more protection to wear through this time!

  If you add shoes when your horse needs some protection, that doesn't mean he'll always need shoes. Sometimes they can be a temporary or seasonal addition. If you trail

[26] Csurhes, S., Paroz, G., and Markula, A., (2009) Feral Horse Risk Assessment. *State of Queensland 2016.* Retrieved from https://www.daf.qld.gov.au/__data/assets/pdf_file/0004/51961/IPA-Feral-Horses-Risk-Assessment.pdf

Rocky environments and hard work might mean extra hoof wear

ride thirty miles a week in the summer but you don't like freezing your tail off in the winter and you only come to the barn long enough to pet him and say "hi," he might be able to be barefoot in the winter and only wear shoes for your marathon trail riding months.

Just be aware that when you pull shoes off, you might see some hoof changes. Hoof walls can break up where the old nail holes were, since that area is already weakened. You'll also want to think of the environment when you pull shoes. If the ground is really hard, like in winter during a deep freeze your horse might have a tougher transition. Pulling shoes during spring or fall when the ground is soft is more likely to go smoothly and although your horse might need a little while to adjust to being barefoot, we're not talking noticeable lameness here. She may try to avoid the gravel on your driveway if her hooves aren't that tough yet, but you shouldn't be experiencing lameness, hot hooves, or rapid pulses. These are signs of inflammation, and that's not part of a healthy transition to being barefoot.

The hoof may break up around the old nail holes when shoes are pulled

- Traction: Another circumstance that calls for shoes is when a horse doesn't have enough traction for the job they are doing. For instance, your barefoot jumper might be doing great with the 2'6", but when you start moving up, she seems to lose the propulsion you need to get over the jumps, and her hind end starts to seem muscle sore. She might just need a shoe with a little bit of traction on her hind feet to help her dig in and push off better. In that case, you might want to go with a shoe that is fully fullered, or has a crease that goes from heel to heel. Depending on your footing, you could even have her set up in a concave shoe.

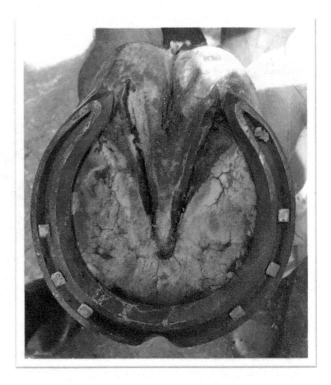

A concave shoe increases traction

Or let's say you have an eventer that is starting to slip a little on cross country, especially when there's some mud on the course or on a dewy morning when the ground is hard and the grass is wet. Maybe he'd like a shoe with drilled and tapped holes for screw in studs. That way, you can have super traction when you need it, but take it out for everything else.

On the other hand, some horses need reduced traction, like reining horses. Smooth plain stamped shoes are a good choice for less traction.

Again, if your horse needs shoes for traction reasons, they may be able to get away with being barefoot if you have an "off season."

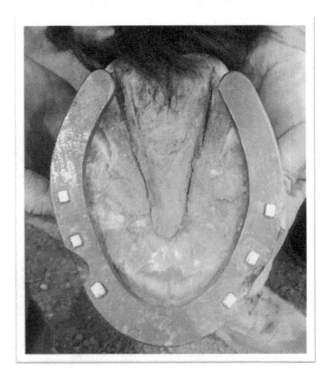

A plain stamped shoe reduces traction

- Therapeutic reasons: A third reason your farrier or vet might suggest shoes is if your horse has an injury or pathology and needs shoes for therapeutic reasons. Maybe your mare pulled a suspensory. Along with treatment from the vet, special shoes can be used that help the foot land and load in a way that puts the least possible amount of stress on the suspensory ligament while it heals. Once she's feeling better and you've got the vet's okay, your farrier can slowly ease her out of the shoe by applying less and less extreme versions of it.

A patten bar is a specialized therapeutic shoe for certain severe injuries

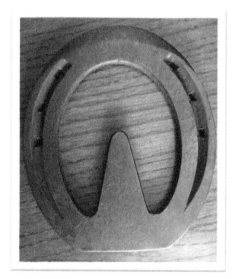

A heart bar shoe is a traditional choice for treating laminitis

Another example would be if your gelding was diagnosed with laminitis. Your farrier could use specific types of shoes that help reduce leverage on his sore hoof walls and transfer some of the load onto his frog instead. We'll talk about that more in Chapter 34, but you get the idea. The earliest farrier textbooks that we have, going back into the late 1500s, show diagrams of many of the exact same therapeutic principles that we use today.

Does that mean that we're behind the times? Actually, since horses were an immensely important part of everyday life and industry in that era, I'd say it probably means we're on the right track. Sound horses determined peoples' livelihood, and if your horse was lame, you might not have any food that week. Horse owners were very motivated to do whatever they could to keep horses up and running, and the blacksmiths of the era, without all the modern diagnostics we have today, were able to do that with some good sound logic and horsemanship. We might know why those shoes work today, but they knew that they *did* work five hundred years ago. Show offs.

So if your horse falls into one of those three categories, talk to your farrier about shoeing. Otherwise, your horse can probably stay sound and healthy barefoot.

Quick Takeaways

- **Horses in nature do have hoof pathologies, so "natural" isn't always the solution.**
- **Horses can often be maintained barefoot, unless they need extra protection, traction, or need therapeutic shoeing.**

15 SHOEING IS CRAZY, BUT THAT'S OKAY

Most people think that the ancient Gauls or Britons invented metal horseshoes around the time of the birth of Christ. It's been around for so long now that we don't really stop to think about it. But if you do think about it, the whole thing is completely insane.

I mean, can you imagine being a fly on the wall when the first blacksmith decided he was going to go ahead and attach a metal shoe to a living animal … by sticking nails through its foot?? I'm assuming the horse owner had a lot of questions. Specifically, how the heck do you expect this thousand-pound animal not to throw you through the wall of this ancient smithy when you start driving nails into it? How come my horse isn't going to bleed out when, you know, you're planning on sticking nails into it and then *leaving them there*? (I'm imagining some shouting in this conversation.)

Luckily, some naïve optimist let that crazy blacksmith give it a try, and all of a sudden a mounted warrior didn't need to take twenty horses with him so that he had at least one sound war horse. All of a sudden, horses' feet didn't break up and fall apart when they had to walk on cobblestones. Cavalries and trade caravans could move farther and faster across rugged terrain. That blacksmith may have possibly been a psychopath, but he changed the course of history.

So how can we drive nails into a living animal, leave them there, and not have blood pouring out or a horse that can't walk?

You already know that there is a protective, insensitive covering around all the sensitive structures in the foot, and you've probably guessed that the nails must be completely in that insensitive hoof capsule.

But let's make this just a little more challenging. The hoof wall might be a prime target for nails -- it's insensitive and it's usually about 3/8 of an inch thick, so it's a nice big surface to hit. Unfortunately, nails driven into the hoof wall alone tend not to be super strong. Why? Remember all those tubules that make up the horn of the hoof wall? Remember the intertubular horn that glues all those tubules together? It's a pretty strong makeup, but if you drive a nail along those tubules, you can split

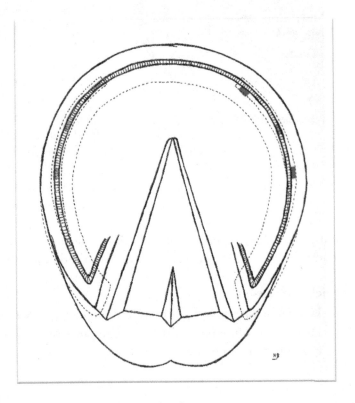

Safe nailing should be in the white line

the intertubuler horn. Plus, if you drive the nail too shallowly in the hoof wall, there's not enough mass to hold it securely.

So, instead of driving nails into a nice, wide 3/8-inch target, farriers shoot for a 2mm target -- the white line. The white line is an ideal place to drive a nail since its flexible makeup doesn't usually split or fracture, and then as the nail drives outward, it goes through the full thickness of the wall, giving it a good strong hold. Downside? Your farrier is trying to hit a 2mm target on a living, possibly moving, thousand pound horse. Easy, right? It's not a stressfully small margin of error at *all*.

As long as the nails hit the white line and angle outward through the hoof wall, nailing on shoes is completely painless for the horse, barring pre-existing pathologies like arthritis or fractures that make the concussion of nailing painful. Since it's important to hit such a small target, farriers usually try to shape their shoes to the shape of

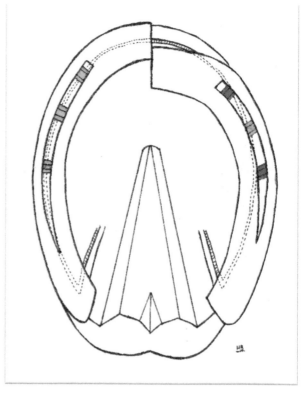

Shoes should be shaped to the white line (left) for safe nailing. Nailing into the hoof wall or the sole (right) causes problems

the white line, unless there's an important therapeutic reason not to. If the shoe is shaped to the white line, all the nails should be safe, and as we learned in our anatomy discussion, the white line matches the shape of the coffin bone. If coffin bones are specifically shaped to do the job that each leg is required to do (front end rounded to be able to move in any direction, hinds pointed to be able to dig in and propel the horse), shouldn't we shape our shoes to mimic the coffin bone and let the horse's feet have the shape to function as they should? I'm voting yes, if anyone is counting.

This is why I take a real issue with people who call a square toed front shoe or trim natural. To me, nature gave us beautiful, functional shapes for horse's coffin bones and feet that are specifically designed to give that horse the best movement possible. Frankly, taking away that design and slapping poorly functioning square toes on everything under the guise of "natural shoeing" seems a little insulting. Just go ahead and tell Mother Nature she messed up, why don't you?

Nature really doesn't do well with squares. Square corners on horses' hooves become leverage points, and leverage points become flares that drag hoof walls and white lines away from coffin bones. In fact, a researcher named Dr. Michael Miller trimmed 21 horses over

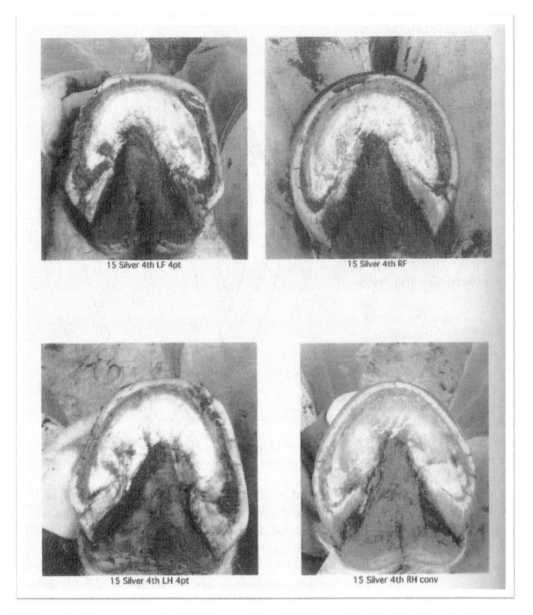

15 Silver 4th LF 4pt

15 Silver 4th RF

15 Silver 4th LH 4pt

15 Silver 4th RH conv

The feet on the left were trimmed with a four point trim and the feet on the right were trimmed with a traditional trim. The distortion on the left is obvious. Photos courtesy of Dr. Mike Miller.

three trim cycles with either conventional trimming methods or a four-point trim and documented the results on the hoof. The photos that he took consistently showed that the four-point trim led to splitting and delaminating of the hoof wall and white line in the toe and heel quarters.[27]. So let's just say that any system that doesn't allow the hoof to function the way

[27] Miller, M. E., (2010). *The Mirage of the Natural Foot.*

nature intended it, and causes actual damage to the hoof, shouldn't be called natural. Moving on!

Next up on the crazy scale is that, not only did we decide to put metal shoes on horses and attach them with nails and somehow that worked, but we also decided that since we had built those shoes out of hot steel (or iron in the early days) we should just go ahead and see if they fit while they were still flaming hot. I'm sure this giant flight animal won't be upset by seeing a cloud of smoke come off of his own foot! Again, I really want to know if the guy who came up with this was mentally unstable, or if life was just that miserable back then.

So why in the heck would we fit horse shoes hot? Originally, a blacksmith couldn't go pick up tools at the shoeing supply store. He was the shoeing supply store and the hardware store, and the mechanic, and often the veterinarian. When it comes to tools that are hard to make, a rasp is pretty high up there. So while most modern farriers use their nippers to clip off the bulk of the hoof that needs to be trimmed, and then smooths it out with a rasp, ancient farriers didn't have the luxury of rasping. Instead, they would cut off what they could, as flat as they could, and then place the hot shoe on the hoof until it burnt off the high spots and flattened it out. Ancient ingenuity for the win.

In the process, they discovered that there were actually some benefits to hot fitting. For one, since the shoe was still hot when they checked it on the foot, they could easily re-shape it if it wasn't right. They also found out that a shoe that fit flush to the hoof stayed on better than a shoe that had some daylight between it and the hoof. Why? Because the hoof flexes every time that it bears weight, so if it's not flat on the shoe, there will be more movement in some areas than others, and the shoe can begin to loosen.

In modern times, we can buy rasps by the case so we don't have to worry about saving money by burning feet flat. We also don't have to make our own shoes anymore, thanks to modern manufacturing, although some of us still choose to handmake some or all of our shoes. Once manufactured rasps and shoes became readily available, plenty of shoers didn't see a need to hot fit or forge shoes anymore. After all, it lowers our profit margin when we have to buy propane to heat a forge, plus you have to buy all kinds of forging tools. So since it's not necessary anymore, and it has a higher overhead, why do so many farriers still hot fit?

It's not because we like to stink up people's barns with burnt hoof smoke (okay, maybe a little). It turns out, when farriers got away from hot shoeing, we started to find out some advantages that we didn't know about.

The fact remains that even if you buy all premade shoes, farriers still need to shape them to each individual horse's hoof. Heating the shoe up makes it significantly easier to shape, especially when you move up to larger shoe sizes. This means less wear and tear on the farrier's hands, elbows, and shoulders.

Although rasps are no longer cost-prohibitive, farriers are humans, not manufacturing robots. We might get feet pretty flat when you look at them with the naked eye, but honestly, we'll never get them micrometer flat. The same goes for our shoes. So even today, the best way to make sure that the shoe and the hoof perfectly align is by hot fitting the shoe.

Plus, it has been shown recently that hot fitting shoes kills a significant amount of bacteria and fungus on the hoof surface, bacteria and fungus that might otherwise travel up nail holes or undermine the hoof wall. Significantly for horses that live in wet environments, hot fitting may also seal the freshly trimmed ends of the horn tubules so that moisture cannot travel up them.

Luckily for the horse, hot fitting isn't painful since the horn is a remarkably poor conductor of heat and cold. We see this all the time when horses stand in the snow all day without showing any discomfort, or go for a nice walk on the blazing hot sand without hurting their feet.

So if your farrier doesn't hot fit, does that mean they're a know-nothing hack and you should run them out of town? Hang on, put the pitchforks and torches down. There are also situations where hot fitting just doesn't work. Although many of us consider it to have a lot of health benefits for the horse, it's also not without challenges.

First off, some horses just can't stand it. Although it isn't painful, most horses do find it concerning the first time that they see it if they haven't been raised around hot fitting. And it makes sense; for a flight animal that has often lived on planes and grasslands, smoke usually means *run like heck*. Prairie fires are fast moving and dangerous, so for a horse to think twice when they see smoke is pretty logical. Most horses decide that it's okay when they realize it doesn't hurt and nobody else is panicking, because they've learned to trust humans about all kinds of weird things. But every so often, there's a horse that just plain can't take it. Most of the time it's an experienced horse who has been shod cold (with no smoke) their whole lives, and the first time someone tries to hot fit them they decide that it's a really bad idea. They know all about shoeing, and they know that smoke is not part of it. Um, heck no!

Another consideration is pure safety. If your horse is being shod in a stall, your farrier definitely doesn't want to bring a hot shoe into an area full of shavings or straw. Likewise, if your horse is being shod next to a big pile of haybales, your farrier probably doesn't want to create a fire hazard. If you live in an area with dangerous weather extremes, your farrier may skip hot fitting to minimize the amount of time they spend exposed to the elements.

Long story short, shoeing horses was probably invented by a lunatic, but amazingly 95% of horses allow us to do it, in what is probably the greatest show of trust that you'll ever see. I mean, really, everything in a horse's flight animal nature says that none of this should work. But through all the time and interactions that your horse has had with you and with other humans throughout her life, she's decided that in general, humans are trustworthy and if you're asking her to do this super weird stuff, it's probably safe (though someone might need to snort at all of it, and she may volunteer for that job).

Crazy, right?

Quick Takeaways
- **Shoes should be shaped and fit so that the nail holes line up over the white line.**
- **Hot shoeing is safe, painless, and often beneficial.**

16 TRIMMING AND SHOEING

In this book, I'm not trying to teach you how to shoe your own horse, and in fact, I don't think trimming or shoeing should be attempted by anyone who hasn't received extensive hands-on training from a professional. That being said, I know you're curious about what your farrier is aiming for during the shoeing process and what they do to get there. So we're going to go over what happens during trimming or shoeing, but again, my intent isn't to give you enough detail to do this yourself. If you're interested in trimming or shoeing your own horse, please find someone to give you professional, hands-on instruction.

We'll start with the trim because whether your horse is barefoot or shod, everything starts with a good trim. Keep in mind that I'm giving you a general overview of the process, but your farrier might do things slightly differently depending on what your horse's hooves look like, any lameness history, and the environment your horse lives and works in.

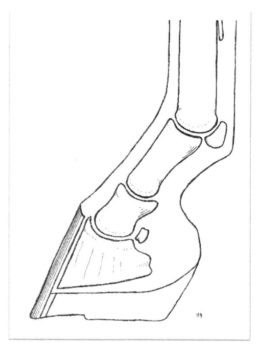

A sole with plenty of depth may be trimmed to increase concavity

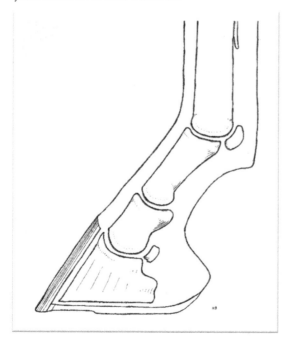

A flat, thin sole cannot be trimmed to create concavity

First, your farrier will assess the balance of the hoof and the way that it relates to the rest of the body, as well as the amount of hoof growth available for the trim. These facts will tell them how to trim the hoof for soundness and performance. Although they're taking in a lot of information, you may not even notice this part of the process. Experienced farriers who are familiar with the horse they are shoeing can often assess the hoof in just a few seconds.

Most farriers begin their trim by using their hoof knife to trim the frog and sole. Once these structures are trimmed, it is easier to see how much hoof wall is available, as well as any imbalances.

Trimming the frog mainly consists of removing any loose, shedding, or undermined frog tissue, and making sure that the collateral sulci are open so that dirt and manure can easily shed out of the frog. Your farrier will also be exploring any crevices or pockets they find to make sure that any thrush is addressed. If your horse doesn't really shed her frogs, your farrier may also have to trim off some healthy frog so that it doesn't become too large. On the other hand, if the frog is clean and tidy, your farrier may not have to trim it at all.

When your farrier trims the sole, they will be removing dead, shedding sole and smoothing out the solar surface since pits and ridges can collect dirt and bacteria or create pressure points. Depending on your region, they may trim the bars almost smooth with the sole or leave them prominent. If your horse has plenty of sole, they may trim to enhance the cup of the sole, but keep in mind that if your horse has a flat, thin sole, they can't carve concavity into it without endangering sensitive structures. While trimming the sole, your farrier will also be observing the shape and thickness of the white line, which gives them clues about the ideal shape for that hoof and its overall health. Again, if your horse cleanly sheds out excess sole or doesn't have a lot of sole to start

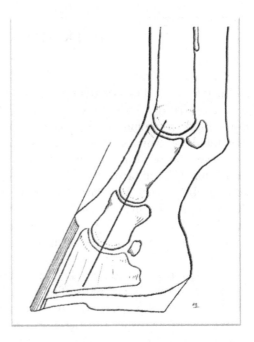

With a straight hoof pastern axis, all the bones line up evenly

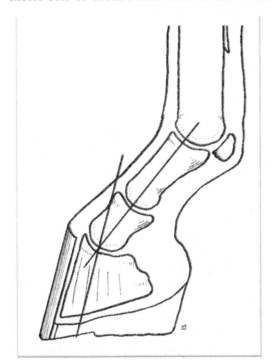

A broken forward hoof pastern axis doesn't allow optimum function.

with, your farrier may not trim any sole at all.

Once the frog and sole are trimmed, your farrier will probably switch over to nippers or a rasp. Both tools remove hoof wall, but your farrier can trim far more efficiently with nippers than with a rasp if there is significant hoof wall to trim. On the other hand, it's much easier to create a smooth finish with a rasp. For this reason, on a hoof with normal growth, most farriers will use nippers to remove the bulk of the excess wall and then use a rasp for the final finish. Again, if your horse hasn't grown much hoof wall, your farrier may not use the nippers at all.

Before trimming wall though, your farrier needs to know where to trim. They may look at the hoof on the ground from the front or the side, and they may pick up the leg and look down the back of the hoof so they can see the balance of the hoof. From the side, they'll be looking to see how the hoof capsule lines up with the pastern bones (hoof pastern axis or HPA). They're shooting for both being at the same angle since that means that the coffin bone is lined up correctly with the bones above it. From the front, they might look for an even, flat coronary band, which shows that one part of the hoof isn't jamming up more than the other.

They'll also be looking for the horse to be standing in the middle of his feet, within the boundaries of individual conformation. While sighting the bottom of the hoof, they're looking for how the hoof relates to the leg, as well as looking for any high or low spots. Once they've established where the longer areas are, they will trim off excess hoof, either from the bottom if there's plenty of depth of foot, or from the top if your horse has a lot of flare. All of this will vary slightly due to individual conformational deviations.

They will probably bring your horse's hoof forward to trim off flare on the outside of the hoof. The goal is to have hoof walls that are straight from top to bottom without bending or flare, but if there's a lot of flare or the hoof wall isn't very thick, it might not be possible to remove all the distortion. If your horse hasn't flared, your farrier may not have to rasp the outside of the wall at all.

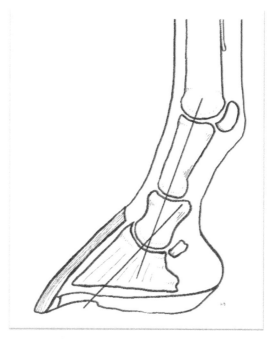

A broken back hoof pastern axis creates unnecessary soft tissue stress

A barefoot trim should be beveled on the bottom edge

On the barefoot horse, once the hoof is flat and level, your farrier will bevel the edges of the hoof so that there aren't any sharp edges to break off. How big of a bevel is necessary? That depends on your environment. Wet hooves typically need a bigger bevel since they are softer and more easily damaged, while hooves in dry areas might just need the sharp edge taken off.

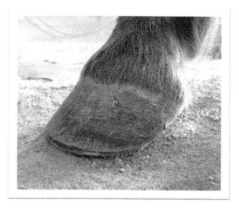

Side view of a barefoot bevel

If they're shoeing your horse, at this point they'll pick out an appropriately sized shoe and shape it to fit your horse's hoof. They'll look for a shoe size that covers the bottom of his hoof wall, including covering both heels. Depending on your environment and your horse's job, they may also fit it a little wider and longer in the back half of the hoof. In wet environments, hooves flare and expand as they grow throughout the cycle, so you need a little extra shoe, called

97

expansion, to allow for that change. In dry environments, it may not be necessary. This is where your farrier's experience with your environment comes into play.

The shoe should also be fit to the shape of the white line. There are exceptions to the rule, but in general, shaping to mimic the shape of the white line will ensure that nail holes in the shoe line up over insensitive structures.

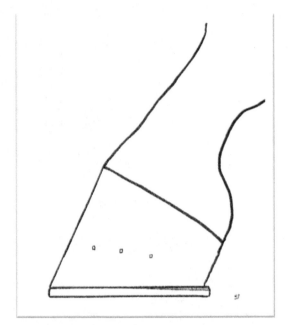

A shoe should be fit slightly longer than the hoof

Once the shoe is fit, it has to be secured to the hoof. Although glue-on shoes are an option (and we'll talk about them in Chapter 17) nailed shoes are still by far the most common option. Your farrier will use specially designed horseshoe nails that have a rectangular head and nail shank and a beveled tip. The beveled tip is so small you may not even notice it if you aren't looking for it, but it directs the nail outward so that it doesn't get into any sensitive tissue. As each nail is driven, your farrier will usually bend over the end that comes out, and twist or clip it off. This is for safety, so that if your horse pulls her hoof, she won't accidently injure herself or her farrier on a sharp nail point.

When all the nails have been driven, there's still a row of sharp nail ends sticking out. To make these safe and help secure the shoe, your farrier will fold them all over neatly, known as clinching. If you've ever heard the phrase *clinching the deal*, this is likely where it originated. Clinching is the final step of the shoeing process, just as clinching a deal means that you've finalized the agreement.

Each nail end is bent over and rasped smooth with the hoof wall. As a finishing step, your farrier will check the hoof for any sharp edges.

Now that you know the basics of the shoeing process, let's get into the nitty gritty of shoeing -- why one shoe is better than another, whether to nail or glue,

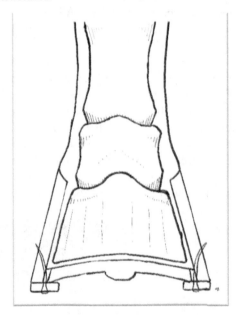

Nails are driven in the white line

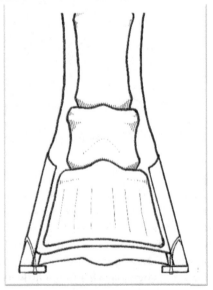

The nail are clinched over for safety

and why your horse might need clips.

Quick Takeaways
- The frog and sole are usually trimmed to remove loose, exfoliating, extra material.
- The hoof wall is trimmed to create a level, flat surface, and balanced to the limb, and flare is addressed.
- Shoes are shaped to the white line and typically attached with nails.
- The finished job should be safe, with all sharp edges and nail end smoothed.

17 DIGGING INTO THE DETAILS

Let's say you've decided your horse needs shoes. Now all of a sudden there are a ton of options, everyone has ideas, and everyone is backing up their opinions with helpful facts like "that's just how it's done." Don't worry, there are legitimate reasons to choose each option, so you don't have to pick your shoeing by throwing darts blindfolded at a list of shoeing styles.

First up, the vast majority of shoes are made out of either steel or aluminum. There are a few other options such as titanium shoes and rubber composites, but titanium is prohibitively expensive and difficult to work with, while composites are often difficult to shape to hooves and create undesirable traction levels on certain footings. Those choices usually aren't considered unless the more common options aren't working well.

So what's the difference between horses that need steel shoes versus horses that need aluminum? Humans like easy, simple classifications, so we like to repeat things like *All hunter-jumper horses wear aluminum.*

Turns out that's a little *too* easy. It's like saying that all baseball players wear cleats. It's true if you make a few assumptions, like that you're talking about professional baseball players in the modern era. But what about kids playing a pickup game in the park? They definitely don't need cleats to have a good game. Plus, there was a pro baseball player called Shoeless Joe Jackson who got blisters from his cleats and finished the game in his socks. The type of shoe used should be based on the needs of the individual horse, not some broad stereotype.

What are the pros and cons? Steel has a lot going for it. It is a much harder material, so it lasts a lot longer and wears less. It is also significantly cheaper than aluminum and allows for the shoe to be hot fit. Aluminum melts by the time it reaches the right temperature for hot fitting, and an aluminum shoe is almost always completely worn out by the end of a shoeing cycle. Steel has the ability to flex and spring back into shape, meaning that it helps absorb some shock without deforming, while aluminum doesn't. But aluminum is also a lighter material, so if a horse needs a special therapeutic shoe that has a lot of material in it, building it out of aluminum will reduce the weight significantly. The biggest deciding factor is what type of footing the horse is working on. Back when sand or dirt were pretty much the only options, people could use either type of metal without worrying too much. But now, with modern synthetic footings becoming popular, the shoe choice makes a huge impact.

Synthetic footings have plenty of advantages, like ease of maintenance and the fact that they aren't as affected by moisture levels, but that comes at a cost. In traditional footings, the hoof hits the ground and then enters a short slide phase before coming to a complete stop. That slide phase acts like a crumple zone in a car, allowing a little deceleration before you come crashing to a halt. Some modern synthetic footings are so sticky that they reduce or completely remove the slide phase[28]. The hoof hits the ground and comes to a dead stop. Horses that haven't trained on synthetic footing and then attend a show where it is used can stumble, crash off of jumps, and dump riders. Research on synthetic tracks show that training in one type of footing and performing in another is a major risk factor for injury[29]. Horses that are on it consistently know

---

[28] Thomason J.J., Peterson M.L. (2008). Biomechanical and mechanical investigations of the hoof-track interface in racing horses. *Vet Clin North Am Equine Pract. Apr;24(1)*: P. 53-77.

[29] Peterson, M., Roepstorff, L., DVM, Thomason, J. J., Mahaffey, C., McIlwraith, C.W., (2012). Racing Surfaces: Current progress and future challenges to optimize consistency and performance of track surfaces for fewer horse injuries. Retrieved from
http://www.racingsurfaces.org/whitepapers/white_paper_1_20120508.pdf

how to handle it, but their bodies are still taking a huge beating.

So what does that have to do with aluminum or steel shoes? It turns out, since aluminum is a more porous material, it slides less in sticky footing than steel does. With the slide phase already shortened in some of the sticky synthetic footings, aluminum adding extra grip isn't going to improve anything, unless you like doing unscheduled dismounts over jumps.

What about weight? As we already discussed, if we have a therapeutic shoe that needs a lot of material in it, weight can become a factor, but what about in normal shoes? If you're in a sport where they like long, low hoof movement, you might have heard that steel will make your horse's movement too big, or make them flex their knees too much.

Let's think proportionally here. The average steel horseshoe weighs about 10 ounces, while an aluminum shoe of the same size weighs in at about 6 ounces. The average weight of a fit horse that would wear that size shoe would be about 1,000 pounds, so as a percentage of her body weight, a steel shoe would be about 0.0625%. Meanwhile as a human, my work boot that I wear every day weighs 1.5 pounds, which comes out to about 1.2% of my body weight (no, I'm not telling you how much I weigh! Do the math for yourself if you really want to know). My comfy sneakers? They weigh 6 ounces, or 0.3% of my body weight. So for a horse, an average sized steel horse shoe isn't the equivalent of wearing work boots all day, or even wearing your comfy sneakers. It might be closer, weight wise, to a pair of flip flops. And yes, maybe there are a few elite athletes who need running shoes that weigh less than an average pair of flip flops, but that's because they've fine tuned every part of their running regime to the point where it matters. Like male Olympic swimmers shaving their chest hair to reduce drag, it might make a difference, but shaving your chest isn't going to turn you into Michael Phelps. Sorry.

One type of glue on shoes

You want my honest opinion? Steel is often the best choice for your horse. There are a few circumstances where aluminum is preferable, but that decision should be based on what is best for your horse as an individual, not on old fashioned stereotypes. If you're on the fence, ask your farrier to look at the type of footing that you normally work on and see what they recommend.

Another ongoing debate has been between traditional shoes that are attached by nails versus modern materials like glues. In the past, there was no debate because the glues that we had to work with were really, really bad. Shoes fell off quickly, so it was more of a Hail Mary than anything. Luckily for us, technology hasn't left adhesives behind, and we now have access to several extremely high quality glues that can keep shoes securely attached for six weeks or more.

Nailing shoes onto horses' feet certainly has its drawbacks. Some horses have shelly, weak walls that fracture when nails are driven, while others are exposed to a lot of bacteria that then thrives in the nail holes and causes issues. Add to that the fact that with a 2mm margin of error and a sometimes moving target, nails can end up too close to sensitive structures (hot nailing). And then there's the occasional thin-walled, sensitive horse that doesn't care for nails in their feet at all and get sore no matter what the farrier tries. Thanks for the sleepless nights, sensitive horse!

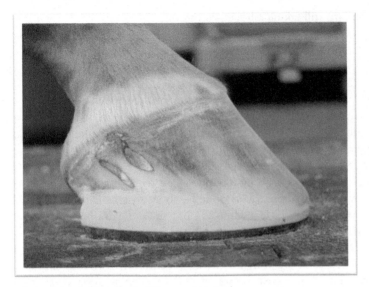

A shoe glued on to a foot with a quarter crack

So why don't we switch to glue? Mainly, because it's still cost prohibitive for a lot of budgets. In 2021, a regular steel shoe costs a farrier about $3.10. Obviously this doesn't include propane, tools, fuel, insurance, or any of the other costs of running a business. This is just for the shoe itself and 8 nails. Meanwhile, to glue a shoe on could cost anywhere from $30 to $55 dollars in actual supply cost. Obviously if you have a horse in four glue-on shoes, you could be tacking on material costs of over $200 in addition to whatever shoeing costs you normally have. Spendy.

Plus, for glue to be successful, the hoof has to be prepped correctly so that it is squeaky clean before the glue hits it. Glue attaches to the first thing it contacts, so if there's dirt or even oil from your skin on the hoof, the glue will adhere to that instead of the hoof, and the shoes won't stay on. Also, bacteria trapped under the glue can wreak quite a bit of havoc in six weeks. That means it's really important to thoroughly clean the hoof before gluing, which requires more time than your farrier would normally spend for a shoeing.

The hoof must be thoroughly cleaned before glue is applied or bacteria can damage the hoof wall

However, if your budget can afford it and your horse is one of those delicate creatures who doesn't handle nailing well, it can be a great option. If your horse doesn't have any problems with nails, nailing shoes on is usually the easiest, most cost effective method.

Now, what's the scoop on clips? Some shoes have clips on the side, some have clips on the front, and some shoes have no clips at all. Is it just for show or is there a method behind the madness?

The biggest reason we put clips on a shoe is to help keep it from shifting on the hoof. The average nail that attaches a shoe to your horse's hoof is about 1/16th of an inch thick by 1/8th of an inch wide, and that's not a whole lot of material to resist all the force of a thousand-pound animal landing, sliding, and taking off again, not to mention constant stomping at flies during the summer. With six or even eight nails, plenty of horses manage to slide their shoe back little by little throughout the cycle, and eventually the nails can shear off or the shoe can slide back far enough that a hind foot can grab it.

The solution? Metal tabs called clips that come up from the shoe onto the front or side of the hoof wall to transfer some of the force off of the nails. In an ideal world they are fit smoothly to the arc and angle of your horse's hoof, allowing the shoe to fit normally and securely. So why do we have different clip placements on different horses?

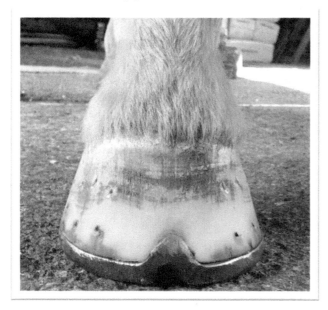

A toe clip

It depends on the shape of the hoof and what kind of force you are trying to protect against. In a normal front foot, a single clip in the toe is usually plenty to keep the shoe from sliding back. However, if your horse hits the ground unevenly, he might be sliding his shoes sideways. If that's the case, clips on either side of the shoe can help.

Side clips also limit hoof expansion[30], which can be good or bad depending on the circumstances. It can be good if your horse has a hoof crack or a coffin bone fracture, and you need to help stabilize the hoof capsule. But it can be a bad thing if you have a tight, contracted hoof that could use some more healthy expansion. In that case, your farrier might choose to go with a toe clip or even no clips to give the hoof a chance to relax.

You might be thinking, *hang on, toe clips? I feel like I've only seen clips on the side of the hoof. That's the way the top show horses are shod so shouldn't my horse have them too?* There's one reason that has nothing to do with function as to why you might see a lot more side clips than toe clips. In North America, the majority of shoes that are pre-manufactured with clips are made with side clips, not toe clips. Farriers can also purchase unclipped shoes and pull their own clips wherever they want, but if they're grabbing one out of the box, there's a good chance its side clipped. It's dictated by convenience, not function.

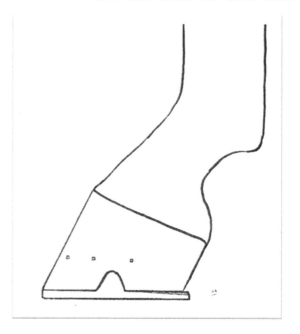

Side clips

---

[30] Hinterhofer, C., Stanek, C. and Haider, H. (2001). Finite element analysis (FEA) as a model to predict effects of farriery on the equine hoof. *Equine Veterinary Journal, 33*: 58-62.

What if you have a question about your horse's shoes that I didn't cover? Ask your farrier! If they are trimming your horse's feet a certain way or putting shoes on your horse, they probably have a logical reason why they think that's the best thing for your horse. So ask, because it's a great chance to learn more.

Quick Takeaways
- Steel shoes are more durable and cost effective, but aluminum has its place if you need to reduce weight in a bulky shoe.
- Aluminum has more drag in some sticky synthetic footings, so steel might be more appropriate for those circumstances.
- Glue is a useful tool for horses who don't have adequate hoof quality to hold nails, but for many horses, nails remain the best choice.
- Clips help prevent shoes from shifting, and their location should be dictated by the individual horse.

18 PADS ON THE BRAIN

Pads are another tool in the farrier's toolbox, and there are a variety to help correct just about every problem imaginable . We already talked a little about how flat pads can help a horse with thin soles with some extra protection, but pads can also protect hoof walls, cushion injured bones, relieve injured areas, or even defend against the weather. Pretty cool, right?

How do pads help hoof walls? Not all pads do, but frog support pads can. Frog support pads are plastic pads that have a thicker section that fits over your horse's frog, which gets the frog into the weightbearing game. This can be useful if your horse has a section of her hoof wall that needs some help. For instance, if she has low, crushed heels, transferring some of the weight off of them and onto the frog can give them a chance to get some new growth going in the right direction. Or if she had a bout of laminitis, your farrier can use frog support pads to take some of the weight off the injured lamina and redistribute it onto the frog. We'll

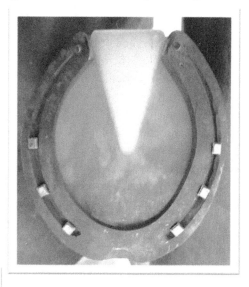

A frog support pad

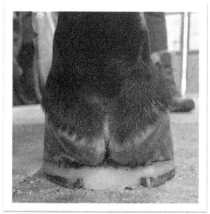

Weight bearing on a normal shoe

Weight bearing on a frog support pad

talk more about why this works in Chapter 34.

Pads can also help reduce concussion since it's essentially a softer layer between the hoof and the shoe. It's not a huge change, but it can make a difference for some horses that just struggle with hard ground. If your horse has a little arthritis or sidebone going, or even an inflamed coffin bone, it can help to take just a little sting out of the concussion.

Wedge pads might be the most commonly prescribed pad type, because they can make a low foot look a little better. This can be useful if there's not enough hoof to trim to get the coffin bone in alignment with the pastern bones, but remember that if the hoof and pastern bones are in a straight line, it's not a good idea to try to raise the coffin bone, even if it looks low. Low but correctly aligned is better than slightly higher but with a broken forward hoof-pastern axis. Also, a big wedge might lift the heels of the hoof capsule, but there is evidence that the coffin bone might actually rock back a little in the hoof capsule. It might look better on the outside, but you could also be pinching sensitive structures and creating bruising or corns. There's

A wedge pad

no magic wand that works for everything, but it can be useful for some circumstances.

If you're going to wedge, please wedge responsibly! Remember when we talked about how the frog and the back half of the hoof are flexible and elastic for shock absorption? That flexibility means that if we wedge the heels without supporting the frog, it can collapse downward between the heels. You might be safe doing it on a strong footed horse in a dry environment where feet are harder, but a soft, wet foot that's already low and weak? You're asking for trouble.

One way we can avoid that trouble is by using full pads instead of rim pads. A full pad covers the entire bottom surface of the hoof, including the frog, while a rim pad only covers the area of the foot already covered by the shoe. A full wedge pad helps support a weak frog rather than allowing it to sink to the ground. You can even use a wedged frog support pad.

Another way we can help frogs cope under pads is by using firm hoof packing or pour-in pads (more on this in a second) under the pads. Again, this fills in any gaps so that the frog can be engaged, even if it is lifted up off the ground.

For the horse who needs intense protection, full metal pads are an option. This can either be removable or

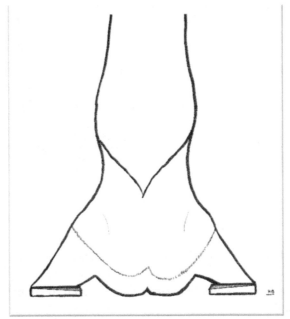

Weak feet may collapse through a shoe or wedge pad

permanently attached to the shoe. The removable version, often attached with small threaded bolts, is known as a hospital plate, and it's great for horses with hoof wounds. The wound is protected under the plate and kept clean, but the plate can also be removed for treatment whenever necessary. Full, non-removable metal pads are less common, but they are sometimes used for urban police horses who may be working on dangerous footing, especially in riot control situations where people may intentionally try to lame up horses.

Metal, though, is the least common pad material. The majority of pads are made of either leather or plastic, and the types of pads we've talked about so far are usually available in both materials. Leather may absorb more concussion and can be more breathable, but plastic pads often hold up to abuse better and can be manufactured with greater variety. There's one type of pad that only comes in plastic though, and that's snow pads.

A removable metal pad known as a hospital plate

Where are my Northerners? If you live somewhere that snow stays on the ground for any length of time, you've probably had to chisel chunks of snow out of your horse's hooves. All that snow packed in there isn't just annoying, it can also be dangerous for your horse. Walking on those big snowballs, your horse is unsteady and his muscles, tendons, and ligaments have to work a lot harder. Moving at speed, he really doesn't have a lot of control over the angle that his feet land

Snowball pad

or load, and pulling ligaments or spraining a tendon is a real risk. Luckily, we have snow pads. Snow pads come in two varieties -- rim pads or full pads. Full pads provide more protection, but both types function on the same principle. They have a flexible plastic bubble that pops snow out as it tries to pack in. This can save you a ton of time picking snow and ice out of your horse's hooves, and save your horse a lot of stress and strain.

There's also a relative newcomer to the world of pads; pour-in pads, which are "poured in" to the hoof as a thick liquid that quickly sets up as a firm gel. There are a ton of options that this invention gives us. We can use it as a flat, all over pour to protect a thin sole; we can do a thick pour all the way to the ground; or we can dam off areas before we pour so that the gel only flows to certain areas. Thanks to this feature, we can use it to protect an injured area by pouring the rest of the bottom of the hoof and leaving the injured area open for treatment so that the rest of the sole takes the weight. We can also pour the back half of a hoof so that the frog takes some weight so that an injured hoof wall can be relieved.

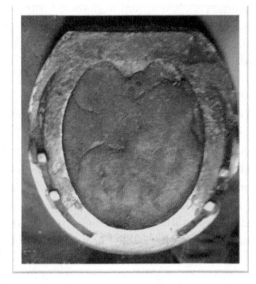

A pour in pad

We can even use a pour-in pad that goes all the way to the ground so that the sole can't flex towards the ground. Normally, sole flexion is a good thing, but if your horse has a broken coffin bone, you would want to limit all the hoof capsule movement that you can.

When it comes to pads, we've got an option for ever season and every lameness. Here's to modern science!

Quick Takeaways

- **Pads can be used to transfer load off of an injured area.**
- **Pads may be used to reduce concussion or hoof movement.**
- **Wedge pads are sometimes used to change hoof angle, but individual conformation should be taken into account.**
- **Snow pads can reduce the amount of ice and snow that ball up in the hoof.**

19 THE B WORD

I was talking about Breakover! Geez, you thought I was going to start cussing?

Breakover is one of those buzzwords that people like to throw around. You've probably heard this one from vets, farriers, even trainers and other horse owners. And people say it so confidently that you don't want to be the dummy who has to ask what it means.

You're not dumb if you don't know the B word. Part of what makes it so confusing is that the word breakover is used to mean a couple of different things, and people rarely define which one they're talking about. They'll just say something like *Bring his breakover back* or, incorrectly, *he needs more breakover.* But no one ever defines what type of breakover they are talking about -- the phase of the stride, breakover distance, or the point of breakover. They may not even know that there are three different meanings to the word. Most people just use it to mean "shorten the toe." It's actually a bit more interesting than that.

The phase of stride known as breakover is the basis for the other two terms, so we'll talk about that first. When we're talking about horse movement, we break the stride up into different chunks so that we can get specific.

- The swing phase, which begins the moment the hoof leaves the ground. The leg then extends forward and the swing phase ends just before the hoof lands again.
- The stance phase, which begins when the hoof impacts the ground, often called heel strike or landing. The hoof slides to a stop and the leg becomes fully loaded, known as midstance. The final section of the stance phase is breakover, where the heels leave the ground and the hoof pivots onto the toe. The stance phase ends as the hoof leaves the ground and re-enters the swing phase.

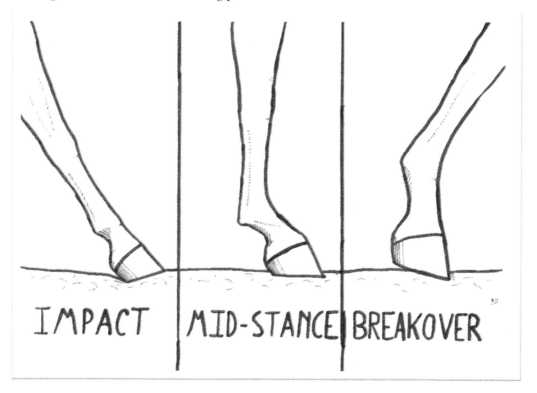

IMPACT | MID-STANCE | BREAKOVER

You can get more specific, but those are the basics.

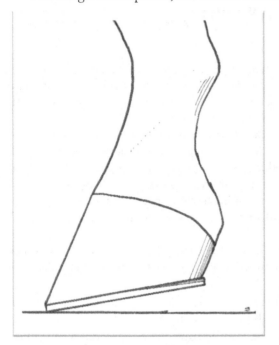

Breakover- the phase of the stride

Point of breakover

Breakover is the part of the stride where your horse's body is shifting forward and momentum, along with the deep digital flexor tendon, and pulling that hoof off the ground. Just before the moment that breakover occurs, the deep digital flexor tendon is under a huge amount of tension, because it's building up power to snap that hoof off the ground. The more difficult it is to breakover, the more that tension has to build before the hoof actually leaves the ground. If we're talking about how long it takes for the hoof to breakover, that's called "time of breakover."

Point of breakover, on the other hand, is a specific point on your horse's hoof, the part of her hoof that is the farthest forward on the ground surface. This is the point that the hoof rotates around as breakover (the phase of the stride) occurs. The point of breakover is something that we can affect through trimming and shoeing. For instance, in a really long toe, low heeled horse, we would have a breakover point that was pretty far forward. However, if we trim off some of the extra toe and fit up a shoe with a beveled or rolled toe, the new breakover point will be quite a bit farther back. Remember, it's the last point touching the ground, so if we bevel the shoe, our breakover point would become the last point of the *unbeveled* surface of the shoe, since the beveled part won't touch the ground.

So what causes extra tension before the moment of breakover? Breakover distance. This is a measurement of the distance between the point of breakover and the center of rotation of the coffin

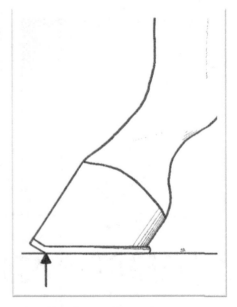

Point of breakover with a rocker toe

joint. Imagine a line drawn straight down from the middle of the coffin joint. That's your center of rotation. A big distance between that point and the point of breakover means more tension on the deep flexor tendon before breakover (the stride phase) happens.

Clear as mud? Now you know why most people don't explain what they're talking about when they say breakover.

When people say that the breakover needs to come back, they are talking about the point of breakover. And what happens when we move the point of breakover back? That's right, the breakover distance gets smaller. Smaller equals less tension before the moment of breakover. So if you have an injury in the deep flexor tendon, or in the navicular bone, which is right under the deep flexor tendon reducing the breakover distance and therefore, the tension on the deep flexor tendon can be really useful.

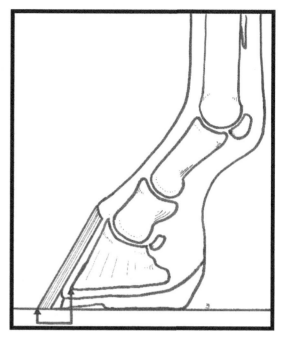

Breakover distance

If reducing the breakover distance reduces tension on the deep flexor tendon, shouldn't we be doing it to all horses as preventative care? Not really. The deep flexor tendon needs to build up a certain amount of tension so that it can do its job and flex the leg for the flight phase. Like a lot of things, it's a good thing up to a point, but it can be overdone.

So what do people mean when they say *he needs more breakover?* It's just another (confusing) way to say that we need to reduce his breakover distance. *Easing breakover* is similar, but it specifically refers to reducing the amount of force necessary to create the movement of breakover. We're still talking about reducing breakover distance, just saying it a little differently.

It's also important to understand that hind feet don't experience breakover the same way that front feet do. On the front feet, breakover occurs as the body moves over the limb and continues forward, lifting the heels off of the ground. The front feet aren't propelling the horse, they are there for balance and steering, so when it comes to the stride, they aren't really "pushing off." On the other hand, hind feet are driving the whole horse. A hind foot

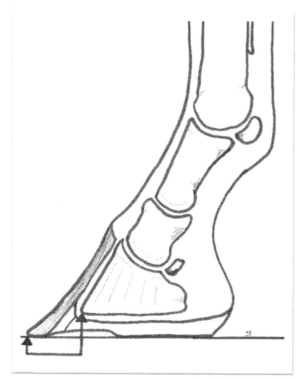

Breakover distance increases with a long toe

111

stays planted on the ground and the hind leg pushes the horse's body forward from that point. If you watch a slow motion video of a horse galloping, the hind feet push off the ground and "break over" after they have left the ground. It can be difficult to get a grasp on, but the important thing to know is that squaring toes or setting back the shoes on the hinds isn't going to speed or ease breakover, but it may affect the horse's ability to push off and drive themselves forward with their hind feet.

There's a lot of talk about breakover these days, and it is an important idea. We just have to make sure that we're all on the same page when we talk about it.

Quick Takeaways

- **Breakover: the stride phase refers to the time between the heels leaving the ground and the toe leaving the ground.**
- **Time of breakover is the amount of time it takes for that action to occur.**
- **Point of breakover is the last point touching the ground when the hoof is leaving the ground, the point that the hoof pivots around.**
- **Breakover distance is a measurement of the amount of distance between the center of rotation of the coffin bone and the point of breakover.**
- **Reducing the breakover distance lowers the amount of force that the deep flexor tendon exerts before breakover occurs.**

20 WHERE'S MY HORSE'S SHOE? ALL ABOUT SHOE LOSS.

If you have a horse that wears shoes, you might have been there … You bring your horse in, planning to go for a ride, but when you pick her hooves you suddenly realize she's missing a shoe. Darn it, no ride for you today, and now you're hoping that your farrier will be able to come out soon to fix it.

It's no fun when it happens, but it gets really frustrating for everyone involved when it happens frequently. If it happens a lot, you might be wondering what's going on. Is your farrier screwing something up? Is there something you can change to help your horse keep her shoes on?

Yes, shoe fit can be an issue, but farriers don't want to come back to fix shoes any more than you want to call them to tell them about it. Occasionally a horse needs a shoe fit longer or wider than normal if they have special hoof concerns like severely crushed heels, but even then, shoe loss usually will have another contributing factor. I've never met a farrier that didn't look for fit issues the first time a shoe comes off, so if you've lost more than one shoe, there's a good chance that there are other factors at play.

So what other factors might be contributing to your horse's shoe loss?

- Turnout in muddy conditions. A lot of people like to say that the mud sucks off the shoes, but it actually works a little differently than that. The nails holding his shoes on are more than strong enough to deal with the suction that the mud produces, but a 250-pound weight pinning the shoe down while the foot tries to leave? That's a different story. When your horse is out moving around in slippery, sticky mud, he's not terribly coordinated, and sometimes his front feet can't get out of the way before his hind feet arrive, or a foot slips and it's in a location that he wasn't expecting. When a hind foot steps on a front shoe, there's a lot of weight holding that shoe down while the forward momentum of your horse keeps the hoof moving forward. The same thing can happen in deep snow, or even working in deep or uneven footing.

- Poor quality hoof. If your horse has genetically thin or weak hoof walls, or has been on a shoe-pulling spree so her hoof looks like a worn out chew toy, there might not be enough mass for the nails to hold on to. Usually this one becomes an issue if one of the other factors on the list is happening, rather than being the only problem. If this is the case, ask your farrier

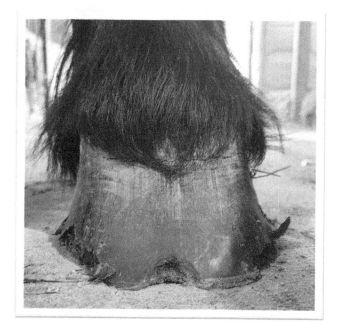

Weak, chipping hoof

and/or vet if they think your horse might benefit from a hoof supplement or nutritional change, and try to remove any other shoe loss risks that you can. Sometimes you can stop the shoe loss cycle if she can just keep a shoe on long enough to grow some fresh, strong hoof.

- Overly energetic play. This one's tough because everyone loves seeing their horse having a great time, playing with his friends, stretching his legs -- right up until that shoe comes flying off. Especially in rambunctious youngsters, it can be hard to keep them from going crazy when turnout time comes.

A chipped hoof doesn't allow for strong nails

Unfortunately, during all those fun games, horses get themselves into some crazy positions and young horses aren't known for their coordination. Or his buddy can even help him pull his shoes by running right beside or behind him and stepping on his shoes. Like a bunch of kids in a ball pit, somebody's going to get hurt but everyone's having fun. Plus, during some phases of growing, horses can go through a gangly-legged phase that doesn't help at all. So what can you do to help? Obviously you can't turn off your horse's playful spirit and you wouldn't want to even if you could. You can, however, keep him from catching his shoe so much with a good pair of bell boots. We'll talk about those in more detail in a couple minutes. You might also have to turn him out with a calmer companion if his buddies like to get a little crazy. He'll still play with a calmer friend but it's less likely to get out of hand. Or if he's a horse that stresses during turnout and bringing in times, it might help to change up the order that horses are brought in or out. Maybe he doesn't like being out there alone and runs the fence line, or maybe he needs to be first to come in when he knows there's food in his stall.

- Pawing or playing near obstacles. The classic is a horse that doesn't like being left alone in the pasture and paws at the gate to come in. It's easy for her to accidently put her foot through the gate while she

Pawing over a door frame is a risk for shoe loss

114

paws, and then hook the shoe as she pulls it back. The same thing can happen if there are tree roots or a rail at ground level in an area where horses eat or play. Pawing or even backing up across these obstacles can pop a shoe off. Pawing or kicking at a stall door that pops out when it's hit can trap a shoe in the door frame too. Some horses will even snag shoes on a wire fence and leave them hanging there. Removing obstacles and making sure that she's not the last one to come out of the field can fix this one. Even baling twine that's buried in the mud can snag a shoe under the right circumstances, so make sure if you're feeding hay outdoors

Conformation or lack of collection can lead to overreaching

that all the twine comes back inside with you. Besides, no one wants to run the risk of their horse accidently ingesting twine.

- Conformation. If your horse has a short back and long legs, it's really easy to catch a front shoe. Likewise, if his hind feet are really close together, he might step on one hind with the other and pull a shoe. There's nothing you can do to change your horse's conformation, but bell boots can help.

- Lack of collection while working. If she's not really paying attention while you're riding, you already know she might stumble or put her feet down in silly places or misjudge her distances to jumps. Fast work like running barrels is also a good way for horses to step on themselves or put a foot wrong. All of that means that she's not thinking about getting her feet out of the way and keeping her legs collected and moving straight. You know what happens next -- feet hit shoes, and shoes go flying.

- Stomping flies or kicking. Repeatedly slamming his feet against hard footings like concrete or hard-packed dirt can raise clinches on shoes, bend nails and spring shoes, and even shear nails off over time. If your horse has this issue, adding fly boots can help a lot. If he's kicking the wall in his stall, see if you can find out when or why. Many horses kick the wall to warn off a neighbor especially while they're eating so if he's particularly concerned about a neighbor, maybe you can switch him to a different stall and see if he gets along better with another horse. You can also alter the stall by adding rubber mats on the wall to reduce concussion. Some people ultimately resort to kicking chains, a padded bracelet that goes on his leg and annoys him with a short chain that rattles against his leg when he kicks, but doesn't hurt him.

- Too much moisture. Hooves don't like excessive moisture, because it softens horn, and that means weaker horn for the nails on your shoes to attach to. Unfortunately, wet conditions are especially damaging to horses that already started out with genetically weak or poor hooves. High moisture content can also give bacteria a good breeding environment. One example is a horse that's always out in wet paddocks or in mud. Early morning turnout in areas with heavy dew can saturate hooves. Humans might be a big factor in this one -- repeated bathing. Obviously, you don't want your horse walking around filthy every day, but try to keep cleaning to drier methods as often as possible if your horse has weaker hooves. If bathing is necessary, try applying a hoof sealant and allowing it to dry before bathing.

Muddy turnout is a big risk for shoe loss

- Too long of a shoeing interval. I probably don't have to say this, but shoeing jobs do have an expiration date. Your horse's hooves are constantly growing, so there will come a point where the shoe won't fit the foot that well, especially since the hoof is constantly expanding and contracting. Eventually that will loosen up nails. If you're concerned because your horse's shoes are coming off at twelve weeks, that's more of a schedule problem than a shoeing problem. Or if your horse has a superpower for growing hoof, you might have to keep her on a shorter shoeing schedule than normal.

- Rider error. I know, I know, this one is nobody's favorite, but it does happen. Riders that sit too far forward on their horse's neck, or riders who are too large for their horse, can cause stumbling and keep their horse from being able to get their feet out of the way in time. Hopefully this isn't you, but if it is, you can fix it! Ask your trainer or an experienced rider to help you make sure your saddle position is correct and that you're sitting in the right spot. And remember, not everyone is the size of a jockey or made to ride a pony. If you're six feet tall, you're going to need a bigger horse to be proportionate than if you are five feet nothing. Luckily, horses, like people, come in all shapes and sizes and there's a perfect match for everyone.

How do you know how your horse is pulling shoes? If you aren't there at the exact moment that shoe goes flying, you might feel like you're in the dark. But there are a lot of clues if you can find the lost shoe.

I know, it's a pain in the butt to go wander around in the field looking for one small needle-in-a-haystack shoe. (Hint -- it's probably near food, water, the gate, or the giant skid marks). But there are a lot of good reasons to find it.

First, its location and the shape that it's in can give you clues as to how your horse is pulling shoes. When you find it, look around for obstacles like tree roots, bent gate bars or deep mud. You can also check out the shoe. If it's bent, your horse or another horse probably stepped on the shoe. If it's not bent, your horse's hoof wall might be on the weaker side. Your farrier might even be able to tell from the direction that the nails are bent how your horse pulled the shoe.

Another reason you want to find shoes is that if you have the lost shoe, your farrier doesn't need as much time to fix it. If they have to shape a new shoe, it takes a little longer, especially if they have any special pads or modifications, and any time a farrier is fixing a shoe, that wasn't a task they scheduled ahead of time. If they have a full schedule, it can be hard to find a big chunk of time in the day to drive to a barn and make a new shoe. It requires a lot less time to pop six nails in a shoe and clinch it, so it's easier to find the time on a busy day.

Last, and most important, you want to find a lost shoe because horses have a habit of trying to self-destruct. If they are turned out in a beautiful field with one hazard in it, they will find that hazard and see how big of a vet bill they can come up with for you. And a lost shoe out in a field is a hazard. Even if it is a flat shoe with no clips, it has six sharp bent nails sticking out of it and they quickly turn into sharp, rusty, bent nails. What happens when your horse steps on the shoe or decides to go for a roll right where the shoe is laying? I'm sure you've seen the super scary, gross pictures on social media so I don't have to tell you that it gets messy and painful.

Okay, maybe I gave you some ideas about where your shoe loss is coming from. Want the super secret magic bullet that helps almost all kinds of shoe loss?

Bell boots. But not just any bell boots. *Bell boots that fit.*

Bell boots work by covering both your horse's heels and the heels of his shoes, so that if (or when) he steps on himself, the bell boot slides his other foot off instead of letting it grab the edge of the shoe. So bell boots only work if the bell boot actually *cover*

Too small a bell boot doesn't help keep shoes on

A well fit bell boot

the back of the shoe. This means that a properly fit bell boot comes down all the way to the ground when your horse is standing. Say it with me, folks. Bell boots should touch the ground.

Oh, and one other little detail: if your bell boot is ripped up and looks like a beaver chewed on it, it may or may not protect the shoe. If one of the ripped out sections happens to be in the area where the hind foot is coming up to catch the shoe, it's going to do no good at all. I don't know if you're a gambler, but I wouldn't like to gamble on whether or not one of the good chunks of the bell boot will cover the

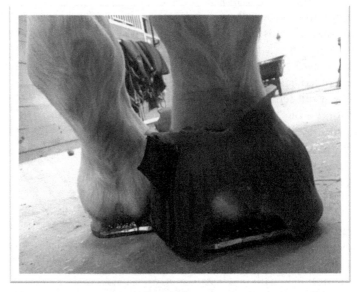

Torn up bell boots need to be replaced

heel when you need it. If you notice damage, save yourself a headache and just buy a new pair.

You might find out that your hard-on-shoes horse is also hard on bell boots. It makes sense that if she likes to pull shoes, that wear and tear is going to go on the bell boots if they're doing their job. If you're constantly finding torn up bell boots, try going with the sturdiest brand you can find, and if that doesn't help, try this: two pairs of bell boots.

I can feel you looking at me weird from here. I'm not crazy (okay, I might be but that's unrelated to the current conversation). For some horses, one pair of bell boots isn't enough. They reach up and pinch a chunk of bell boot between the front hoof and the back hoof, and it gets ripped off. If you put a larger pair of bell boots on top of your normal pair, it puts a softer surface under the top pair of bell boots so there's less of a chance of pinching and ripping a chunk of the bell boot out. Sounds nuts? Don't knock it 'till you try it.

Remember, there's rarely just one factor to shoe loss. Just because you see one thing that makes sense on the list above, don't discount the rest of the list. Give it a read and consider all the options. The more shoe loss causes you can remove, the better your chances are of keeping shoes on. Plus your farrier will be happy, your horse's hooves will be healthier, and you won't have to miss any more rides!

Quick Takeaways
- **There is always a reason for shoe loss, and sometimes more than one factor.**
- **For the safety of the horse and the convenience of the farrier, lost shoes should always be found if possible.**
- **Well fitted bell boots can prevent a large percentage of lost shoes.**

Part 4
Nutrition, Environment, And Management:
Factors For Hoof Health

21 WATER AND WEATHER

If you live in an area that has four distinct seasons, I'm betting you've noticed a difference between how much your horse's hooves grow in the winter versus the summer. You might also notice that your horse's hooves get softer and shed sole and frog during the wetter seasons.

And if you live somewhere with weather that's pretty consistent all year round, your horse's hooves are still adjusting to the weather, even if it's not as obvious.

Horses that live in consistently wet environments have higher moisture contents in their hooves. There's been some disagreement between researchers whether the hoof wall moisture content changes when it's exposed to a lot of water, or if it's just the sole and frog that are affected[31]. We do know that the elasticity of horn samples changed between wet and dry hooves[32]. Hooves with higher moisture contents are more flexible but softer, which makes it tougher for the hoof to resist all the compression that it's exposed to. Even if the hoof wall isn't as affected by moisture as the frog and sole, the hoof wall needs help from the frog and sole to keep everything working in the hoof. If they aren't doing their part, the hoof wall has to put in overtime. Wet hooves show overload like flare and distortion a lot easier than dry ones do.

Also, wet environments are hospitable to bacteria and fungus that can attack the hoof (think thrush and white line disease). If you don't believe me, think back to that experiment we all did in middle school with the slices of bread. The usual method was to take slices of bread from a loaf and sprinkle them with water, then put them in different places. One would be put on a sunny windowsill. One slice went in the refrigerator, and one went in a dark closet. Remember which one went nuts and grew a big, fuzzy moldy jungle? The one that was in the dark closet. Bacteria and fungus dig moist environments with plenty of food and no sunlight. We're going to talk more about why that's important when we

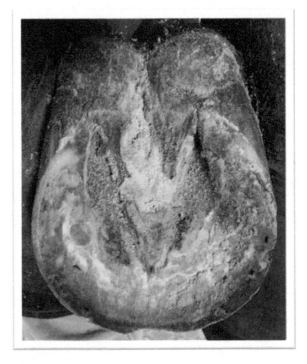

Exfoliating frog is white in color

---

[31] Hampson, B.A., de Laat, M.A., Mills, P.C., Pollitt, C.C., (2012). Effect of environmental conditions on degree of hoof wall hydration in horses. *Am J Vet Res. 73(3):*435-8.

[32] Hinterhofer C., Stanek C., Binder K. (1998). Elastic modulus of equine hoof horn, tested in wall samples, sole samples and frog samples at varying levels of moisture. *Berl Munch Tierarztl Wochenschr; 111(6):* P. 217-21.

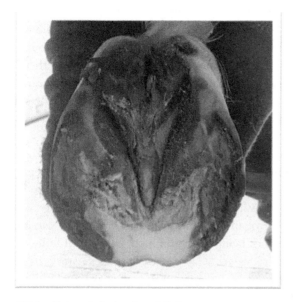

White, flaky sole is simply exfoliating

get into treating white line disease in Chapter 28 and thrush in Chapter 26. For now, just remember that super gross piece of bread with all the mold, and think about how we don't want that to be your horse's hoof.

High moisture content and bacteria can also help separate the layers of the sole and frog that are ready to exfoliate. That's why we typically see sole and frog shedding in the rainy times in spring and fall. In areas with four distinct seasons, sole and frog retention and shedding usually go in cycles, with horses building up and retaining sole in summer when the ground is hard and dry and in winter when the hoof needs extra protection against the frozen ground, and then shedding out all that extra retained sole in spring and fall.

How do you know if what you're seeing is a healthy exfoliation or something scarier? As long as there is good, healthy sole or frog underneath the shedding tissue, you're probably in the clear. On the other hand, if the horse is in pain or if you see any blood, you should give your farrier and/or vet a call.

For those of us that live in wet environments, it's easy to feel like moisture is the enemy. Hooves usually get stronger and have higher angles in the dry seasons. On the other hand, for those that never get moisture, hooves can have very different problems.

Remember how too much moisture makes your horse's hooves too soft and flexible? Well, some flexibility is a good thing, and super dry feet are missing that.

Dry feet, especially those in extremely hot environments that suck the moisture out of everything, can get tight and contracted, instead of flexing open and closed like the back half of the hoof should. That's one of the important shock absorbing mechanisms of your horse's hoof, so now there's more concussion traveling up the leg.

Frog often sheds in layers

The same goes for the cupped sole flexing to absorb shock. A lot of horses in dry environments have really cupped, upright feet, which is great, but what if that cup isn't allowed to function correctly? It's still keeping the coffin bone up off the ground, so that's good, but if it's super dry and hard, it isn't going to be very flexible. If there's no flexion, where does that force go now? A lot of it goes into joints and bones above it, and over time that's extra wear and tear. The same goes for the foot that has a lot of retained sole. If there is no cup to the sole because it's full of sole all the way to the ground, the hoof is getting a lot of protection but not as much shock absorption.

The frog is a similar story. Remember when we talked about the function of the frog way back in Chapter 5? The frog is all about absorbing shock, allowing movement, and keeping blood pumping back up the leg. If you live in an excessively dry place, you've seen the frog your horse gets during dry seasons. That thing turns into concrete, and it is definitely not flexing or acting like a cushion! The outside of a frog in dry country gets so hard that it can only be trimmed with a pair of nippers if at all, instead of being easily trimmed with a hoof knife.

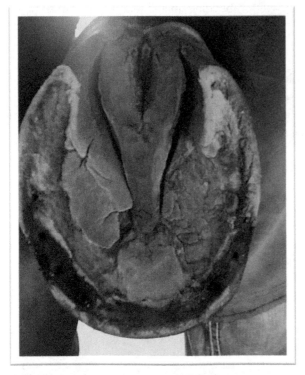

Dry feet retain sole and frog

Whether it's a smart adaptation to really hard, rocky ground or just the natural results of not seeing a drop of moisture for six months, sometimes hooves like that just don't shed sole. They just keep adding layer after layer until it's flat with the ground, while the solar corium is in there like a little hoarder making more sole *just in case*. Whether it needs extra protection or not, it's not in the best interest of the coffin bone or the solar corium to have a big flat block of sole that goes all the way to the ground instead of having a cupped, concaved sole. If the sole is super hard, your farrier might be able to use their nippers to cut through some of it, or they might have to use a small torch to scorch the outer layer of horn so that it temporarily becomes soft enough to trim. And it's not just horses in hot, dry environments that can get this way. If your horse is on stall rest in clean, dry shavings, he can get really hard, dry feet too.

If any of this sounds like your horse, ask your farrier if they would like you to soak your horse's feet before the appointment. It can make a huge difference in how easily your farrier can trim out impacted sole. Soaking can mean overflowing the water trough a little so that she stands in some mud or doing an actual soak like you would for an abscess. Not sure what that would look like? Check out Chapter 40 for more on soaking.

So there are pros and cons to both wet and dry feet. But do you want to know what environment is the absolute worst for your horse's feet? An environment where the feet are constantly going back and forth between wet and dry. Hooves can adapt to wet environments, and hooves can adapt to dry environments. But when they're going from wet to dry every five seconds? The hoof just can't keep up.

If we've learned anything from the Covid-19 pandemic, it's that when you suddenly start washing your hands 348 times per day, your skin is going to become more dry and cracked than the Sahara Desert. Why did adding more water to your hands make them drier? Because they weren't just getting wet, they were getting wet, getting the protective oils washed off them, and then being dried. Repeating that process over and over broke down the natural moisture barrier that your skin has and left it reacting to whatever you were exposing it to. (To be fair, all the alcohol-based sanitizers probably weren't helping either). But you can create the same conditions in your horse's hooves with too much wet and dry.

The main culprit for this problem isn't Mother Nature -- it's us. The horses that go through the most wet and dry switches are usually performance horses who live in barns. Think about the schedule of a horse who lives in this kind of setting. They wake up in the morning in their nicely bedded stall (dry) and then after breakfast they get turned out in the dewy grass (wet) or worse yet, in the mud

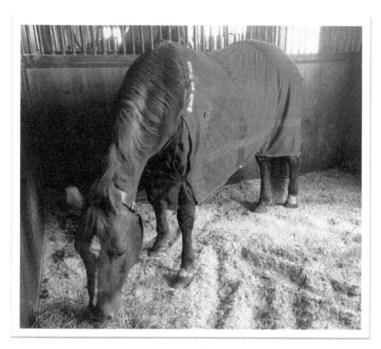

Domestic horses live in very different environments than horses in the wild

(super wet!). Then after an hour or two, they head back into the freshly cleaned stall (dry). A little later, you come out to ride them, but first you give them a good grooming and paint on some of that nice shiny hoof conditioner (wet) before you head into the sand arena to ride (dry). After your ride, you take them to the wash rack and give them a good bath (wet) and then they head back to their stall for the night (dry). In this scenario, they go from wet to dry seven times in one day. That's a lot more change than their hooves would ever see in nature.

And their hooves do show the effects of all that change. It's typical to see small, vertical surface cracks from all the expanding and contracting that the hoof is doing, along with weak, shelly areas around the clinches. You might experience more shoe loss than normal since the hooves are weakened. It's also fairly common to see bacterial and fungal infections in the hoof structures.

What's worse, there's research that suggests that hooves that are already lower quality might be less resistant to the effects of moisture. In a study using hoof samples from horses with good quality horn and poor quality, brittle horn, hoof samples were soaked in water for two weeks. Then the hoof samples were treated with a traceable fluid with the goal of seeing how far the fluid penetrated into the horn. In the hoof samples that they considered to be good horn, soaking the feet didn't change how far the fluid permeated (3-20 cells deep, depending on if it was a cut section of the wall or the outer surface). On the other hand, the brittle hoof showed permeation deep within the section, and soaking the sections made the fluid permeate even farther[33]. The researchers concluded that brittle, poor quality feet don't have a strong permeability barrier though they didn't offer an opinion on whether that was the chicken or the egg in this scenario.

So what can you do to prevent your horse's hooves from being damaged by this kind of wet and dry back and forth? It's not like you can stop turning your horse out or keeping him in a stall, right?

Don't worry, there are less extreme options than releasing him into the wild or keeping a hair dryer pointed at his feet at all times.

Your best game plan is to reduce the number of switches back and forth by taking out some of the unnecessary wet parts of his day. If he normally goes out in a muddy paddock, is there a drier area he could be turned out in? If he's normally on morning turnout in a grassy field that soaks your shoes and the bottom of your jeans when you walk out to get him, see if you can switch his turnout time to a little later in the day when some of the dew has burned off.

Hooves can develop superficial cracks from extreme moisture changes

And if he does go out somewhere wet (I know, sometimes it's unavoidable) make sure to pick out his feet and wipe down the outsides of his hooves when he comes in. The last thing you want are big globs of mud on his hooves that never totally dry. You'll not only have extra moisture exposure, but you're also keeping a nice layer of bacteria against his foot and giving it plenty of time to find a place to colonize. No thanks.

Skip hoof conditioners in favor of a sealant. He's got plenty of exposure to moisture already, so he doesn't need you to throw more on there. Instead, use a sealant that will protect his hooves from moisture, and give it time to dry before you take him into the arena.

---

[33] Kempson S.A., Campbell E.H. (1998). A permeability barrier in the dorsal wall of the equine hoof capsule. *Equine Vet J Suppl. (26):* P. 15-21.

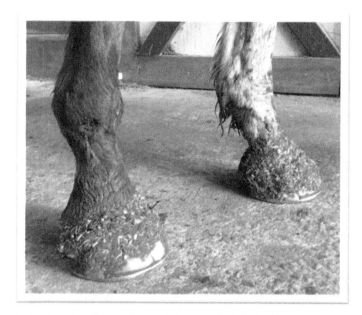

Muddy feet should be picked and cleaned when the horse comes in

I hate to be the one to say it, but your horse really doesn't need a bath every day. Yes, you want to groom him thoroughly and make sure he's not covered in sweat and dirt, but bathing too often isn't healthy either. Hooves aside, bathing frequently can deplete the natural oils in your horse's coat and skin and lead to skin sensitivity and dryness. If he is really sweaty, you can opt for a hose down without using soap or shampoo to reduce the amount of oil you are stripping away. In a lot of cases, you can skip a bath in favor of a dry grooming or even a sponge-bath style spot cleaning. If you do have to bathe (I hear you, show people!) you can apply a sealant to your horse's hooves before you do. Then, after the bath, get as much water off him as possible, especially his legs. Go ahead and grab a towel and dry his legs and hooves. The less time his feet are getting saturated, the better.

What if you're not sure if your horse's feet are suffering from too much wet, too much dry, or too much of both? Ask your farrier! Remember, they are the professional that you hired to keep an eye on your horse's hooves, and they want to have the healthiest feet possible to work on. Plus, they are intimately acquainted with the weather conditions in your area, because they have to deal with them every day. They will be able to show you any symptoms of moisture related issues, or maybe give you the all clear. Either way, they can help make sure that your moisture management program is on point and right for your horse.

Quick Takeaways

- **Environmental moisture plays a huge role in hoof health.**
- **Frequent, rapid changes in environmental moisture are detrimental to the hoof.**

22 HOT AND COLD

Apparently, there's a few magically temperate places in California and Oregon where the temperature range is always between 75 and 40 degrees Fahrenheit and it's sunny most of the time. For the rest of us, we have to deal with either hot summers or cold winters, and if you live in a particularly pleasant corner of the world, you and your horse's hooves might have to deal with both. Awesome!

If you live in an area with hot or humid summers, you are probably more than familiar with the swarms of flies, mosquitos, and other stinging insects that come with it. There's nothing like heading out on a ride only to be swarmed by bugs until you go home covered in itchy bug bites -- and your horse doesn't care for it either. They are often hounded from morning to night by flies and they spend the whole time out in the field swishing their tails, stomping their hooves, and moving around to get away.

All that stomping can be tough on your horse's hooves. If they are on hard ground like dry, packed dirt, rocks, or concrete there's a lot of concussion every time she stomps her hoof. She might bruise her feet if she stomps hard enough or often enough to damage the tiny capillaries in her coriums. If she has white hooves, you might even be able to see red or purple bruising in her hoof walls or soles when her feet are really clean.

Excessive stomping can cause bruising

If she keeps it up, she could actually bruise her coffin bone, which, like any bone bruise, takes a lot longer to heel than a little soft-tissue bruise. You might notice that she's acting a little foot sore or short. She could even inflame her coffin bone, known as pedal osteitis. This can permanently damage her coffin bone, since the bottom edge of the bone will degrade and be easier to fracture in the future.

It's not just internal structures that can be damaged by constant stomping for flies. She can also chip her hoof wall if she's barefoot. Worse, the chipped hoof could rip up into sensitive tissue like a hang nail. Plus, chipping leaves sharp edges that she might cut herself on, and could leave her hoof unevenly balanced.

Horses that wear shoes aren't immune either. When your shod horse stomps at those pesky flies, he puts a ton of shear force on the nails which can either snap nails off or shove the shoe back off of the toe. It can also raise clinches or weaken the hoof wall around the nails, which makes it easier for nails and shoes to loosen up.

So basically, there's nothing good about flies, but you already knew that. So what can you do about it?

The best way to reduce flies is to change the way that manure is managed on your property. If you've ever left a pile of manure in the sun for longer than a few minutes, you know that flies will swarm to that sweet smell. They also love to lay their eggs in it, which is a real bummer if it's going to stay on the property for long enough to let them hatch. Obviously, the less manure is near the horses, the less they will be bothered by flies. So keeping stalls and paddocks clean and frequently emptying muck buckets can help a lot.

What about that giant pile of manure that seems to be attracting every fly in your county? If you have enough space, spread it. Flies don't breed on manure that is dry and broken apart, so if you can get it spread and drying in the sun, you can put the kibosh on the next generation of flies. You do need a lot of space though, with some sources suggesting that the manure from one horse needs to be spread over five acres, minimum. Best case scenario? Find a local farmer that's interested in manure to spread on their fields. The manure is off your land, not breeding flies, and is actually improving a farm field. Win-win-win (as long as the farmer is able to use it frequently enough).

What if you have to keep the manure on your property? Build your pile as far away as possible from the areas where horses live. You probably came up with this on your own from sheer common sense and not wanting a super smelly pile of manure close to the barn.

You can also use traps to trim the fly population. Since one fly can lay about a thousand eggs each season, getting rid of a few flies now could have big impacts next hatching cycle! Traps can be placed near windows and doors into the barn, areas that flies must pass through to get to your horse. Alternatively, place them near areas where there is manure or near paddocks. Any fly that heads into the trap isn't biting your horse.

Use air flow and shade to your advantage, too. Flies love warm sun and still air, so give your horses a shady spot in their turnout where there may be fewer flies. If your horse is stuck in a stall, fans don't just keep him cool, they'll also keep some of the flies off.

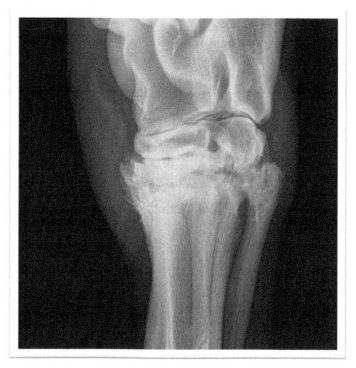

Excessive stomping can lead to arthritis in the hock and other joints

What if it's not your barn, so you can't change how often manure is picked up or whether they use fly traps? The most effective method to protect your horse from flies is by using fly boots and sheets. Look for sturdy, good quality fly boots, because they can take a beating, but they will be your horse's best friend (okay, second only to you, the super nice human who bought her the fly boots). This is the simplest way to reduce the amount of stomping your horse does in the fastest amount of time. It's well worth the cost when you consider how much healthier her feet and legs will be.

Of course, you can also use fly sprays, which are great as a short-term solution but not usually very effective in the long term. You can't spray it on in the morning and expect your horse to stay fly free all day.

Even if it weren't for flies, there's still some concussion related problems that you might face in hot, dry environments. Since the ground is often really dry and hard, every step has more concussion than what you might find in a wetter environment. This means your horse might be more prone to getting arthritic conditions like ringbone or hock arthritis. If you need to reduce concussion on hard ground, talk to your farrier about putting pads on your horse to help.

As we talked about in Chapter 20, you might also see issues with soles and frogs losing flexibility and not shedding out, which doesn't help with concussion issues. But you might also see differences in how much new hoof is produced, depending on whether you have dry summers or wet summers.

Since the amount of hoof your horse grows is dependent on the amount of nutrients available to build from, you can expect to see more hoof growth during seasons where grass is abundant. If you live somewhere that has consistent rains throughout summer, your horse will be getting plenty of green grass during pasture time. That means plenty of extra nutrition for hoof building. However, if you live in an area where rain pretty much stops by July, any grass will be crunchy and dry within a few weeks. That means less fresh forage for your horse, so you might see hoof growth slow down once the grass quits growing. It's not uncommon for horses to grow hoof quickly during spring, slow down a little during a dry summer, pick back up during a rainy fall, and then slow again during winter. If your horse grows hoof really fast, you might have to shorten your shoeing cycle during warm wet seasons.

So what happens when winter rolls around? The flies die off, thank goodness, but before we get to enjoy it, the weather turns cold and snow starts blowing in.

If your horse is outside most of the time, or in an unheated barn, he'll be using a lot of his calories staying warm and growing that super thick coat, so he won't have as much extra energy for growing hoof. You might see his hoof growth rate drop off. And, if he's barefoot, he might wear off foot on the ice and snow too.

If your horse goes outside when it's snowy, you're probably familiar with the frozen snowballs that she brings in on the bottom of her hooves. You've probably chipped them out while cursing Mother Nature and wondering why you live where you do. They're not only annoying for you but they can also be dangerous for your horse. Those big snowballs make uneven footing for her, and if she likes to run around out in the field, she could easily strain a tendon or ligament. If your horse wears shoes, ask your farrier if she can have snow pads. Snow pads are a plastic pad with a bubble that pops snow out of her feet as it tries to pack in.

Even without snow, there's one problem that really throws horses and their humans for a loop every year. That's the magical time of year when mud and winter collide and we end up

Frozen, ridgey mud is very hard on hooves

128

with frozen, churned up mud that's hard as rock, ridgey, and uneven. Fantastic!

When we're having a wet, muddy fall and the paddocks are trampled up and then the bottom drops out of the temperature, horses can get sore quickly. For one, they are forced to walk on extremely uneven, hard ground, which will make joints and soft tissue sore just from all the extra torque.

The worst part for most horses is that the mud is extremely hard, so much so that it's similar to walking on large, uneven rocks. A lot of horses bruise their soles, especially if their hooves are soft from all the mud. If your horse bruises her soles on the frozen mud, and then temps warm up and the mud melts, those bruises are exposed to a lot of bacteria. Bacteria loves nutrient rich sources like blood so it can breed like crazy. It's a perfect storm for creating and feeding abscesses.

You can't prevent mud from freezing, but there are a few things you can do to keep you horse healthy.

If you know that you've got a muddy paddock and it's supposed to freeze hard, see if you can flatten the worst of it out, usually around gates, water troughs, and feeding areas. If you are lucky enough to have access to a roller, that's a super quick way to get it done. Otherwise, you might be stuck doing the most important parts by hand.

If you already know that you have a thin-soled horse, consider throwing snowpads on early so his hooves have some extra protection before he gets sore. And if you have another turnout area that isn't so muddy and uneven, that can be another good option.

Icy conditions can also be very dangerous for horses, with slip and fall injuries ranging from pulled soft tissues to broken bones. Luckily for the shod horse, your farrier may be able to add traction to your shoes with options like borium, drilltech, or tungsten ice pins.

Summer and winter both come with their own struggles, but if you plan ahead, you can still enjoy time with your horse and keep her healthy and sound.

Quick Takeaways

- **Reducing the fly population can alleviate some of the detrimental effects of warm weather.**
- **The challenges of cold weather can often be reduced with a little planning and forethought.**

23 ALL THE THINGS THE HOOF HAS TO PUT UP WITH...

You already know that your horse's hooves put up with a lot of crap ... literally. Every time your horse poops while you're tacking up, you know he's sticking his hooves in it if he can beat you to it.

So what happens when your horse keeps his hooves packed full of manure? It's not just unpleasant when you pick it out, it's also harboring a lot of bacteria. If you've ever wondered why it's hard to stay ahead of thrush in his hooves, you might be interested to know that many of the common bacteria found in thrush infections are also found in manure. You're cleaning out his hooves and trying to kill bacteria, and then he steps in that nice fresh pile of manure and sticks all that bacteria right back in there. Thanks, buddy!

You can't stop him from stepping in his manure as soon as he drops it, but you can prevent him from stepping in it over and over. The more you can keep the areas that he lives in cleaned up, the less opportunity he has to get that bacteria in his feet. If we go back to that bread mold experiment we talked about in Chapter 20, we know that bacteria loves a wet, warm environment, so clean and dry is the name of the game for thrush prevention. Using good quality, absorptive bedding is an important step, since a study performed on horses in Norway found that the biggest risk factors for thrush were wet bedding, using straw as bedding (we'll talk about this in a second), and spending all their time in a stall[34]. Thrush prevention isn't just limited to keeping his stall clean though. If you can get manure picked up in paddocks before he has a chance to trample it into the ground, especially if you live in a wet area where his paddock turns into a mud puddle, you can keep the paddock significantly cleaner.

Manure isn't the only challenge to the hoof that your horse creates for herself. She also has to deal with ammonia and hydrogen sulfide rich urine. It doesn't just smell; it also can seriously affect her hoof strength. A study performed on cow hooves showed that by exposing horn to ammonia and hydrogen sulfide, hardness and elasticity of horn was reduced significantly. Hooves soaked in ammonia and hydrogen sulfide also lost a lot of their moisture barrier, because they broke down one of the most important lipids that helps waterproof the hoof[35].

If you are already struggling with moisture management like we talked about in Chapter 20, managing urine can also be a really helpful factor. This usually comes down to bedding type and cleanliness. Frequent stall cleaning helps, as well as pushing back bedding to allow the stall floor to dry. The type of bedding used also makes a difference. A study performed in 2016 compared the moisture absorption of pine shavings, straw, hemp, and spruce bedding. Each type of bedding was exposed to urine and researchers measured how much each type of bedding absorbed. The clear winner? Pine shavings absorbed the most urine and continued to absorb more for the full 24-hour test period.

---

[34] Holzhauer, M., Bremer, R., Santman-Berends, I., Smink, O., Janssens, I., Back, W. (2017). Cross-sectional study of the prevalence of and risk factors for hoof disorders in horses in The Netherlands. *Prev Vet Med. 140*: P. 53-59.

[35] Higuchi, H., Kurumado, H., Mori, M., Degawa, A., Fujisawa, H., Kuwano, A., Nagahata, H. (2009). Effects of ammonia and hydrogen sulfide on physical and biochemical properties of the claw horn of Holstein cows. *Can J Vet Res. ;73(1)*: P. 15-20.

Another big advantage to pine shavings was that they not only absorbed more moisture, but they also hosted less bacteria than the other types of bedding. The study also looked at four types of bacteria that commonly infect horses: *Streptococcus equi,* which causes Strangles; *Streptococcus zooepidemicus,* a bacteria that causes equine respiratory and reproductive infections; *Fusobacterium necrophorum,* which is one of the primary thrush causing bacteria; and *Dermatophilus congolensis* or Mudfever bacteria. Pine bedding actually showed less bacterial growth than the other types of bedding tested[36]. Some researchers have suggested that pine wood actually has an antibacterial and antifungal effect, but it could also be tied to the better moisture absorption. Whatever the reason, it's definitely good to have less from that list of bacteria in your horse's house.

That said, pine shaving aren't a magic bullet. The study above only looked at moisture absorption and bacterial growth over 24 hours, since it's recommended that manure and urine be removed every 24 hours from stalls. There are no shaving on earth that can keep bacteria from growing if manure and urine aren't cleaned up regularly. Still, if you're doing your part and cleaning up after your horse, using pine shavings instead of straw can make a big difference when it comes to exposing your horse's hooves to less bacteria and urine.

Manure and urine might be the most destructive things your horse's hooves have to put up with, but there are plenty of other things that he walks around on that affect his hooves, for better and for worse. You already know from riding that your horse feels a lot different when she's working on soft footing like deep grass or sand, versus hard footing, like a packed dirt trail, concrete, or even a sand arena that hasn't been consistently maintained and has a hard track around the rail. It feels different because her feet interact differently with different footings, and she has to use her body differently to compensate.

If you do a lot of work on firmer footings, you'll probably see a lot of wear on your horse's shoes or his feet if he's barefoot. This isn't too

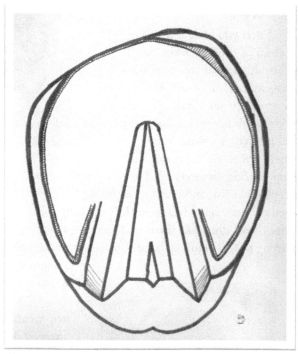

Uneven wear

bad if he's got stellar conformation, but if he doesn't move perfectly straight, you'll see more wear on one side than the other.

[36] Yarnell, K., Le Bon, M., Turton, N., Savova, M., McGlennon, A. and Forsythe, S. (2017). Reducing exposure to pathogens in the horse: a preliminary study into the survival of bacteria on a range of equine bedding types. *J Appl Microbiol, 122*: P. 23-29.

You might also see this type of wear if your horse is turned out in a limestone paddock, or in a hard, rocky area. These types of turnouts can be great for managing moisture issues, but they do come with the downside of extra wear. Again, not as much of an issue if your horse has pretty straight legs, but something to keep an eye on if she's got less-than-textbook ideal conformation. With enough wear, even a well conformed hoof can just get too short.

There's one school of thought that says that since your horse wore his feet that way, that's how he wants them and how he'll be the most comfortable. There is certainly something to be said for easing breakover in the direction that he likes to move. The problem with him self-trimming in that direction is that he doesn't know when to stop.

If you look at the bottom of your sneakers, you'll probably see that you wear some spots more than others. I usually wear off the outside of my heels in my work boots. It's fine at first but I don't hit a magic point where it feels the best and then stop wearing my heels off. I just

Conformation issues lead to uneven and excessive wear

keep on wearing more and more until I have to stand and walk differently to compensate, and then my back starts feeling stiff. Eventually, I buy a new pair of boots, and for the first two or three days I don't like them at all because they feel weird, but before the end of the week, I'm starting to feel better because I'm standing and walking more squarely. I sure wouldn't be taking my new boots and grinding off the heel to match my old one!

Most horses don't have a point at which they stop wearing either, so if you don't reset every so often by doing a balanced trim of the hoof and addressing any distortion, they will keep wearing out of balance until they get to a point where they move more crookedly just to compensate … and when they compensate, they wear their hooves even more out of whack. This is why if your horse is barefoot and working on hard ground, you might need to think about shoes to help imbalanced hooves. He might be growing plenty of foot, and if we put a shoe on to

Joint issues can cause excessive shoe wear

132

protect it, he'll stay a lot more even. Usually a simple, no-frills shoe will do the job just fine.

Hard footings also send more concussion up your horse's legs when her hooves hit the ground, so you might want to keep an eye out for arthritic changes. Although you can't see the coffin joint, you can look for soft, puffy swelling at the pastern and fetlock joints, as well as knees and hocks. This can be a warning sign that her joints are trying to cushion themselves by adding extra joint fluid, which is one of the first steps in arthritis, and definitely the step where you want to catch things. You might be able to change up a few factors to help her out, like changing workload, improving the footing that she works or lives on, or changing turnout. You can talk to your vet about a maintenance plan for her joints, and talk to your farrier about a shoeing plan to help reduce concussion, which usually involves some kind of pads.

Another type of concussion-related injury you may see is in the form of coffin bone inflammation or inflammation of the sensitive lamina, usually called road founder. These would both be indicated by severe lameness, usually after a hard ride on firm surface, and is a good time to pump the breaks.

Coffin bone inflammation, or Pedal Osteitis, is usually seen in horses with flat feet, where the coffin bone is directly bearing weight on the bottom surface of the bone (instead of being held up by the comfy laminar hammock like we talked about way back in Chapter 2). So all that force is going straight into the bone. And if there's one thing the coffin bone doesn't care for, it's direct force. Pedal Osteitis usually shows up in an x-ray looking like a ragged edge on the coffin bone instead of a nice smooth border. This is because some of the bone has actually been reabsorbed into the body, which seriously weakens the remaining bone. A lot of times this can even lead to coffin bone fractures.

If you've got a case of Pedal Osteitis, you need to get your vet on board right away so that you can limit the amount of bone loss. Your vet might prescribe NSAIDs to reduce the inflammation, but you also need to make some management changes to remove the cause of the inflammation. (It doesn't help to stick a bandaid on a cut if you haven't pulled the knife out!) This means plenty of rest and staying off hard ground for a while. You should also talk to your farrier about options for getting that sole up off of the ground, which might mean shoes and pads or boots if your horse is barefoot, or adding some kind of sole protection if your horse already has shoes.

Road founder, or mechanical laminitis (mechanical referring to outside forces as opposed to metabolic or other internal causes), is also a serious concern that you want to get on top of quickly. It's essentially an overloading of the lamina, usually from too much concussion. As you might guess from the name, it is seen classically in horses working hard on paved roads, especially when they're working at high speed. Remember, adding velocity increases the amount of force on the hooves. Like any other stressed tissue, the lamina become inflamed creating internal swelling, heat, and pain. You'd start to see these symptoms shortly after the incident of overwork on hard ground.

No matter what kind of structure you're talking about, there are two basic reasons that structures fail. Either a normal structure is placed under abnormal load, or an abnormal structure is placed under normal load. The third, and most catastrophic option would be to place an abnormal structure under abnormal load, but most abnormal structures don't really make it past a normal load, so we don't see this one too often. Example: Let's say I build a house. I'm not a carpenter, so my building skills aren't great and the house looks okay, but it's got a pretty shoddy foundation and I didn't really reinforce anything. This would be an abnormally weak structure because I had no idea what I was doing. On the first windy day, half my roof blows off. This is an example of an abnormal structure failing under normal load.

Now let's say I learned my lesson. I pay actual contractors to construct a good quality home for me. I'm super excited because the walls don't shake when I slam a door now. This house will last forever! Then, the tornado sirens come on and a tornado comes through and rips the roof off my new house. There was nothing wrong with my house's construction (normal structure), but the force applied to it was definitely abnormal (gale force winds). Both structures end up roofless, but the reason why is different each time. And if my poorly built house had faced the tornado, we'd be looking at picking up matchsticks from all over the county. The destruction would have been much worse.

So in the case of road founder, we're usually looking at a normal structure (healthy lamina) that has been exposed to abnormal load (several hours of severe concussion doing high speed road work). We're going to talk a lot more about how laminitis works in Chapter 34, so flip over there if you want to know more. For now, if you are experiencing road founder, call your vet right away so they can help you get the inflammation under control, and make sure that you put your horse in nice, soft footing so that they aren't taking any more concussion in the meantime.

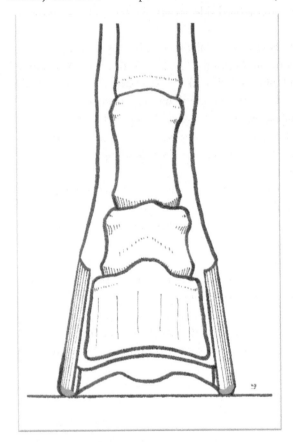

Weight bearing on hard surface is primarily on the hoof wall

At this point, you might be thinking working on hard ground is the devil, and we should all be riding horses in super deep sand arenas. However, if you've ever been one of those really motivated people who likes to go running on the beach during a vacation, you'll know that soft footing comes with its own set of issues. Even if you haven't tried to go for a run on the beach, if you've ever seen anyone running by (from your comfy beach chair with a cold drink in your hand) you may have noticed that they tend to stick to the strip of wet sand. Why? Because it is freaking hard to run in deep, loose sand.

Landing in deep footing might be nice and cushioned, so your horse doesn't have to deal with nearly as much concussion as they would on a firm surface. The problem comes in when it's time to push off, which is the part where a horse gets that forward momentum going. If she's on hard footing, the ground stays firmly underneath her hoof and she can drive forward off of it, but on soft, loose footing, the dirt or sand shifts as she tries to push off of it. She has to push a lot harder to get the same amount of forward momentum. This means much more muscular effort for the same amount of forward movement.

If you ride in arena, you know that there's a big difference between a nicely maintained arena and one that has hard, packed down spots and deep, soft spots. Turns out, that's also a big risk factor for injury. One study testing dirt and synthetic racetracks found that there was a big difference between pre-compacted footing, like that hard ring around the edge of your arena, and normal footing when it came to the way that it reacted with the hoof[37]. And if the reaction with the hoof is different from one step to the next, your horse is going to have a hard time adjusting and being prepared for where and how his feet are landing, leading to stumbling and tripping.

From current research, it looks like a well-maintained soft footing that isn't too deep is the best option. Not only does a soft footing have significantly lower concussion than a hard footing, but it also helps to even out weight bearing, even if your horse doesn't land perfectly flat. This is because the footing can shift slightly and pack in to load areas that might not be able to bear weight on hard surfaces[38]. A study done on French trotters found that a group of horses trained on a hard surface for four months showed significantly more serious injuries than a matching group that trained on a softer surface[39]. Of course, like any study that comes out of the racing industry, keep in mind that those horses were working on hard footing *at speed*, and pretty frequently. Taking a trail ride once a week on a hard packed trail won't trigger results as extreme as what this study showed.

One other thing to keep in mind when you're deciding what kind of footing to ride on is your horse's history. Every horse is an individual so there's no one right answer that fits every single horse. If your horse has had an injury in the past, or has an ongoing degenerative condition, take that into account as well.

You know when your horse is a little off, sometimes it's easy to see in soft footing but almost invisible on a firm surface, or vice versa? That's because certain injuries are more bothered by one type of force than another. In general, bone and cartilage injuries are most obvious on firm footing, because hard tissue has to deal with a lot of concussion. Soft tissue injuries like tendon, ligament and muscle damage are usually more apparent in soft footing, because muscle and tendons have to work harder to create movement in soft footing, and the ligaments and tendons are more likely to have to compensate for uneven footing. So, if your horse is dealing with long term arthritis problems, like hock arthritis or ringbone, you probably aren't going to want to do a lot of riding on hard ground. On the other hand, if she's

---

[37] Setterbo, J.J., Fyhrie, P.B., Hubbard, M., Upadhyaya, S.K., Stover, S.M. (2012). Dynamic properties of a dirt and a synthetic equine racetrack surface measured by a track-testing device. *Equine Vet J. 45(1)*: P. 25-30.

[38] Oosterlinck, M., Royaux, E., Back, W., Pille, F. (2014). A preliminary study on pressure-plate evaluation of forelimb toe-heel and mediolateral hoof balance on a hard vs. a soft surface in sound ponies at the walk and trot. *Equine Vet J. 46(6)*: P. 751-5.

[39] Crevier-Denoix, N., Audigié, F., Emond, A.L., Dupays, A.G., Pourcelot, P., Desquilbet, L., Chateau, H., Denoix, J.M. (2017). Effect of track surface firmness on the development of musculoskeletal injuries in French Trotters during four months of harness race training. *Am J Vet Res. 78(11)*: P. 1293-1304.

recovering from a soft tissue injury, like a strained collateral ligament or a pulled suspensory ligament, you aren't going to want to work in a deep arena, at least until she has recovered fully.

What if the only option you have available for riding is one that isn't ideal for your horse's situation? Talk to your farrier and see if they can help you come up with a shoeing plan that will help your horse. Letting your farrier know what type of footing you usually work on can be an important piece to the puzzle of keeping your horse sound. Sometimes a smart shoeing plan can compensate for a less than ideal riding surface.

We talked in depth in this chapter about all the things that come out of your horse, probably in more detail than you ever wanted to know, that can affect his hoof health, but what about what goes in? Let's dig into the world of equine nutrition and how we can build a better hoof from the inside out.

Quick Takeaways

- **Urine and manure are hard on hooves, so reducing the amount of exposure will improve hoof health.**
- **Firm or abrasive footings may lead to heavy hoof or shoe wear and increase concussion.**
- **Soft or deep footings create more stress on muscles and tendons.**

24 FEEDING THE FOOT

Feeding sounded simple before you actually got a horse. Throw some hay, maybe a scoop or two of grain, no problems. But then you went to the feed store to grab a bag of grain, and *holy cow* there are five hundred different options. Some of them say they are the only right choice for a young horse, an old horse, or a show horse. How do you compare them all? Then you turn around and there's another hundred supplement options claiming to fix everything from a runny nose to laminitis. Does your horse need a supplement? To make matters worse, the FDA doesn't test or regulate claims that supplements make, so companies can literally print on the bag that their supplement will make your horse grow wings if they want to. And what about those mineral blocks, salt licks, and all-in-one mineral and salt blocks? Hay isn't all that simple either, and it's even harder to tell what you're getting since different weather conditions might give you a very different hay from the same field in different years, and depending on where you live, hay shortages might mean you have to take what you can get.

It's not like feeding doesn't really matter to your horse's health. Obesity can lead to a whole host of issues, from joint pain to navicular disease and laminitis. Speaking of which, too much sugar and your horse could get laminitis. Supplementing can be scary too, because for many vitamins and minerals, having too little can lead to weak feet but having too much can also cause problems. Take selenium as a pretty extreme example: horses need selenium to keep their muscles healthy, but a few milligrams more than the recommended daily dose is highly toxic and can lead to horses sluffing their hoof capsules. Yikes!

Good news: there are lovely people called equine nutritionists who have done a ton of research so that we don't have to have a panic attack every time we try to buy feed for our horses. Plus, there are a number of reputable feed and supplement companies that invest in research and horse owner education, and I mean actual education, not just a glorified sales pitch. There have been whole books written and courses designed around equine nutrition, so in this book we're only going to talk about nutrition as it affects the hoof.

Extremely underweight horses may not have enough caloric energy or nutrients to build a strong hoof

Finding the right amount of feed to maintain a healthy body weight is vital for your horse's overall health, and that includes the hooves. We've all seen the pictures of underweight, neglected rescue horses with their curled up hooves, but that's not the only hoof challenge they face. If you've rescued a neglected horse yourself, you know that it takes a while for them to regain their health and strength, even after they've been fed a good quality diet, and the hooves take a while to catch up as well. If the horse hasn't been trimmed for a long time, her feet are trying to deal with the mechanical stresses of super long hooves as well as the fact that she hasn't been getting the right nutritional building blocks to create healthy hooves. In fact, you'll often be able to see a ring on her hooves marking when she started getting enough good food, and the horn above it will be growing stronger and healthier. Usually it's just a waiting game once you get her diet balanced, watching the healthy hoof get closer and closer to the ground with every trim.

You might also see horses who lose weight as they get older. Sometimes this can just be from tooth problems making it hard for them to chew and digest forage and grain. In this case, regular dentistry and soaking food or feeding a soft mash instead of hard to chew food might help him get some extra nutrients on board. If that doesn't make a difference, talk to your vet because they might be able to diagnose another digestive issue like ulcers or allergies that are messing with your horse.

The other side of the coin is one you'll know all about if you have an easy keeper. Being overweight puts a lot of extra stress on your horse's hooves, and creates a constant low grade inflammatory response in his body. We'll talk a lot more about how this works in Chapter 34 when we talk about laminitis, but it's really important to get that weight off him as soon as you can. The Equine Management Extension from Rutgers University explains that for the majority of horses that aren't pregnant, nursing, or in heavy work, the only feed they need is good quality forage and a mineral block. No grain or concentrates necessary. Keep in mind, heavy work doesn't mean a half hour lesson five

Obesity leads to many health concerns

times a week, it's more like at least an hour of high speed work per day. They also suggest that horses should be fed forage at a rate of 1.5-2% of their body weight per day for maintenance, but if your horse needs to lose weight, you need to feed 1.5-2% of their *ideal* body weight[40]. This means if a healthy body weight for your horse is 1000 pounds, but he's weighing in at a chubby 1200 pounds, you would want to feed a maximum of 20 pounds of forage (2% of 1000 lbs), not 24 pounds (2% of 1200 lbs). Make sense? We're feeding for the weight we want, not the weight we have. As always with dietary changes, make sure to talk to your vet about the best method for your horse. Some horses have sensitive systems and need to slowly ease into a new diet instead of going cold turkey. Plus, vets are a really good resource for weight loss ideas.

So if your horse has a healthy body weight, what signs can you look for to see if your horse needs a supplement for her hooves?

Since hoof horn is mostly made from the protein keratin, if there's a deficiency in the building blocks for keratin it will show up not just in the hooves, but also in your horse's coat, mane, and tail. If you notice that your horse has a dull hair coat or brittle hair in her mane and tail, that might be a clue that she's not getting complete nutrition.

Looking at hooves, if your horse has crumbly, shelly hooves that chip up around the nail holes and have trouble holding shoes on, she might be short on some nutrients. You can also check hooves for cracks, flaring, hooves that seem dull and weak, or that grow slowly. Ask your farrier if the horn feels strong when they are trimming or nailing, or if it feels soft. Since they are handling a lot of feet every day, farriers can be a good resource if you have questions about whether or not your horse's hooves are normal for your area.

If those signs sound familiar, how do you know what nutrients your horse is lacking? Should you just feed a general hoof supplement or target with a specific vitamin or mineral?

Unless you know for a fact that your horse isn't getting a specific nutrient (for instance if a

[40] Williams, C.A. (2004) *The Basics of Equine Nutrition*. Retrieved from
https://esc.rutgers.edu/fact_sheet/the-basics-of-equine-nutrition/

specific mineral isn't found in the soil in your area and your feed doesn't contain it) you're probably better off feeding a hoof supplement that covers all the vitamins and minerals that hooves need. This partially makes sense because horses that are short on one building block are often missing other nutrients as well. There are also several nutrients that need to be fed in the correct proportion with another nutrient to be absorbed correctly, or seem to work a lot better with another nutrient.

For those of us who don't have degrees in biochemistry or equine nutrition, it can be hard to know which supplements are going to actually help your horse, and which ones might as well be a placebo. Luckily, reputable supplement companies will list the nutrition facts of their

Guaranteed Analysis:

	Guarantee	Per 2.5 oz.
Crude Protein (min)	25.0%	17.7 g
Lysine (min)	1.8%	1.27 g
Methionine (min)	7.2%	5.1 g
Crude Fat (min)	6.4%	4.5 g
Crude Fiber (max)	13.0%	9.2 g
Acid Detergent Fiber (max)	18.0%	12.7 g
Neutral Detergent Fiber (max)	26.0%	18.4 g
Calcium (min)	1.2%	850 mg
Calcium (max)	1.7%	1.204 mg
Phosphorus (min)	0.6%	425 mg
Copper (min)	1.700 ppm	120 mg
Zinc (min)	5.077 ppm	300 mg
Biotin (min)	200 mg/lb	30 mg
Vitamin C (min)	2.800 mg/lb	435 mg
Vitamin E (min)	60 IU/lb	9 IU

Feeding Instructions (1.100 lb. horse):

- The enclosed scoop holds approximately 2.5 oz.
- Feed 1 scoop (2.5 oz.) per day for 6-8 months.
- After 6-8 months you can change to a maintenance level of ½ scoop (1.25 oz.) per day.
- If problems persist, resume feeding at 2.5 oz. per day.
- The product can be given as a top-dress to daily feed or grain ration.
- Adjust the amount given based on the weight of the animal. Higher amounts to larger horses, and lower amounts to smaller horses.

Sample guaranteed analysis sheet

supplement on the packaging, which you'll find under the title *Guaranteed Analysis.*

So what are the nutrients you should look for when you're reading the labels?

There are three basic nutritional components that your horse needs for healthy hooves: amino acids, minerals, and vitamins.

Amino acids are important building blocks for proteins like keratin, and *essential* amino acids are the ones that horses bodies can't create for themselves, so they need get them through their diet instead. Methionine is the most commonly supplemented amino acid for hoof growth because it is a sulfur-based amino acid, and sulfur helps form the links in the connective tissue of the hoof. It's also an element that's often in low supply in grasses and feeds. Most hoof supplements contain between 1,000 and 5,300mg of methionine. You'll probably want to aim for the higher end of that range if you're trying to manage problem hooves, but you don't want go over the recommended dosage, because too much methionine can actually damage intertubular horn by bonding to zinc so that the zinc can't be used in horn production[41].

Other amino acids you might see in hoof supplements are lysine, proline, tyrosine, iodine, and threonine. Tyrosine and iodine are important for thyroid function, so if your horse has low thyroid function, usually indicated by obesity and poor quality horn and coat hair, you might want

---

[41] Steward, J., (2013) Understanding the Horse's Feet. The Stable Block, Crowood Lane, Ramsbury, Wiltshire, SN8 2HR. Crowood Press.

to make sure he's getting enough tyrosine and iodine[42].

Minerals are usually found in your horse's diet thanks to your soil. Plants growing in the soil use some of the minerals from the dirt, and when your horse eats the grass or hay, she absorbs those minerals through her digestive tract. Sometimes minerals are also supplemented by combination mineral and salt blocks, but this can actually cause some problems for your horse. Her mineral needs are pretty consistent, but her salt needs change depending on exercise and sweating. If you give her a combination mineral and salt block, she can't eat more salt without getting more minerals too. Since extra minerals are hard for the body to shed, she can end up with a mineral toxicity if she's eating a lot of the block to get the salt. It's safer to offer plain salt and then supplement minerals separately. Plus, then you can make sure she's getting the recommended daily dosage of important minerals.

So what minerals should you be looking for in a hoof supplement? Calcium, phosphorus, zinc, copper, and sulfur are all important. Calcium and phosphorus are one example of minerals that need to be fed in the correct ratio if they're going to work correctly. If you want strong hoof walls, calcium helps form strong connections between cells, and calcium deficiencies have been linked to crumbly, soft hoof walls and shoe loss. Where does phosphorus factor in? Phosphorous is necessary for strong bones in horses, but too much of it can actually block calcium absorption. According to Oklahoma State University's Equine Extension, calcium and phosphorous should be fed at an ideal ratio of two parts calcium to one part phosphorous. It can be fed up to six parts calcium to one part phosphorous, but you definitely don't want to get down to a one to one ratio, or feed more phosphorous than calcium. Don't forget to factor in the whole diet including hay and grain, not just the supplement in question[43].

According to research from Life Data Labs, the maker of the supplement Farrier's Formula, feeding bran can mess up that calcium to phosphorus ratio pretty quickly. All types of bran contain phytate, which is high in phosphorus, so if it looks like you might have a calcium deficiency on your hands (or hooves), skip the bran mash[44].

Copper is another important mineral and if you live in an area with high rainfall, your forage might be pretty low on this one. It is a factor in hoof strength so you'll want to check that your supplement has between 25 and 100 mg of copper if your forage could be copper deficient.

Sometimes, soft crumbly hooves are the result of a zinc shortage, since zinc is necessary for keratin to harden. 250-400 mg of zinc will usually meet your horse's dietary needs if your horse isn't getting enough zinc from their forage alone.

Though we mentioned it briefly earlier in this chapter, it's important to remember that the mineral selenium should be fed with care. It is absolutely necessary for healthy muscles, and it has also been suggested that it can prevent tying up. Selenium is what's known as a trace mineral, meaning horses only need a tiny amount, 3 mg per day to be exact. Depending on what area you live in, your horse may be getting plenty of selenium through her forage. 10 mg a day can cause selenium toxicity which is extremely dangerous for horses. If you live in an area where there's a lot of selenium in the soil, like areas with alkali water you want to make sure that your supplement doesn't contain selenium so you don't go over the recommended amount[45].

---

[42] Gravlee, J.F., and Gravlee, H.S. *Nutrients that Influence Hoof Health*. Retrieved from https://www.lifedatalabs.com/hoof-and-joint-articles/nutrients-that-influence-hoof-health

[43] Hiney, K., (May 2017). Minerals for Horses: Calcium and Phosphorus. Retrieved from https://extension.okstate.edu/fact-sheets/minerals-for-horses-calcium-and-phosphorus.html

[44] Gravlee, F. (2017). A Guide to Proper Care and Nutrition For the Equine Hoof. Retrieved from https://www.lifedatalabs.com/docs/Hoof%20Booklet%20US%202017_Web.pdf

[45] J. R., (June, 2014). *Selenium Levels for Horses*. Retrieved from https://www.horsefeedblog.com/2014/06/selenium-levels-for-horses/

What about vitamins? Vitamins A, C and D are all important for hoof growth, although C usually only needs to be supplemented in horses who are stressed or stall bound. Your horse usually gets enough vitamin D from the sun just like us, but if he's stuck inside, you might need to supplement.

Unhelpfully, vitamin A deficiencies and excesses both show the same symptoms -- a break down in the intertubular horn of the hoof wall. You'll actually see the tiny tubules like little threads or tiny fingers coming out of the bottom of the hoof wall. If you see the signs, check your current feed and supplements to find out if your horse is getting enough or too much vitamin A.

And now, the most famous vitamin in a horse's feed... biotin, hero or disappointment depending on your experience.

There has been a huge focus on biotin in research for the last thirty years, but the studies aren't all saying the same things. For instance, in 1995, a study of 152 Lipizzaners looked at feeding 20 mg of biotin every day, with a control group that took a placebo. Hoof growth rates were no different between the two groups, but the quality of growth did improve[46]. Another study performed in 1994 found the same result[47]. But studies in 1992 and 1998 showed an increase in hoof growth as well[48],[49].

Biotin is a necessary ingredient for keratin production, as well as collagen and elastin, which are both important for healthy skin. It also seems to be one of the few nutrients where a little is good, and a lot is better. When researchers looked at biotin levels in horses with unhealthy hooves, many of them had totally normal biotin levels in their blood. That didn't stop their hooves from improving when they were fed large doses of biotin. Since biotin is a water-soluble vitamin so if your horse can't use it, it will just filter out of his system. It might be a waste of money if he didn't need it, but it's not going to hurt him.

So should you just grab a pure biotin supplement and load your horse up if he's got bad feet? Not necessarily. Unless you know for sure that biotin is the *only* missing piece of the nutritional puzzle, you'll probably want to look for a hoof supplement that hits all the vitamins, minerals, and amino acids that his hooves need. Besides ensuring that you're not skipping something, it's also been shown that biotin works better when it's eaten with zinc, methionine, and calcium.

Remember that whatever supplement you feed, you won't see immediate results since you have to wait for new growth to replace the old, weaker growth. You might be able to see the difference near the top of the hoof wall within a month or so, but it'll probably be around a year before you see a completely replaced hoof. So if you decide to feed a hoof supplement, you're going to have to continue to feed the supplement for a year or so until it grows down far enough to see the difference at the ground surface of the hoof. It won't really help anything if you feed for a month and then quit on it because you haven't seen results.

Also, thanks to the fact that some nutrients are dangerous in larger doses, you'll want to make sure you only feed one supplement unless the supplements in question were designed to be fed

---

[46] Josseck, H., Zenker, W., Geyer, H. (1995). Hoof horn abnormalities in Lipizzaner horses and the effect of dietary biotin on macroscopic aspects of hoof horn quality. *Equine Vet J.27(3):* P. 175-82.
[47] Geyer, H., Schulze, J. (1994) The long-term influence of biotin supplementation on hoof horn quality in horses. *Schweiz Arch Tierheilkd 136(4):* P.137-49.
[48] Buffa, E.A., Van Den Berg, S.S., Verstraete, F.J., Swart, N.G. (1992). Effect of dietary biotin supplement on equine hoof horn growth rate and hardness. *Equine Vet J. ;24(6):* P. 472-4
[49] Reilly, J.D., Cottrell, D.F., Martin, R.J., Cuddeford, D.J.(1998). Effect of supplementary dietary biotin on hoof growth and hoof growth rate in ponies: a controlled trial. *Equine Vet J Suppl. (26):51-7.*

together or a nutritionist has given them the okay.

Finally, you can put all the nutrients into your horse that you want, but if those building blocks aren't making it to the hoof, it's not going to help you. You need to have enough blood flow getting to the coriums of the hoof to carry the nutrients there. If you have damaged or compromised blood flow such as if your horse has lower circulation thanks to old age or has a rotated coffin bone that is compressing blood vessels, you might have plenty of building blocks for the hoof floating around in the blood stream, but not enough actually making it there.

This could be the issue if your horse grows really slowly or unevenly, in which case a supplement for circulatory health might benefit your horse.

Circulatory supplements are focused on getting good blood flow, not on nutrients to build hooves. They may contain ingredients like arginine, an amino acid that helps support healthy circulation, antioxidants like resveratrol, grape seed extract, and N-acetyl cystine, which fight oxidative stress and support a healthy inflammatory response, and herbs like yucca and turmeric, which are thought to help fight inflammation. If you're thinking about using a circulatory supplement, talk to your vet to find out what options would be healthy choices for your horse.

If you're feeling overwhelmed by the options, consider hiring a professional to come up with a personalized game plan for your horse. You can ask your vet if they recommend a particular equine nutritionist or call your local county extension office. There are also easily google-able companies that offer to create personalized feed plans for your horse.

If your horse has hoof issues and you want to know for sure if there's a nutrition problem, you can submit a blood sample to Life Data Labs for testing. This is part of an ongoing, large scale research project in which they are testing blood from a wide variety of horses with health problems, looking for nutritional links. From the perspective of furthering science, your horse's blood sample could help further research about any health problems she has. From a health perspective, you can get a full analysis of your horse's nutritional needs for free if your horse is accepted into the study. Especially for the horse with hard to pin down hoof problems, this could be seriously beneficial. You can find out more at: https://lifedatalabs.com/hoof-care-and-research/nutrition-research-program. And no, I'm not being paid by Life Data Labs to promote this service. I'm only telling you this because I think it could help your horse and the state of equine nutrition research as a whole.

For the most part, though, feeding isn't rocket science. If your horse isn't having any hoof problems, you probably don't even need a hoof supplement. But if she is, you've got the knowledge to make informed decisions by reading the guaranteed analysis on the supplements you're considering, and you've got the resources to get help if you're having a hard time finding the right balance for your horse.

Quick Takeaways

- **Horses need the correct nutrients in order to build strong hooves. A balanced hoof supplement may be necessary to get them there.**
- **Complete nutrition includes amino acids, minerals, and vitamins, in the correct proportions.**
- **Never combine supplements or use more than the suggested amount since some nutrients are dangerous in large quantities.**

Part 5
Pathologies, Problems, and Prevention.

25 CATCH IT QUICK

Since this next section is going to be all about bad stuff that happens to feet, I think we should start by talking about ways to spot problems *before* they get serious. In each chapter, we'll be talking about recognizing symptoms of each type of pathology or disease, but here we'll just be talking about the basics of keeping an eye on things. A lot of this chapter might sound like common sense, but sometimes we all need a reminder on just how important the simple things can be.

Just like they say when you head to the doctor for your yearly checkup, early detection improves the success rates for nearly every condition. There are plenty of hoof conditions that can be resolved within a few weeks or a month if you catch them early, but could do permanent damage if you let them progress. Even with degenerative conditions that we can't cure yet, noticing the signs early can help you manage symptoms and slow the disease process, giving your horse more years of being healthy and serviceably sound. All good stuff!

So how can you keep tabs on your horse's hoof health?

The most important tools you have are your eyes and your hands. Every time you see your horse, you should be picking up his hooves and picking them out. The only exception would be if you are seeing your horse multiple times a day, but you should definitely be picking hooves out when your horse comes in from the pasture and before and after riding.

This is really good for your horse's hoof hygiene, since a lot of the bacteria and fungi that attack hooves are anaerobic, which means they don't like oxygen. And killing bacteria and fungi should definitely be a daily hygiene habit, like brushing your teeth. If you only brushed your teeth once a week, you'd get cavities pretty quickly, and the same goes for picking horse's hooves. Once a week doesn't really cut it.

If this is your view of the hoof, you have no idea what could be going on under all that

Not only does picking out your horse's hooves actually prevent a lot of issues by killing bacteria and fungus, it's also a chance for you to check his hooves for foreign objects, injuries, or changes. More than once, I've been asked to check a horse out because of a lameness, and found a roofing nail stuck in the frog, while the owners were unaware. This should never, *ever* happen. If your horse goes lame, the first thing you should do is pick out her hooves, looking for things in there that shouldn't be there. Even rocks or wood chips wedged in a hoof can be painful. If you're looking at a foreign object in your horse's hoof and there's blood involved or it looks like it's stuck into sensitive tissue, stop and call your vet. Don't pull the object until you get your vet's okay, because your vet might need to take an x-ray to see what structures it is damaging. We'll talk about what other steps you should take in Chapter 37.

You should also be checking out his hooves for chips, cracks, or changes in shape, and while you've got your eyes and hands on his hooves, check their temperature too. Knowing what a normal hoof temperature feels like for your horse can help you notice if they're abnormally hot.

What can you do if you notice a change? Talk to your farrier or vet (we'll talk more in Chapter 38 about how to know whether you should be directing a question to your vet or to your farrier) and ask them if you should be concerned. Not every change or chip in the hoof is cause for anxiety.

Speaking of talking to your farrier, they are also a good resource for keeping an eye on your horse's hooves. If you can, be present when your horse is being shod. Ask your farrier how your horse is looking and if there's anything they notice. Since they see your horse every six weeks, they are pretty familiar with what her hooves look like and what "normal" is for her. They can tell you whether changes are good, bad, or just different, and help you come up with a plan.

If your schedule doesn't allow you to be there when your horse is being shod, you can still get the latest updates from your farrier. Call, text, or leave a note at the barn before your appointment if you have any questions or concerns. You can also check in after the appointment and ask how your horse's hooves are looking.

If you can't be there very often to see your horse, you'll want to make sure someone else is checking in on your horse's hooves. Depending on the situation at the facility your horse is at, this might be a groom, trainer, or a

Even if you're picking out hooves but not doing it thoroughly, you could still be missing thrush

The same hoof, thoroughly picked out

friend at the barn. They may not be able to give your horse the level of care and attention that you would, but you can ask them to pick out and look at your horse's hooves when they can. Even a few extra check-ins can make a difference.

What if your horse *does* have a hoof issue and you have a vet diagnosis? A lot of the time your vet and farrier can come up with a treatment plan to help, but it's really important that the whole team is on the same page.

Ever play the game Telephone when you were a kid? You know, the one where all the kids sit in a line and the kid on the end whispers a message that's passed along and distorted until it gets to the last kid? Remember how much different the message ended up? That's exactly what you *don't* want happening when your horse has a hoof issue. If your vet diagnoses a problem, and then tells you, and then you tell your trainer, and your trainer tells your farrier, your farrier might be getting a different diagnosis and shoeing prescription than what your vet came up with. Make sure that your vet and farrier are communicating with each other directly.

The main ideas for keeping an eye on your horse's hooves are observation and communication. But what if all that observation and communication leads you to realize that there's something off about his hooves? Don't ignore it! Learn more about what's going on so you can make the best choices for your horse. Let's find out more about common hoof problems and what you can do to help them.

Quick Takeaways

- **Daily hoof picking is good for early detection of problems as well as hoof hygiene.**
- **Ask your farrier if they notice any changes or have concerns about your horse's hooves.**
- **Direct communication between the entire team is extremely important when dealing with a hoof issue.**

26 THRUSH

According to a 2016 survey by the *American Farrier's Journal*, a whopping 41% of farriers saw thrush on a weekly basis, while another 19% of farriers saw it monthly[50]. That's a lot of thrush going around!

So what is thrush anyway and why is it so ridiculously common? Thrush is an anaerobic bacterial infection that attacks the frog. Anaerobic means that thrush bacteria thrive in an oxygen-free environment. When the hoof gets packed full of manure or dirt, there's no air getting to the frog or the bacteria and the bacteria can go crazy. Of course, getting manure or dirt in her hooves is nothing out of the ordinary for your horse. If she's outside, she's finding a muddy spot to stand, and if she's in a stall, you know she's stepping in her manure as soon as it hits the ground. The more stuff there is for her to pack in her feet (like when she's in a muddy field, or if her stall isn't cleaned very often) the more time that bacteria has to multiply.

The real down side is that thrush bacteria destroys formerly healthy frog tissue. It's

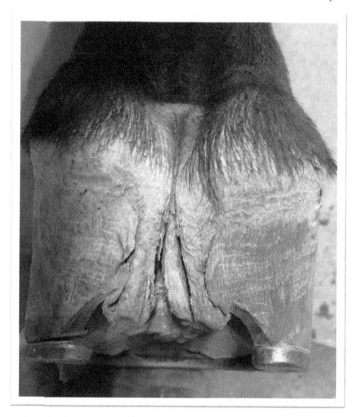

When the frog is split and thrushy the whole hoof capsule looses strength

actually caused by keratolytic bacteria, which means that the bacteria eats away keratin, which is the major building block of the frog[51]. It especially likes to attack the central sulcus and the collateral sulci on either side of the frog. As you know from Chapter 5, a strong frog plays a huge role in the health and function of the hoof, from protection, to shock absorption, to blood circulation. So if the frog has been eaten away by bacteria, it isn't able to perform any of those functions. In upright feet, you might see the hoof get even tighter and start to contract because the frog isn't helping push the heels apart under load. If your horse has lower angled hooves, you might see her heels collapsing and crushing because the frog isn't able to help with weight

[50]American Farriers Journal. (2017). *Tackling Those Nasty Thrush Concerns.* Retrieved from https://www.americanfarriers.com/articles/9218-tackling-thrush-barn-call-charges

[51] Ross, M.W., Dyson, S.J., (2010). *Diagnosis and Management of Lameness in the Horse.* W.B. Saunders, Elsevier, Health Sciences Division 11830 Westline Industrial Drive, St. Louis MO 63146-3313 USA.

bearing and shock absorption. Plus, no matter what type of conformation your horse has, if you lose strength in the frog, you also lose the connection between the heels of the hoof, so each of them is forced to function independently instead of working together. For instance, if your horse lands on one heel first, that heel might jam up if it's not solidly connected to the other heel. Let's just say the frog is important, and we'd like to keep it around!

So where does the thrush bacteria come from? *Fusobacterium Necrophorum* is the most common thrush bacteria[52] (although there are a range of different bacteria that are found in thrushy feet) and it's also unfortunately found in manure, so it's always around. Even super clean, dry stalls will have manure in them eventually, and we all know horses step in manure like it's their job.

How do you know if you have a case of thrush brewing? If you're not picking out his hooves, you really won't know until it gets super bad. Thrush doesn't cause pain or lameness until it has eaten down to sensitive tissue, and that doesn't happen overnight. Notice that I also said that *you* need to pick out your horse's hooves if you want to catch thrush early. Even if you have your horse at a full service barn where someone else is grooming and tacking up your horse, you should still be checking his hooves regularly. Grooms can be overworked, and they typically have a lot of horses to get ready, so things can get missed in spite of their best intentions. Plus, depending on the skill and experience of the person in question, they may or may not be trained to recognize thrush, and they probably won't be comfortable starting a treatment regime without your permission. Remember,

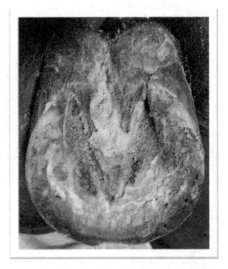

White, mealy frog tissue is not thrush

ultimately *you* are responsible for your horse's wellbeing, whether you've delegated some of the daily tasks or not.

Let's say you're picking out your horse's hooves, and you notice white, cheesy looking stuff on her frogs, along with some chunks of loose looking frog. Should you start treating for thrush? Actually, what you're looking at there is probably just exfoliation. Remember back in Chapter 5 when we talked about how frogs

A layer of frog peeling off with a clean smooth layer underneath it is just shedding frog

don't typically wear away, so they have to shed instead? If you're seeing white frog tissue, that's what's going on.

---

[52] Petrov, K.K., Dicks, L.M. (2013). Fusobacterium necrophorum, and not Dichelobacter nodosus, is associated with equine hoof thrush. *Vet Microbiol 161(3-4):* P. 350-2.

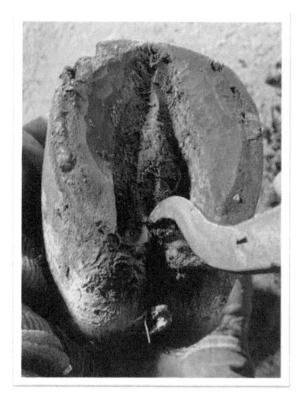

A deep central sulcus full of black goo indicates a serious thrush infection

Once you've seen thrush, it's easy to tell the difference. It looks like black gooey stuff in any crevices or pockets in the frog, and it smells awful, unlike shedding frog, which has little to no odor. That sticky black stuff is actually a mixture of bacteria, necrotic frog tissue, and usually manure or mud. Given that composition, you can see why nobody is making thrush scented candles. It smells a lot worse than regular manure packed in a hoof.

All that black goo is also pretty thick, which makes a nice anaerobic environment for the thrush bacteria, so if you see it, you definitely want to get it out of your horse's frog, ASAP. If you catch it early, you might be able to kill it with regular hoof picking, but if it's had the chance to really get into the frog, you might have to use a topical thrush treatment. Since *fusobacterium necrophorum* is anaerobic and keratolytic, it likes to find a little crevice and then eat itself a pocket to safely feed and multiply in, so if you've had thrush for a little while, you might see ragged edges and pockets surrounding the area that was first infected. All these little pockets can be hard to totally clean out, and they can become anaerobic again pretty quickly, so that's where a thrush treatment that gets into every little corner can really help.

Environment is one of the biggest factors that predispose horses to thrush. As you've probably already guessed, since the bacteria that causes thrush is found in manure, cleaning up after your horse regularly definitely lowers your risk of thrush, especially if your horse is in a stall most of the time or in a small paddock. Remember that study we talked about in Chapter 23 about different beddings? There was less thrush-causing bacteria present in stalls that stayed drier than in the stalls with less absorbent beddings. That's pretty typical for all the different infections we can get in hooves: clean and dry helps.

Since moisture and manure carry a higher risk of thrush infections, you've probably already guessed that a muddy paddock where manure gets churned up into the mud before it can be picked up isn't going to be ideal. In fact, it's kind of the ideal environment for breeding bacteria, since it's constantly wet and has a nice distribution of bacteria throughout the mud, so no matter where your horse steps, they are being exposed (or submerged, in severe cases) to bacteria.

If you're at a barn with less-than-ideal manure management or muddy paddocks, you might notice that your horse gets constant thrush infections, while some of the other horses stay healthy. What factors make one horse get thrush all the time while another horse never has a problem with it, when they're both in the same iffy environment?

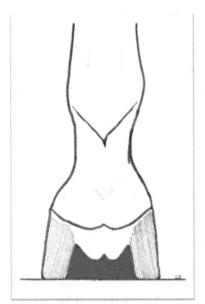

Upright feet have more space to pack in manure, so they are more prone to thrush

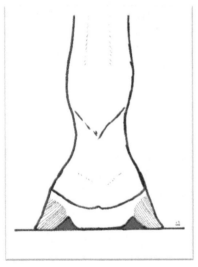

Low feet tend to self-clean better than upright feet

Turns out hoof conformation plays a big role. If your horse has naturally upright hooves, that comes with a lot of benefits that people with flat footed horses can only dream of, but it also comes with a negative. Higher heels mean deeper collateral sulci, so stuff really packs in there. Some flat hooves do a decent job of self-cleaning, but your upright footed horse isn't going to a very good job of cleaning out his hooves. If your horse has the type of conformation that puts a lot more stress on one heel than the other, like toeing in or out severely, having an offset hoof capsule, or being really base wide or base narrow, you might already have a deep central sulcus in the frog which can be a great environment for thrush. We'll talk more about these types of conformation and the sheared heels that can go along with them in Chapter 31.

You might also see your horse's personal habits make a difference too. Some horses like to stand by the gate all day in turnout, usually one of the muddiest areas of the field. A horse that is pushed away from the rest of the group might not end up in the busiest, most trampled areas. If your horse is calm in her stall, she's going to keep a cleaner stall than a horse that paces constantly and tramples manure all over the area.

If you're looking at a foot lameness, and you see thrush in your horse's frog, is there a chance that the thrush is making her lame? That's going to depend on the details of the lameness.

Thrush usually causes lameness when it eats away enough of the frog to expose sensitive frog tissue to the environment. We're talking either a really thin layer of frog or *no* insensitive frog left, usually in the area of the central sulcus or the collateral sulci. If you're picking out her hooves, a case of thrush this severe is going to be very noticeable, because she'll be flinching when you pick out the area, and it may bleed from even gentle hoof picking. (Side note: if your horse flinches when you're picking her frogs or you see blood, start treating for thrush right away, because a healthy frog *never* acts that way.) If your horse is lame because of thrush, the lameness will show up in soft or deep footings where sand and grit is working itself into the wound, or uneven footings like rocks or wood chips, since they can put pressure on the sensitive area.

Remember how protection is one of the functions of the frog? If it's not doing that job, it can not only make your horse sore, but you're also risking serious internal infection since there's no barrier between her bloodstream and the bacteria found in the outside environment. You would never rub manure in an open wound, but that's what's happening every day if she has exposed sensitive frog tissue.

Obviously, if you're in that situation, priority number one has to be getting rid of the thrush. Even if you have a less severe case, you want to jump on it before it has the chance to do any more damage.

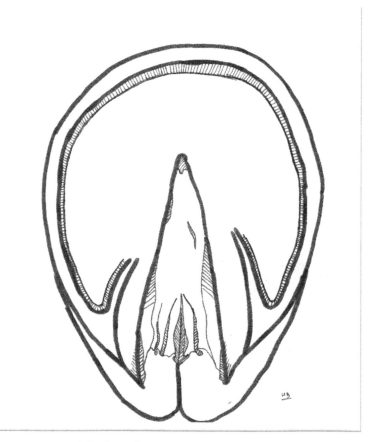

Be sure to carefully clean all aspects of the frog, including as far into the sulci as you can go

Your first job is to completely clean out the frog so you know *exactly* what you're dealing with. You'll want to firmly but carefully pick out all the dirt, debris, and thrush that you can with your hoof pick. This means getting in all those little pockets and under all the little flaps. If you have a deep central sulcus that's too narrow for your hoof pick, try turning it sideways and carefully sliding it into the central sulcus. If you still can't reach the bottom of the sulcus, try using a Q-tip to get down in there. You can also gently "floss" the central sulcus with a gauze 4x4, available in the first aid section of most pharmacies. If you're *still* not getting all the way in there, grab a syringe with a plastic tip (not a needle!) and flush with clean water until it runs out clear. If your horse seems sensitive to flushing, try flushing with lukewarm water instead of cold. Remember, the cleaner you get that foot, the more thrush bacteria you're exposing to oxygen.

Now that you've gotten all the big stuff out, it's time to target the bacteria that's left. There is a huge range of thrush treatments on the market, and you've probably heard a number of brand names thrown around. They can also come with a fairly hefty price tag, but there are plenty of very effective remedies that won't break the bank.

There are two basic ways that thrush treatments can work. The most common are antiseptic treatments, including some big names like Thrushbuster and Kopertox. Another extremely useful antiseptic that's cost effective and gentle on exposed sensitive tissue? Pick up a bottle of the nasty brown Listerine (not the mint one, that's just confusing to your horse when his feet smell like peppermints but he can't eat them). It's designed to kill bacteria and it isn't too caustic for a thin frog although it may sting if sensitive frog tissue is exposed. Any thrush treatment that says not to get it on your skin is probably too strong for exposed sensitive tissue.

A quick word about one commonly recommended treatment that falls into this category -- bleach. Quite a few people have recommended or tried this one over the years, and some people have had success. I wouldn't recommend it though, because it is actually damaging to the hoof (and damage to the hoof is what we're trying to prevent here). Bleach might be a really effective bacteria killer, but as anyone who has tried to go platinum blonde can tell you, keratin, which makes up hair and horn, doesn't like bleach much. Bleach and peroxide are both degrading to keratin, so let's avoid this one since we don't want to damage an already weakened hoof. Plus, bleach is much too strong to use on sensitive tissue.

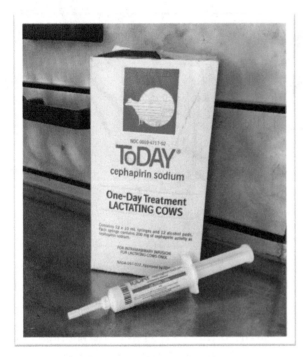

Another extremely effective type of thrush treatment is antibiotics, such as Today or Tomorrow Ointment. These are available in the cow section of your local farm store and are also easily found online. They are manufactured as a treatment for cow mastitis[53], and they come in a syringe with a soft rubbery tip that's easy to fit into the deepest central sulcus. I'm not paid to recommend it (although I wish it was, it's probably the hoof care product I recommend to clients the most often) but it is one that I have seen consistently successful. One word of warning before you grab a box -- it is an antibiotic, so you don't want to use it preventatively. At this point we all know that over-using antibiotics tends to create new, antibiotic resistant strains of common bacteria, so let's not do that. Antibiotics should only be used if you have an active case of thrush.

That said, there doesn't seem to be a lot of truth to the old saying that you need to switch up your thrush treatment because the thrush gets used to one type of treatment and develops immunity. It takes a long time to develop a strain of bacteria that has resistance to a treatment, and if you are effectively killing off the colony, the thrush doesn't have enough time

---

[53] This product is frequently recommended by vets and farriers for thrush treatment, however it is not labeled for equine use. Obviously since I haven't seen your horse, I can't recommend that you purchase or use any medication, so although I do believe very strongly in this product, you should consult your farrier and vet before using any antibiotics. Cool?

to fight it. Of course, if it seems like the treatment you are using isn't working, it is worth trying something else since some products work better in different circumstances.

At this point you might be thinking *okay, I've already tried those types of treatments, and they didn't work at all. Give me a different product that's going to actually work!* A lot of people struggle with thrush treatment but I'm going to let you in on a little trade secret here.

Most unsuccessful thrush treatments aren't because the product wasn't any good, but because of incorrect application. Even if you followed the label, there are some steps that aren't spelled out there.

The absolutely *most* important step to any thrush treatment is to get the frog totally picked out and clean before you apply *any* medication, especially down in all the little pockets and the sulci. If you don't do this all-important step, the bacteria still has a dirt and manure barrier protecting it, and it really doesn't matter what you put on the hoof next. If your medication isn't actually getting to the infection, you might as well dump it on the ground.

Okay so you've super cleaned the hoof, now you pour the treatment on the frog, right? You can, but again, it really needs to get to the areas that are going to be the first to become

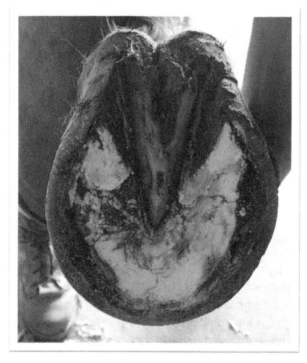

It is important to clean and treat the actual area of infection in a thrushy frog

anaerobic and any actively infected areas. Usually these are little pockets and very narrow fissures, and a general splash of medication on the outside of the frog rarely gets into all those places. You need to make sure it's getting all the way to the base of the infection, so if you have a lot of deep areas, get yourself a syringe with a long rubber or plastic tip and use it to pull up some of the medication in the bottle. Next, pick up the hoof and try to hold it flat so that the meds don't run off right away. Now gently insert the plastic or rubber tip as deep as it will go, and press the plunger on your syringe until you see the liquid coming out of the sulci. Repeat with any other areas of infection. Not only is this method a little neater, it also targets the areas that actually need medication.

Now you've done a really thorough cleaning and applied the medication to the area that needs it. What next? You have to keep on doing it. You are going to treat that thrush every day until it goes away. Thrush bacteria works fast, and if you're treating once a week, you're doing too little, too late. I know this sounds like a lot of work, but if you're like me, you'd rather do a little more work and see actual results than do some work and get nothing back for it. Plan on treating every day until you don't have any more deep cracks or pockets, and then continuing treatment every other day until the damaged areas are completely grown out or until your farrier gives you the okay to stop.

Once you stop using the thrush treatment, this does not mean you stop picking the hooves! Picking hooves is like brushing your teeth -- you don't just do it if you have a cavity. Prevention is way better than trying to fix an infection once it happens, so keep picking the feet every time you see your horse.

Many people question whether it's worth the time to pick out their horses' feet if they are just going back in the mud. When I was a kid, I questioned the necessity of making my bed every day if I was just going to mess it up again, so I get it!

But the answer goes back to the nature of bacterial growth. Since bacteria reproduce through cell division, the number of bacteria in a population doubles every time that reproduction occurs, called exponential growth. So if your horse gets say, ten thrush germs in his hoof by going out in the mud, those ten

Even hooves with beautiful, healthy frogs should be picked regularly

cells turn into twenty, which turns into forty, and so on. Within ten generations, your ten bacteria have turned into a thriving colony of 10,240.

Now let's say at this point, you pull your horse in from the mud and give the hoof a good cleaning, exposing the bacteria to oxygen and killing off the majority of the thrush. If you do a really good job, let's say you reset the bacteria population all the way back to 10, the number we started with. Now as he goes back into the mud, the population growth starts again, but it starts back from the beginning, instead of starting at 10,240 and doubling from there. It's the same reason that people sanitize surfaces at a hospital. They can't prevent germs from getting on the surface, but they can keep the bacterial load in check by knocking it down as frequently as possible.

Thanks to the nature of hoof growth, the frog can't grow back together once the tissue has been damaged. You'll have to wait for new frog growth to come in, and this will take some time. You will probably see your farrier at least once during this process, and they will clean up some of the flaps and pockets on the frog as it grows out. Make sure you share with them what you've seen so far and what you've been doing for treatment. They might have recommendations based on your horse's specific situation, and they probably have a favorite thrush treatment that they find works well in your environment.

As we've seen, thrush is a super common infection, but luckily it rarely causes lameness and is readily treatable with over-the-counter medications and a little effort. It also has a really good prognosis, and rarely has any long-lasting complications if it's correctly treated. So grab your hoof pick and get out there!

Quick Takeaways

- **Thrush is caused by anaerobic bacteria commonly found in manure, and frequent hoof picking and exposure to oxygen is your first line of defense.**
- **Thrush is characterized by foul smelling, black, necrotic tissue in the frog.**
- **A thrush infection causes damage to the hoof structure and function and may cause lameness in extreme cases. It should be taken seriously.**

- When treating thrush, the frog must be thoroughly picked out and thrush treatment applied directly into any pockets of infection.

27 ABSCESSES

If you've ever walked out to get your horse and seen him standing on three legs, you know the panic that an abscess can cause. You try to walk him in and he's barely toe-touching on the bad hoof, hopping along like he has a broken leg. How could this happen? He was totally fine when you saw him yesterday!

Abscesses can flare up overnight, and they can be so painful that your horse refuses to bear weight on that leg at all. But luckily, they are usually resolved with no lasting damage, so they are usually the best possible diagnosis for a really lame horse, and one of the most common.

An abscess is a bacterial infection that occurs when bacteria finds its way past the protective horn structures of the hoof. Once it's inside the hoof capsule, it starts to multiply, and the body kicks off an inflammatory response to deal with the infection. Some of the most common signs of inflammation are heat and swelling, but inside the hoof capsule, there's really nowhere for the swelling to go. In some severe abscesses, bacteria can even form gas pockets which creates intense pressure and pain. The body also creates pus (a mixture of dead leukocytes from the immune response, serum, and necrotic tissue) which adds more pressure. That's where all that pain in an abscess comes from: swelling and pus inside the hoof capsule presses on the sensitive tissue.

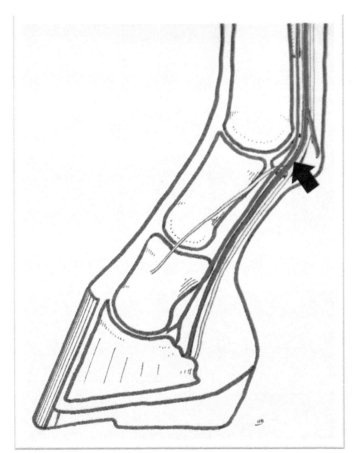

So what other symptoms can you look for besides a lameness with a sudden onset? Abscesses can be hard to pinpoint because the severity of the lameness can fluctuate. Some cases will go from extremely lame one day, to more comfortable the next, and then back to severe lameness the next, since some abscesses can drain slightly, then become sealed up again thanks to dirt packing into the drainage tract. On the other hand, some abscesses never cause extreme lameness, while others consistently get worse until they are opened up or blow out on their own.

Heat and a bounding pulse are also common signs, thanks to the inflammatory response (heat and bounding pulses also are symptoms of laminitis, but it is very uncommon for laminitis to occur in only one hoof). You don't need a thermometer to check your horse's hoof temperature, you

Where the neuro-vascular bundle passes over the sesamoid bones in the back of the fetlock is an easy place to take a pulse

only need to see if the lame hoof is hotter than the other hooves, and the back of your hand should work just fine. Taking pulses is also pretty easy if you know the right place to do it. The blood flow to the hoof comes though a neuro-vascular bundle that runs over the sesamoid bones in the fetlock, which makes it a great place to check for a pulse. If you wrap your thumb and forefinger around the back of the fetlock, you should be able to feel the pulse in the tips of your thumb and finger. You'll want to practice this before there's a problem, so you'll know what a normal pulse strength is for your horse. You should always be able to feel a pulse, but for an abscess you're looking for a stronger, rapid pulse.

There are also a few risk factors for abscesses that might also give you a clue whether this is what you're dealing with. Abscesses are common at times when the hoof has been bruised and exposed to excessive bacteria. A good example of this is taking a ride on a rocky trail that leaves your horse a little sore, so you give him some time off in his paddock, which is pretty wet and muddy. He could easily have bruised his feet on the rocky trail and then when his hooves are soaked in the bacteria rich mud, an abscess could easily start. Or if your horse is turned out in a muddy paddock, a sudden freeze can turn churned up mud into hard, ridgey obstacles. When the weather warms up enough to thaw the mud, her bruised hooves are exposed to all kinds of abscess-causing bacteria.

Another cause of abscesses is a close nail, hot nail, or nail prick. These are all terms for a nail being too close (or in) sensitive tissue. When this is the cause of the abscess, it is usually soon after the shoeing, within a couple of days and certainly not more than a week after the shoeing. These abscess are sometimes the easiest to resolve, because the farrier or vet can hoof test each nail and pull out the offending one, or simply pull the shoe and let the abscess drain for a few days before replacing the shoe.

A related cause of an abscess can be a puncture wound or foreign object in the hoof, but we'll talk about that separately in Chapter 37.

If these symptoms sound like your horse, it's time to give your farrier or vet a call. There's plenty of debate as to whether you should call your farrier or vet for a suspected abscess, and we'll talk more about how to decide in Chapter 38, but either one is an appropriate resource for this particular issue. Typically, farriers are the first call for an abscess, and the vet is called for further diagnostics if the farrier doesn't find an abscess, or they find proof that the lameness is caused by a different issue.

While you're waiting for them to arrive, you can soak your horse's hoof, since this will sometimes allow dirt packed into the abscess tract to wash out and give the abscess some drainage. It can also soften up the horn and may allow the abscess to break out on its own. There are some tips for soaking hooves in Chapter 40 if your horse isn't super cooperative. You can also apply a poultice pad like Animalintex under a hoof wrap, which might start an abscess draining. If you're not sure how to make a durable hoof wrap, check out Chapter 39.

Two things you want to avoid before your farrier or vet arrives: sticky hoof packings and pain meds. Packings like ichthammol or Magic Cushion do reduce inflammation, but once it's in your horse's hoof, it makes it really hard for your

Soaking may help release the pressure in an abscess via a small tract in the sole or white line

farrier to find the subtle black lines and specks that could indicate an abscess tract, plus it's really messy so it's hard to get out of the hoof.

Your vet or farrier may hoof test for the source of the lameness

Pain meds like Bute might be your first thought when you see your horse limping and in obvious discomfort, but they also make it harder for your vet or farrier to pinpoint the area of pain, since the pain response is reduced. Hold off on the Bute until after your farrier or vet has seen your horse.

Your farrier or vet will probably use hoof testers to make sure that the lameness is in your horse's hoof and not farther up the leg. You might be tempted to get a pair of hoof testers and try to locate the abscess for yourself, but this may not be a good idea. According to a study completed in 2013, vets and farriers used hoof testers differently than novices (participants who hadn't consistently used hoof testers before). Vets and farriers applied more force to areas of the hoof that tend to be thicker and more protected, and less force in thinner areas, where novices were less specific[54]. Add to that the fact that some horses have really thin soles and react to hoof testers whether they are lame or not, and you've got a recipe for confusion and possibly inaccurate results. Plus, overly aggressive hoof testing on thin soled horses could actually *cause* bruising.

Most of the time, when your farrier or vet hoof tests, they will be able to pinpoint an area where your horse reacts the most, and they'll look in that area for an abscess tract, which is the entry point for the bacteria. If they see something, they'll try to follow it and open up drainage for the abscess, which usually gives your horse some immediate relief. Often when an active abscess is opened, grayish or black pus begins draining (or even squirting out depending on how much pressure was built up) out of the tract. You'll want to soak the hoof a least once after the abscess is opened to make sure that the area is completely flushed out. Keep it clean, which will help prevent a relapse. Similarly, if an abscess becomes painful again after draining, a soak to clear out any dirt that might have resealed the tract could help.

If they aren't able to find or drain the abscess, you might have to wait a little longer. Sometimes abscesses in their early stages are difficult to locate since there isn't much pressure built up yet. In fact, a study done in Pennsylvania on abscesses showed that severe lameness in an abscess (meaning lots of pressure) indicated a shorter healing time afterwards, probably

A solar abscess opened by a farrier

---

[54] Arndt, J.L., Pfau, T., Day, P., Pardoe, C., Bolt, D.M., Weller, R. (2013). Forces applied with a hoof tester to cadaver feet vary widely between users. *Vet Rec. 172(7):* P. 182.

because the abscess was easily found and opened[55]. If your horse isn't super lame yet, soaking and wrapping might help the abscess blow out sooner too.

Some abscesses vent on their own, usually out of the coronary band. Abscesses always follow the path of least resistance, so if there's no available tract on the bottom of the hoof, it will travel up the sensitive lamina, which is extremely painful, until it reaches the top of the hoof wall and then drain from there. This process usually takes a lot longer to resolve. It also briefly interrupts the new wall growth at the coronary band where it blows out, which leaves a small horizontal crack in the wall which then usually grows out without issue.

If you have a really big abscess blow out on the sole, your horse might need some protection while the new sole grows. This could mean a wrap and a boot on a barefoot horse, or a shoe with a pad or hospital plate for a longer term solution.

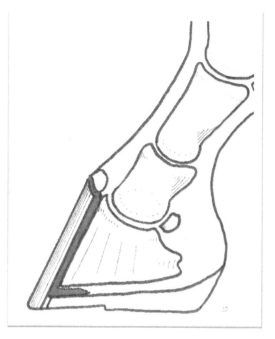

Abscesses may travel up the lamina to the coronary band to vent

Most of the time, once an abscess is opened it resolves without a problem. But if your horse has a lot of abscesses, especially in the same area of the hoof, it might be a good idea to look deeper. There are a few bigger issues that can cause repeated abscessing. If your horse has really thin soles and bruises her hooves on hard ground, you might have to add shoes or pads to help her cope. She could be experiencing a bone infection or a foreign object causing repeated infections. On the other hand, if her feet look pretty healthy and there are no signs of bruising, but she gets repeated abscesses in the same spot on her hoof, it could be caused by a keratoma,

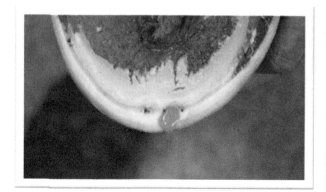

Fluid draining from an abscess

The horizontal line in the heel indicates where an abscess vented at the coronary band

[55] Cole, S.D., Stefanovski, D., Towl, S., Boyle, A.G. (2019). Factors associated with prolonged treatment days, increased veterinary visits and complications in horses with subsolar abscesses. *Vet Rec.; 184(8):* P. 251.

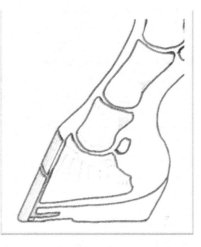

A cross section of an abscess growing out

The small horizontal line indicates where an abscess vented at the coronary band, a few months ago

which is a keratin growth, often on the inside of the hoof wall. They usually don't cause lameness unless they get too big, or if there's a small gap between the sole and the keratoma where dirt and bacteria can get to sensitive tissue. Keratomas can be diagnosed by looking at the bottom of the hoof while it's freshly trimmed, where you will often be able to see a round deviation on the inside of the wall, or by x-ray, where keratomas show up as a smooth indentation on the coffin bone. Dealing with a keratoma, you'll need a team effort between your vet and farrier. Sometimes the abscessing problem may be resolved by protecting the area with a shoe or pad, but sometimes surgery is necessary to remove the keratoma. Ask your vet and farrier if you think you might have a keratoma.

Repeated abscessing can also be seen in severe cases of laminitis. We'll be getting into laminitis

Laminitic bruising causing repeated solar abscesses

in Chapter 34, but the short story is that rotating coffin bones can tear blood vessels in the sole. This leads to a lot of bruising, and if bacteria gets into it, all that blood is a super nutrient-rich environment for an abscess. This typically occurs in either both front hooves or in all four feet, in really severe cases. It also is accompanied by lasting lameness that doesn't completely go away when the abscesses are opened, thanks to the active rotation of the bone and damage to sensitive structures. The good news is, this is very rarely the first sign of laminitis, so if your horse is abscessing but hasn't had any history of laminitis, that's probably not what's happening. We usually see this type of abscessing a lot more with horses who have long term, chronic laminitis.

Abscesses can be scary because of the fast onset and the severity of the pain, but they are usually resolved relatively quickly and don't leave any permanent damage. Now that you know the signs and treatments, you don't need to panic next time that your horse is limping. Just get your soaking gear and go check for heat!

Quick Takeaways
- **Abscesses are infections within the hoof capsule, which result in painful pressure and inflammation.**
- **Common symptoms include severe and worsening pain, localized heat, a bounding pulse, and swelling low in the affected limb.**
- **Treatment involves draining the abscess, usually by cutting out a drainage track. Soaking may speed drainage and clean out any remaining infection once it is opened.**

28 WHITE LINE DISEASE

White line disease -- the disease oddly named after a structure that it doesn't affect. Way to go, scientists who name things, way to go. It is actually a fungal and bacterial infection of the hoof wall, not the white line.

Upside: white line disease isn't painful until it has progressed to a point where the coffin bone doesn't have enough attachment to the wall to be stable. This means that a small infection that's caught early won't cause your horse any pain.

Downside: as a horse owner, there's nothing you can do to recognize a white line disease infection. Since there's no lameness and no external signs, the best way to spot a case is to make sure your horse gets regular farrier care. When your farrier is trimming, they'll be able to see any damage to the wall.

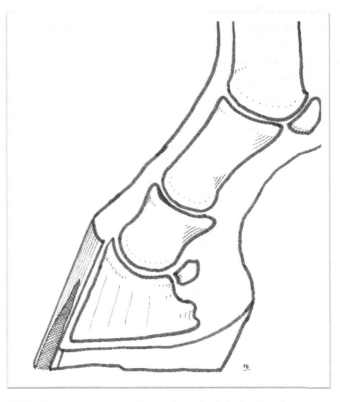

White line disease destroys the main body of the hoof wall

So how does white line disease work? It's an opportunistic keratinopathogenic bacteria and fungus combo. Keratinopathogenic means that they degrade and eat the keratin that makes up the hoof wall, and opportunistic means that they look for weak spots in the wall to attack. Once it gets in there, it starts eating the hoof wall and turning it into crumbly mush that doesn't function at all like healthy hoof wall. It keeps on eating away until it has destroyed the hoof wall all the way up to the coronary band.

When cultures are taken of hooves with white line disease, there are usually a lot of different bacteria and fungi present because the defect usually gets packed full of dirt and manure, but there are a couple strains of fungus that are almost always present. In one study of horses that showed signs of WLD infections, the worst samples came from hooves with fungi called *Trichophyton spp* and *Scopulariopsis brevicaulis*, which are both found in the

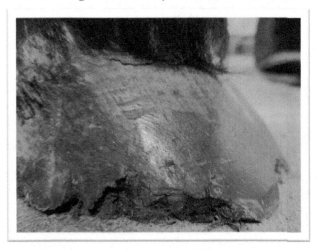

Weak walls are a prime target for white line disease

soil[56]. That means it's going to be almost impossible to prevent your horse from ever being exposed to the fungus.

Since WLD takes the easy route (which is what opportunistic means), it usually attacks the softer, higher moisture section of the hoof wall -- the inside of the stratum medium, where tubules are less densely packed and the moisture content is higher. The outside of the wall might look totally fine, but it can be just a thin shell of normal wall hiding a pocket of crumbly, eaten up horn.

If that sounds like a pretty scary thing to be growing in your horse's hooves, you're not wrong, but this nasty disease does have a soft underbelly -- it's another anaerobic infection, so oxygen exposure stops white line disease in its tracks. This is why if your farrier finds a pocket of WLD in the hoof, they will usually cut it open so that oxygen can get to every part of the defect. Occasionally, people will try leaving the outer shell of the wall intact and just scrape out the crumbly wall and throw some medication into the gap. This isn't usually a good idea since it's almost impossible to know if you got all the way to the edges of the infected area, and if it gets packed full of dirt, the infection will quickly flare up again.

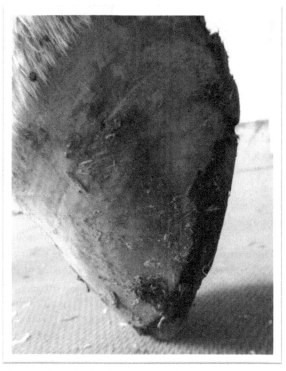

The outside of the hoof wall may look solid, but it is hollow

A debrided white line disease infection

If your farrier spots a crumbly, soft area that looks like a white line disease infection, they will probably start by cutting away the hoof wall that is covering the infected area. This part can look really crazy and extreme, but it is very important to expose the *entire* infected area to oxygen. Your farrier will continue to trim around the margins of the defect until they get to solid, connected hoof wall. If your farrier suspects that the infected area is pretty large, they may ask you to get your

[56] Apprich, V., Spergser, J., Rosengarten, R., Hinterhofer, C., Stanek, C. (2010). Scanning electron microscopy and fungal culture of hoof horn from horses suffering from onychomycosis. *Vet Dermatol. 21(4):* P. 335-40.

vet involved. Vets can use x-ray images to see exactly how big the infected area is before they start debriding. Plus some horses lack the patience to stand still for a slow and careful debridement of the area, so sedation might be called for.

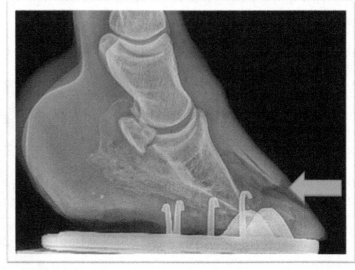

If the defect is pretty big, your farrier might need to add a shoe or even a plate to bridge the debrided area and help stabilize the hoof capsule while the defect grows out. Smaller cases might not require any extra

X-rays show the extent of the white line disease infection

help, but this is also going to partly depend on how strong your horse's hooves are to start with.

Once the entire undermined area has been cut open, it's time to kill any remaining spores or bacteria that might be hiding in tiny fissures or along the edge of the debrided area. You'll want to apply a topical antimicrobial agent as soon as your farrier is done debriding the area, because that's probably the cleanest that hoof will be until the next trim, so this could be the most effective treatment you do. Plus, why give that fungus time to start spreading again?

There are quite a few treatments on the market for white line disease, such as White Lightning and Clean Trax which are applied as a hoof soak, but also create gas that can find its way into all

After a debridement, the defect should be treated topically

the smallest fissures to kill bacteria and fungus. This type of treatment is very effective but does require some time to do the hoof soak. You can also use a strong iodine solution to paint or squirt into the defect, but you will need to make sure that it's getting all the way to the edges, and apply plenty to soak in. You can also mix copper sulfate and vinegar to make a sprayable treatment which is very effective at killing bacteria and fungus[57]. It is important to avoid getting copper sulfate on sensitive

---

[57] Copper sulfate is a very effective antimicrobial agent, but it should also be used with extreme caution since it is poisonous to humans and animals. Follow all the warnings on the label, and never get it on your skin or in your eyes. Keep away from children and pets. You'll also need to make sure that you are *only* spraying it on your horse's hoof, never on his skin or hair. Copper sulfate is available online and at your local hardware store in the pool and pond chemical section.

tissue like the coronary band or your own skin. It's great at killing microbes but not great to absorb into your bloodstream.

So what's the most effective topical treatment? Try hitting the infection with one of the gas-producing soaks immediately after the debridement, and then treat with iodine or copper sulfate solution daily until the next trimming appointment. This way, you'll get the benefits of both types of treatment. For safety's sake, you should never apply more than one treatment at once, since it could affect the chemical composition of the treatments and either make them ineffective or create unintended side effects.

Your best friend for treating white line disease is a clean and dry hoof. Remember, fungus and bacteria love warm, anaerobic environments, so you'll want to be letting the hoof dry and expose it to oxygen as often as possible. Ideally, the horse should be turned out in a dry environment until the defect has grown out, but if this isn't possible, you'll have to work a little harder.

Regardless of whether you have a wet or dry environment, you'll need to clean out the debrided area as often as you can. Getting oxygen in there to any spores or bacteria that might be making themselves comfortable is your daily goal. And you will have to be thorough with the cleaning. You can use your hoof pick to clean out the majority of the dirt, but that's not going to be enough to get all the dirt out from around the edges and the tiny cracks. You'll have to grab a stiff brush, such as a small wire welders brush, and really get the dirt knocked out of there. If you're thinking about the nylon brush on the back of your hoof pick, forget it. That sucker is too soft for a serious job like this.

Once you've got the defect nice and clean, that's the time to spray, squirt, or paint your topical white line disease treatment onto the defect, paying special attention to the edges. Good work! Now tomorrow, do it again. This one's a little like taking antibiotics: If your doctor prescribes them, you need to take the recommended dose for the recommended amount of time. You don't take them for three days, feel a little better, and quit taking them, or else you'll be back to see your doctor with the same problem in a week or so.

When your farrier comes back for the next appointment, they will clean out the defect again and probably have to trim a little more off of some of the edges. It is normal for there to be some slight progression of the infection, usually one or two small pockets off of the main area, but it should be significantly less progression than the first time.

Once the infection is under control, it's just a waiting game of keeping it healthy while the defect grows out. If you had a big infection, you could be looking at six months or more before it's completely gone, but stay vigilant. You don't want to do everything right for the first five months and then waste all that hard work by letting it re-infect in month six. Stay strong and stay on top of it. Then one visit, you'll watch your farrier trim off the last little bit of the defect, leaving a nice, strong, working hoof wall from top to bottom.

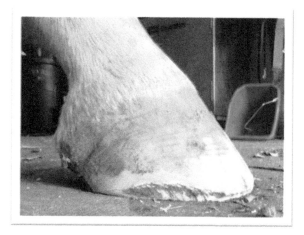

Continue treatment as the defect grows out

Take a second to pat yourself on the back, you did it! White line disease is one of the few hoof problems where the prognosis is almost entirely up to you once the original debridement is done. It's all your hard work and consistency that will save your horse's hoof, but once you do, you can feel good about yourself every time you look at his healthy hoof.

Quick Takeaways

- **White line disease is a keratinopathogenic fungal and bacterial infection of the hoof wall, destroying the inner section of the wall.**
- **It is most commonly diagnosed by farriers during routine trimming and shoeing.**
- **White line disease is anaerobic, so treatment typically necessitates the removal of all affected hoof wall so that oxygen can reach the entire defect, followed by topical treatment.**

29 CRACKS, SPLITS, AND SCARS

Given everything we've said about the anatomy of the hoof wall and how it's strong and elastic and generally shoulders the majority of the weight bearing for the hoof, what makes a hoof wall fail? It's normally the structure your horse counts on day in and day out, so why does it wake up one day and decide to quit?

Like we talked about in Chapter 23, there are two basic reasons that structures fail. One is that an abnormally weak structure was put under normal load, and the other is that a normal structure is put under abnormal

Small superficial cracks can be caused by rapid changes between wet and dry

load. If you learn one thing from this chapter, it should be the fact that structures don't fail just *because*. There is *always* a reason for a failure, even if we don't know what it is at the time. So don't accept "that's just how it is." We might not even be able to fix the reason why things are failing, like poor genetics or conformation, but knowing what the most likely reasons are will help you make informed decisions about treatment and what your expectations should be.

So what are some common reasons that hoof walls crack? If we're categorizing the reasons, here are some that fall under "abnormally weak structure taking normal load;"

- Incomplete or imbalanced nutrition leading to poor quality horn. For more on feeding the hoof, flip back to Chapter 24.

- Extremely wet environments causing soft hoof walls that lack the rigidity we'd like to see. We talked about this in depth in Chapter 23.

- Quick changes between wet and dry, causing superficial splits in the hoof wall. This is caused by rapid expansion during wet conditions, and then rapid drying that leads to shrinking.

- Flared or dished hoof walls, which have a lot less structural strength than straight walls.

- Stretched white lines where dirt and debris can pack between the sole and the wall. This can work against your horse in both categories. Separated structures don't have the same strength and ability to share load as well-attached structures, so that's a weakened structure. But it's also abnormal load because that dirt and debris actually pushes the wall out and acts like a wedge driving up the inside of

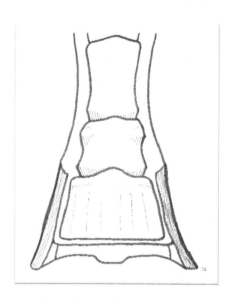

Flared hoof walls increase leverage

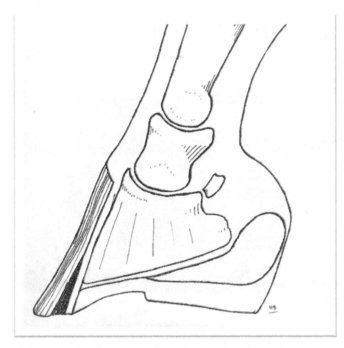

Debris in the white line can pry the wall away from internal structures

the hoof wall, which is not the type of stress that the hoof wall is designed to deal with: abnormal stress.

• Thin hoof walls. This could be totally natural, since some horses genetically have thinner walls than the ideal (thoroughbreds are notorious for this) and young horses typically have thinner hoof walls too. Their hoof walls are supposed to get thicker and stronger in proportion to their body growth and weight gain, but if a young horse is overfed to aim for an arbitrary size or weight, they can put on weight faster than what their hooves compensate for. Hoof walls can also be thin thanks to human interference, if your farrier rasped the outside of the hoof wall aggressively, usually to try to get rid of a flare.

• Already weakened areas of the hoof wall, like an area that's infected with white line disease or an area with an old scar which we'll talk about a little later in this chapter.

What about abnormal loads placed on normal structures?

• Overweight horses. This one sounds obvious, but it's extremely common and affects every part of your horse's health. The hooves don't get proportionally thicker and stronger when your horse gains weight, and in fact they may get weaker as they flare and try to deal with metabolic changes.

• Conformation can be a problem because if a horse's legs aren't straight, the load isn't equally shared across the hoof. One area might be overloaded while the others aren't helping out much. It can be even more of an issue if your horse's front or hind legs don't match each other, like a high/low conformation, or one leg being toed-in and the other being toed-out.

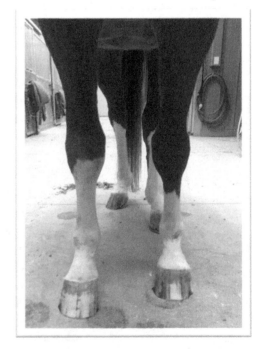

Conformations that create uneven weight bearing set the hoof up for damage

168

- Long or imbalanced hooves. The longer the hoof gets, the more leverage there is on the wall. Even with perfect conformation, there will come a point where the leverage is more than what the wall can put up with. If your horse also has less-than-ideal conformation, he'll probably hit that point of overload sooner.
- Short shoeing. Sometimes in a last ditch effort to keep a horse from pulling shoes, farriers will fit a shoe very short or tight, and the hoof overgrows the shoe. This makes a pressure point where the shoe ends, and it can be enough stress in some severe cases to crack the hoof wall. Sometimes well-meaning horse owners or trainers who are sick of their horse pulling shoes may request this style of shoeing, but it could do long term damage to the foot.
- High impact work, like working at speed on a hard surface, can be enough concussion to cause cracks.

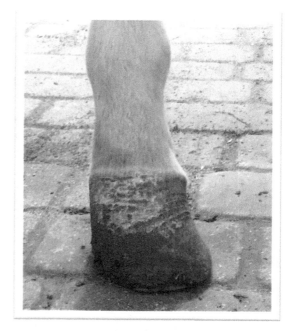

A long, imbalanced hoof creates abnormal stress

The same hoof, trimmed and balanced is subject to far less stress

It's important to realize, too, that there are two different types of hoof cracks, superficial cracks that only go part of the way through the wall, and deep or full thickness cracks that go all the way through the wall. Superficial cracks tend to be caused by things like nutrition and moisture changes, while full thickness cracks are more likely to be caused by force. Obviously, full thickness cracks are a lot more concerning than superficial cracks, since deep cracks actually destabilize the hoof capsule and can involve the sensitive tissues inside the hoof.

So what should you do if you notice a hoof crack starting? If the crack is starting from the top of the hoof wall and traveling down, you will want to call your farrier immediately. This type of crack usually results from imbalance, often related to conformation, and the coronary band in the area of the crack is often pushed upwards. The hoof wall tries to compensate for imbalance by flexing and twisting, but there are limits to how far it can go before it cracks. If you have this type of crack, your farrier will probably trim the hoof to even out the balance of the hoof so that force is applied more evenly, and they may also "float" the area. Since the coronary band is pushed up

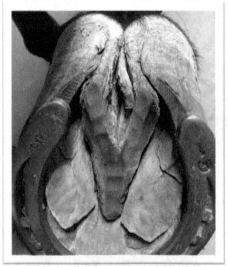

A shoe that does not cover the heels creates pressure points at the back of the shoe

from all the force applied to it, floating is when the hoof wall is trimmed so that the pushed up area of the wall isn't touching the shoe, so that it can settle downward and have a break from that force. Sometimes, when your farrier floats an area, the hoof wall may settle all the way to the floor in ten or twenty minutes, and then they may float it again before applying the shoe.

If you have a hoof crack at the bottom of the hoof, it may not be an emergency, depending on if it seems to

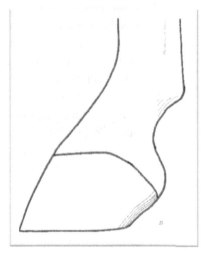

The coronary band may displace upward in the area of stress

be staying the same size or if it is getting longer, moving towards the coronary band. If it's not progressing and you have a farrier appointment coming up soon, you're probably fine to just wait until your regular appointment. If it is growing or you don't have an appointment scheduled for a while, you might want to get your farrier out sooner than later, especially if her hooves are on the long side already.

Hoof cracks starting at the top of the hoof are very serious

Hoof cracks that start at the bottom of the hoof are usually related to leverage, like hooves growing too long or dirt and debris packing into the white line. A lot of the time, your farrier will open this type of crack up to get all that stuff out so it doesn't keep on pushing the wall apart. Plus, these types of cracks are ideal for opportunistic infections like white line disease.

Once the hoof has been trimmed to the best possible length and balance for your horse, and the crack has been opened up if necessary, your farrier might add a few other things depending on how severe the crack is.

If your horse is barefoot, you might have to add shoes until the crack is healed up. With cracks starting from the bottom, a shoe can help keep the hoof wall from prying outward, and it can protect the crack from the bottom so that nothing else shoves in there. If

A hoof crack starting from the bottom may not be as severe, but should still be addressed

the crack seems to be caused by uneven weight bearing, your farrier might choose to use a bar shoe, which is a shoe that is connected in the heels and reduces the amount that each heel can move.

Your farrier could also add clips on either side of the crack to reduce movement of the hoof wall. Clips are simple metal tabs that come up from the shoe onto the hoof, and they can be placed anywhere around the hoof wall. Since they are stiff metal, they don't allow

Your farrier may have to remove material from around the crack to prevent debris from packing into it

the hoof to expand as much in that area. This is helpful for times when you'd like the hoof not to move quite as much, like with cracks or even coffin bone fractures.

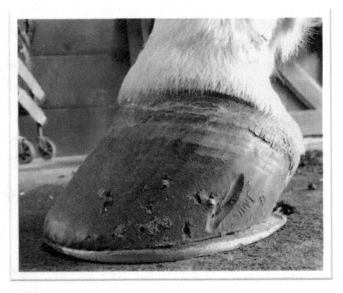

This crack started out at the coronary band and has been growing out for a few months

If the crack is pretty severe, or if it is an ongoing problem that your horse has struggled with for a while, such as if your horse has conformation that really stresses one part of his hoof, your farrier might use some different techniques to take load off of the hoof wall and put it on other structures. They might use a pour in pad or a frog support pad like we talked about in Chapter 18, or a heartbar shoe, which transfers some load onto the frog and limits the amount of independent motion in the heels.

Remember, the hoof wall grows from the coronary band down, so once the hoof wall is split, it can't grow back together. It has to be replaced by new growth from top to bottom.

For the hoof wall to function correctly, it needs to function as one solid but flexible piece. A big enough hoof crack changes that and turns the hoof wall into two independently moving pieces, which not only doesn't handle shock well, but also makes it hard for new solid hoof wall to grow above the crack.

If you have a crack that has a lot of movement in it, your farrier will probably choose to stabilize it with some sort of patch or plate. One quick safety warning though: if your horse has a crack in her hoof that is bleeding, you *never* want to totally seal that crack up until the bleeding has completely stopped. It's tempting to want to cover it up with glue so that it looks better, but it's really easy to breed infection and create an abscess if you seal up injured sensitive tissue. If you do have a bleeding crack, you still have options. Your farrier can make a metal plate that is glued or screwed on either side of the crack but doesn't completely cover it, or

A glue on patch that still allows the crack to be flushed with disinfectant

they can glue on a patch that includes a drain, with no glue in the actual crack. If the crack isn't bleeding, they will have more options for totally covering up the crack.

If you're the kind of person that makes use of Google (probably all of us!) you might have looked up hoof crack treatments, and you might have seen people touting a method of stopping cracks that involves rasping a line over the crack, in the hopes of deflecting force to the sides of the crack or preventing the crack from going up farther. This may work on a superficial crack, but there's no way that rasping an eighth inch groove into the wall is going to stop a crack that is going all the way through the hoof wall. All it does is leave a series of hash marks going through the crack that show all the times this trick didn't work. I think it's about time this one was retired, folks.

Depending on how severe the crack is, your farrier might recommend that you take some time off from riding, especially if you and your horse participate in a high-stress sport. You might need to wait until you've got some good horn grown down before you try stressing the hoof wall again.

Healing a crack is all about setting the crack up for success, and then giving it time. Aside from keeping the hoof as clean and dry as possible, and following any activity recommendations your farrier might make, your biggest contribution to the healing process is making sure that your horse is getting quality hoof care at frequent intervals, and that might have to be a little shorter interval than normal while you're trying to get the crack under control. Keeping the hoof consistently balanced is the best thing

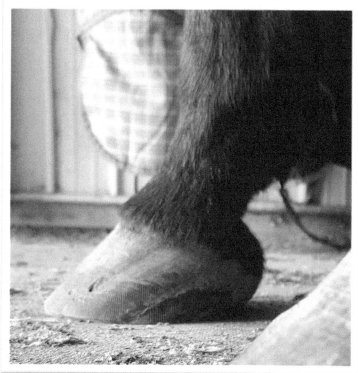

Two indentations in the hoof wall indicate weak spots which could be caused by coronary band scarring

you can do for a crack. Once your farrier has come up with a shoeing package that is working for your horse, it's a waiting game while the crack grows out.

But there are a few circumstances where you're not out of the woods yet when the crack is gone. If your horse has a really uneven conformation that puts a lot of extra stress on one area of the hoof, or if your horse has a scar in their coronary band that causes abnormal hoof growth, your horse is at a higher risk for reoccurring cracks.

Scars in the coronary band are a little bit like damaging your nail bed: there's always an area of your fingernail that grows out weird. Only, if you're a horse, you're walking around on that fingernail and it's not as strong as the rest of your hoof.

If you do have a horse that is predisposed to cracks, you'll want to make sure that he stays on a consistent hoof care schedule, most likely being trimmed or shod every six weeks or less, because it's important to keep the hoof in balance and keep him from putting extra leverage on the weakened areas. Your farrier may also have ideas about shoeing that might prevent further cracks.

Listen to your farrier, take your time, and keep your horse on a tight shoeing schedule. Cracks are a pain for you and your horse, but they will heal, and you *can* prevent them from happening in the future.

Quick Takeaways

- **There are a wide range of reasons why cracks and chips can occur, but essentially it is a sign that the hoof wall is overloaded.**
- **Treatment of a serious crack usually involves balancing the hoof and stabilizing the crack through shoeing and/or patching.**

30 CHIPS, FLAPS, AND AVULSIONS

Okay, nobody likes a hang nail. But what if that hang nail is a hundred times bigger than yours and that nail happens to be what your horse walks around on? Not cool at all. Especially if your horse is barefoot, you may have seen what looks like a flap of hoof wall sticking out near the bottom of the hoof. If it's on the inside of the hoof and your horse travels pretty close, she might even be scraping her opposite leg with it. And although most of these flaps are fairly small, they can also start peeling up higher and potentially get into sensitive tissue.

So what's going on here? Why does your horse's hoof want to break off in chunks? Let's take a look at what happens in nature. According to the Brumby research we talked about in the beginning of this book, wild horses in dry areas self-trim by wearing their hooves off on their 11 miles of daily travel on hard ground, and sometimes wear them off too much. But what

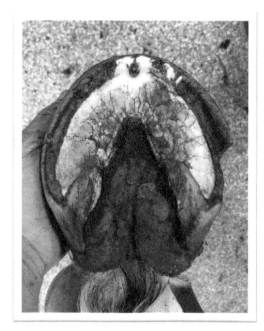

Horses chip up to "self trim"

do the horses in areas with wet, soft ground do? They aren't wearing as much hoof off because they don't have to travel as far to find food and water, plus the ground that their walking on is a lot less abrasive. So just like the domestic horses that we see in neglect cases, their hooves get longer and longer, flaring out, distorting, and dishing in the toe[58]. Eventually, there's so much leverage on the wall that the weakest area or the area under the most stress breaks off. Once a section breaks out, there's less hoof wall to distribute force to, so there's even more stress on the horn that's left. Soon, another section of the wall will break out

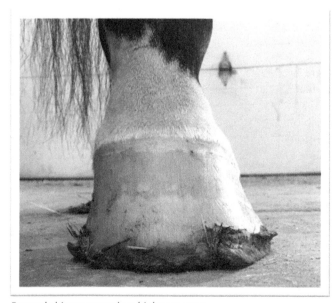

Ragged chips may peel up higher or snag

---

[58] Hampson, B.A. and Pollitt, C.C. (November, 2011). *Improving the Foot Health of the Domestic Horse: The Relevance of the Feral Horse Foot Model.* Retrieved from http://horsefx.com.au/wp-content/uploads/2015/07/Pollitt-and-Hamson-Improving-health-of-domestic-horse-hoof.pdf

too, until the hoof has "self-trimmed" back to a shorter length. It's a ragged, uneven trim, and the horse has no way of controlling how short the trim is, but it gets rid of the extra length. Hey, I never said horses were very good at trimming their hooves. This is the same type of force that is acting on your horse's hooves, just in a less extreme form.

Since you don't want your horse to try his hand at self-trimming (again, the results are not good!) you'll want to control the way that any hoof wall flaps come off. Like when you try to peel a hangnail instead of grabbing nail clippers to snip it off, you never know what direction it will peel or if it will peel up into the sensitive tissue of your nail bed. Plus, just like when you have a hangnail and it gets caught on everything, you don't want your horse snagging it on things or hurting his other legs with the jagged edge.

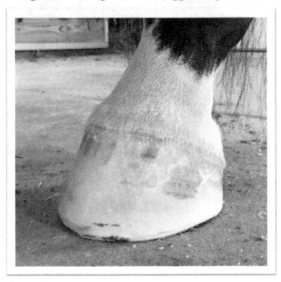

The same hoof from the previous page, trimmed by a farrier shows very little sign of the flaps

Unless your farrier is coming out tomorrow, now's the time to be the competent, multi-talented horse owner you are and go get a rasp. You can always ask your farrier if they have a used, dull rasp that you can have on hand just in case.

Before you freak out, I'm not asking you to do a full trim on your horse's hoof. Right now, you're going to be doing some quick and easy first aid. If you can cut off a hangnail on yourself, you can get rid of one on your horse. It's a pretty similar process, just on a bigger scale.

And if your first response to that statement was "I'm supposed to have a rasp?", flip over to Chapter 41, where we'll talk about the emergency hoof care kit that I'd like to see in every barn that has a horse in it.

All that you want to do is use that rasp on the outside of the hoof, not on the bottom of the hoof, to remove the horn that's already fracturing off. You don't want to hit the good, still-attached hoof wall with your rasp, just the flap that is sticking out. You're going to bring your horse's leg forward just like your farrier does and rest it on your legs while you use both hands to control the rasp. If your horse is pretty heavy coming forward, you can try putting her hoof on the edge of haybale instead of your knee, so that you can focus on trimming off that flap instead of arm-wrestling her. In a human-horse arm wrestling match, the horse is always going to win.

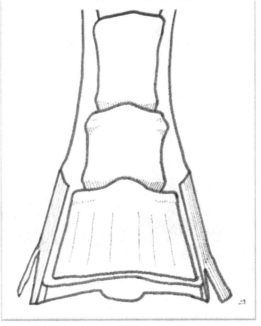

Flaps that do not impinge on sensitive tissue are safe to remove

Once you've gotten the loose flap removed, use the fine side of your rasp to take off any sharp, jagged corners, because you don't want them breaking off, or injuring her other legs. Use your fingers to check for a sharp edge and bevel the area as smooth as you can. Just make sure this doesn't turn into a cutting-your-own-bangs incident, where you keep on going shorter to try to even it up. You shouldn't be removing significant amounts of hoof in this step, just smoothing out the edges.

Now stand up, stretch your back out, and high five yourself because you just helped your horse, saved your farrier a trip out, and handled that one like a boss! Alternatively, if all that sounded like a really bad time, give your farrier a call and ask them to come out to trim it. Just be prepared to pay them for their time.

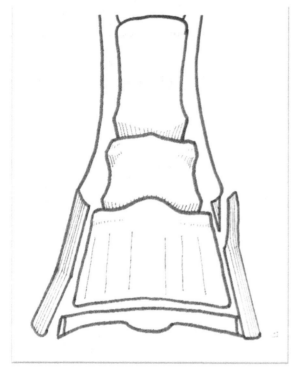

Splits or chips that effect sensitive tissue call for a professional

When should you *not* try to remove the flap yourself? This one is important: If there's blood or your horse is lame on that foot, call a pro. When sensitive tissue is involved, you need more than just that flap of horn removed, you need someone with professional experience and anatomical knowledge, who knows if this is a serious issue or not. Sure, you could rasp it off yourself, but you'll want another set of eyes on this one, because it might need longer term treatment, like a shoe or a patch to help stabilize and protect the area, or even systemic antibiotics to prevent infection. Also, with any hoof wound, you'll want to make sure that your horse has a recent tetanus shot[59], since the *Clostridium tetani* bacteria is found in soil and can easily infect an injury in the hoof[60].

If sensitive tissue is involved, you'll want to keep your horse's hoof clean until your vet or farrier can arrive. If that's going to be a little while, try to get the wound clean and then wrap it. Cleaning the wound can help reduce the risk of infection and wrapping it will not only keep it clean but also help stabilize the flap temporarily. Depending on how painful the wound is, you might be able

[59] Green, S.L., Little, C.B., Baird, J.D., Tremblay, R.R., Smith-Maxie, L.L. (1994). Tetanus in the horse: a review of 20 cases (1970 to 1990). *J Vet Intern Med. 8(2):* P. 128-32.

[60] van Galen, G., Saegerman, C., Rijckaert, J., Amory, H., Armengou, L., Bezdekova, B., Durie, I., Findshøj, D. R., Fouché, N., Haley, L., Hewetson, M., van den Hoven, R., Kendall, A., Malalana, F., Muller Cavalleri, J., Picavet, T., Roscher, K., Verwilghen, D., Wehrli Eser, M., Westermann, C., Mair, T. (2017). Retrospective evaluation of 155 adult equids and 21 foals with tetanus in Western, Northern, and Central Europe (2000-2014). Part 1: Description of history and clinical evolution. *J Vet Emerg Crit Care (San Antonio);27(6):* P. 684-696.

to pick out the area, but you might have to flush it with water instead if your horse is really uncomfortable. Don't put any medication in the wound unless your vet tells you to. If you want some tips on building a sturdy hoof wrap, check out Chapter 39.

Sometimes if you see a flap of hoof and it's bleeding, it could actually be a partial wall avulsion. That's when a section of wall breaks off and is completely independent of the rest of the wall, which usually only happens if there was some severe trauma to the hoof. It's most commonly seen in the back half of the hoof, and it can be caused by things like wire cuts, kicking something that doesn't move like a sturdy fence post, or even stomping on a rock just right. An avulsion is usually a kind of freak accident, and it's pretty uncommon.

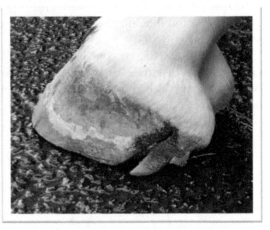

A partial avulsion. The heel is completely independent of the rest of the hoof wall

If that is what you have going on, you're going to want your vet and farrier both involved. Your vet will check for bone involvement and make sure that no other sensitive structures were damaged. Depending on how severe the incident was, they might have to treat some of the soft tissue damage before the farrier can work on the hoof. Then your vet and farrier will come up with a plan together for how to stabilize the hoof capsule. Just like with a hoof crack, it's important to get the broken of section of the hoof locked down so that it's not moving around on its own. Depending on the size of the avulsion, there are a variety of different shoes they can use to protect the hoof. They may also have to float the avulsed section by cutting off some of the hoof wall so that it's not bearing weight, and they will probably plate or patch it. At least for the first shoeing

after the injury, the vet may need to sedate your horse or anesthetize the hoof so that your horse can have a pain-free shoeing. Your vet may also prescribe antibiotics or give you antiseptic to put in the wound, and you will be taking some time off from riding.

It's critical to get the avulsed section stabilized and healed up as quickly as possible, not just because it's pretty painful to your horse, but also because the longer it is moving independently, the more damage and scarring it can cause in the coronary band. As we talked about in Chapter 29, scars in the coronary band are bad news because the horn that grows from that area will be permanently weaker. Since permanently weaker feet isn't what we're shooting for here, let's get that hoof healed up quickly!

Avulsions are definitely the extreme side of hoof wall damage. The much more manageable, but still troublesome side, is hoof wall loss around the nail holes in a shod horse. There are a couple reasons this can be happening. One is that your horse might have some opportunistic white line disease-type infection sneaking in at the nail holes and weakening the horn. This could be the case if you're noticing hoof wall chipping out around the nail holes during your regular shoeing cycle. If this sounds like your horse, ask your farrier if they think a topical disinfectant might help, and try to manage any moisture extremes that your horse has to deal with. Remember that fungus and bacteria love a moist environment (sorry, people who hate the word moist, I said it), so keeping hooves clean and dry can help.

Another common reason for hoof wall loss around the nail holes is the chronic shoe puller. If your horse pulls shoes frequently, they can tear off some hoof wall with the nails when they pull the shoe. If this happens once, it's annoying. If this happens multiple times per shoeing cycle, it can be devastating to the hoof, and to your chances of riding. If that's the case, your horse's hoof wall growth just can't keep up with the rate that it's being destroyed, and each time he pulls off more wall, there's less solid wall to nail into.

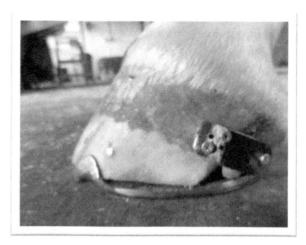

An avulsion may be stabilized with a shoe and a plate across the defect

If this sounds like your horse, for everyone's sake, *please* go back and reread Chapter 20 and see if there's any part of the picture that you could improve on. Sometimes one small element can be the missing piece that changes everything for your horse.

In the meantime, your farrier may end up having to glue shoes on or nail a shoe on and fill in the torn up areas with glue so that there's less shoe for your horse to step on. Sometimes if you can keep shoes on for just one cycle without a pulled shoe, you can get ahead of the hoof wall destruction and actually make some progress.

Dealing with chronic shoe loss can be one of the most frustrating aspects of having a horse, but don't give up. If you and your farrier work together, you can improve the situation, and small improvements add up to big changes for your horse.

Speaking of small changes making a big difference, let's talk about hoof problems that come from conformation, and what we can do to manage them.

Quick Takeaways
- **If a hoof flap is not bleeding or sensitive, you may remove it to prevent it from ripping up higher.**
- **If a hoof flap is bleeding or sensitive, you should call your farrier right away so that they can stabilize the hoof.**

31 CONFORMATIONAL CAUSES, HOOF EFFECTS

In this chapter, we're going to be talking all about the one thing none of us can do anything about: conformation. We know it's important. We know it can either have positive or negative effects on movement, soft tissue, how the limbs load, and definitely on the hooves. The easiest solution would be to only buy a horse with textbook perfect conformation. *But* we all know that there is no perfectly put together horse out there, and if there were, he probably wouldn't have the perfect mind, or he wouldn't have any heart. We're all out there looking for a horse with the right personality, a horse we enjoy being around, and hopefully a body that will allow him to stay sound doing whatever discipline or activities we'd like to share with him.

So what can you expect if your perfect horse has not-quite-perfect conformation? As we've mentioned before, a horse with straight legs is bearing weight pretty evenly on her hooves. She stands and moves squarely so all the parts of her hoof are able to do their job and help absorb shock together. A horse with crooked legs? Not so much. He will stand and move in ways that make one part of the hoof work harder than the others. This is easy to envision if you think about dropping a plumb line from the point of your horse's shoulder in the front limbs, or the point of the hip in the hinds. You want that plumb line to equally divide the leg, but on a horse that isn't built square, it's a good bet that your plumb line will fall to one side or

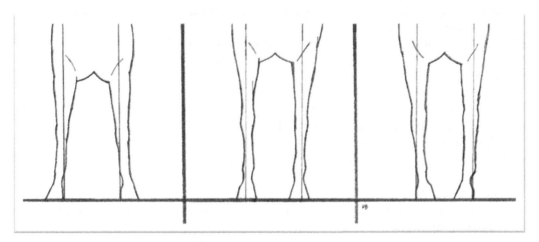

the other. Wherever that line is falling, so is your horse's weight. So if the plumb line hits the inside of your horse's hoof, like if she stands base wide, with her feet farther apart than her shoulders, you'll probably see a straight up and down hoof wall on the inside, maybe even with a higher coronary band. If it falls to the outside, you'd expect just the opposite.

The plumb line weight principle also works from the side. If your horse is standing farther forward than square, the plumb line will be farther behind the heels, which means extra weight being placed on them. Your horse's hoof might react by crushing or bending in the heels, since they're taking more than their fair share of the weight, and you might see a longer

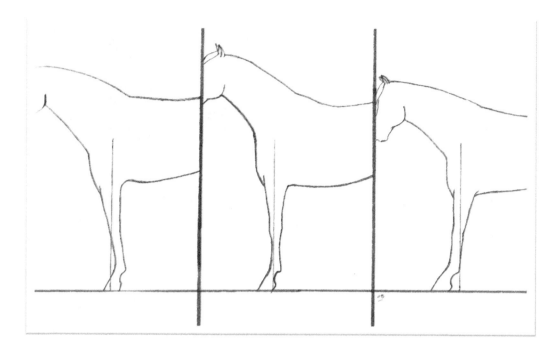

toe. If the line falls closer to the toe than the heels, you could see a dished toe from extra stress, and higher heels since they aren't taking much weight.

Usually the first compensation we see in the hoof is that the hoof wall flares in some areas and straightens in others. If the hoof straightens or rolls under in one area, it has to flare in another area since the entire hoof is connected. If you're curious how this works, grab a big rubber band and stick it on the table in front of you. Push one side in and the other side moves out. Push two sides in, and the front and back squish out. Your horse's hoof functions like that, except that it's not as flexible as the rubber band, so once it distorts past a certain point, it breaks.

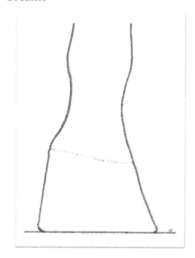

Luckily for your horse, the hoof sacrifices itself in a lot of ways before it finally cracks. It can move in or out by flaring or straightening, and up or down, like when you see the coronary band is higher in one area than another. The coronary band itself can even flatten and stretch to help balance the hoof, but by doing so, it can compromise blood flow and angle of new hoof wall growth.

If you see a lot of flaring on one side of your horse's hoof, or a coronary band that has high points, look up and see if there is a conformational abnormality in that leg. I say abnormality, but less than perfect conformation is probably more normal than good conformation. You can also ask your farrier about this one, because if they've been dealing with the results of the conformation in your horse's hooves, they are probably aware of where the deviation starts.

Uneven loading causes coronary band displacement and hoof wall flare

If your horse is prone to flaring and/or uneven coronary bands, it's really important to keep her on a consistent trimming or shoeing cycle to help maintain the best possible balance for that hoof and prevent more distortion. Like pruning a plant, you'll get better results from frequent, small adjustments than by repeatedly letting it get out of control and then having to get the chain saw out to hack it back into shape. I'm talking about a schedule no longer than six weeks, even shorter if your horse is a fast grower.

Allowing distortions to go unchecked puts way more stress on both the hoof and the structures above it. If you've read Chapter 29, you know that you don't want a hoof crack telling you that there was too much stress on the hoof, but you can also cause bruising in the hoof, pull ligaments especially collateral ligaments, the small ones in charge of keeping joints stable, and even

One side of the hoof straightens while the other flares

create permanent joint damage through repeated uneven loading. And yes, if your horse has really uneven conformation, his joints are already going to be loading unevenly no matter what you do, but you can control the severity of that uneven loading through frequent trimming. Once the hoof has compensated as far as it can for uneven loading, something else has to go. With mediolateral imbalance (side to side), a lot of the time it's the frog. The frog is a pretty soft, flexible structure, but that also means it lacks the rigidity that might give it the strength to resist a lot of torque. Especially if your horse is already battling a little thrush, the central sulcus becomes the weak point that invites failure, and your horse develops a deep split that goes all the way up between her heel bulbs. If you notice this, jump on treating for thrush right away. Even if the cause is primarily uneven loading, you want the frog to be as strong and healthy as it can be to resist that force. If the cause of the split is uneven loading, you'll usually see that one heel bulb looks higher than the other when you view it from the back. This is called sheared heels, and your farrier may float the jammed-up heel, apply a bar shoe to prevent uneven loading, use load sharing devices like pour-in pads, or some combination of the above. Remember, since it is almost always caused by

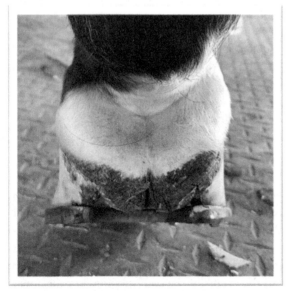

One heel may displace upward

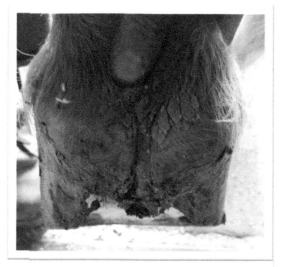

A large split between the heels may be related to thrush or shearing from imbalance

conformation, even once the sheared heels are stabilized and healthy again, you will always want to be on the alert, because we can't fix the conformation problem.

Another effect of long-term imbalance on the hoof is ossification of the collateral cartilages, commonly known as sidebone. This is the process of the springy cartilage plates in the back half of the hoof turning to bone trying to compensate for forces that were beyond what they could handle. Sidebone itself doesn't cause lameness, and you should look at it as a symptom of uneven loading

more than as a disease. It's less like a broken bone and more like the hoof saying, "Help, I've fallen and I can't get up!"

Horses that are actively developing sidebone might show some lameness, but once it's ossified, your horse should be as sound as ever. Of course, bone is much less flexible than cartilage, so sidebone carries a

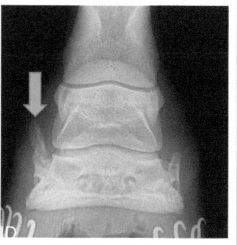

Xrays show the extent of the sidebone

risk of fracture that your horse didn't have back when it was cartilage. You will see severe, sudden onset lameness in the case of a fractured sidebone, but other than that, you shouldn't expect a lot of issues from sidebone.

On the other hand, it is a good idea to see sidebone as a warning light on your horse's dashboard. You know that if your horse has sidebone, that hoof is being loaded to a degree that it can't handle. Usually, you'll want to avoid high concussion activities like riding on pavement or jumping on hard footings with a horse that has sidebone, and you'll want to make sure that he's being

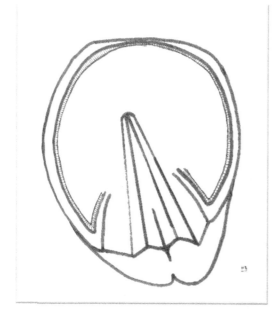

Uneven conformation may lead to uneven wear

trimmed on a regular schedule so that the hoof stays in balance. If he is shod, sometimes a pad can help reduce concussion just a little bit.

Another enemy of balanced hooves is the uneven hoof wear that often comes with uneven conformation. It doesn't take a rocket scientist to realize that if your horse is standing and moving unevenly, the hoof won't be breaking over in the center and it probably won't be landing flat either. That means that one side or even one quarter of the hoof is going to be wearing more than the others, especially if your horse has arthritis or stiffness higher up that lead her to drag her hooves a little. Most of the time, she's not wearing her hooves into perfect balance. Like we talked about in Chapter 23, horses don't know when to stop, so an uneven wear pattern can get pretty extreme and completely change the function of the hoof. It can also throw the hoof even more out of balance and force your horse to stand in a way that actually exaggerates her

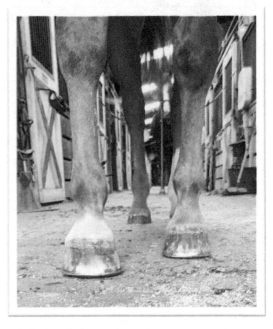

Toed in conformation may cause uneven wear, but shoeing will reduce wear

conformational issues. If your horse wears her hooves unevenly, your farrier can trim the hoof into balance, but the biggest help will be from adding shoes that prevent her from wearing so far out of balance in the six weeks in between trims.

Conformation in the adult horse is locked in. We can't change it by trimming or shoeing, no matter how extreme we get, and trying to change it will usually result in lameness. What we *can* often change is your horse's posture, which adapts and gets worse as the hoof distorts and grows out of balance. Postural adaptation can make a conformational issue look much worse than it needs to be, and sometimes balancing the hoof and removing distortion

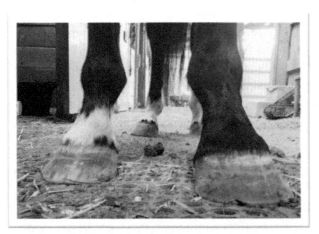

can help improve posture. Better still, posture influences the way your horse moves, so we can sometimes also improve movement, which improves the evenness of hoof loading. This turns into a cycle of improvement where the hoof is loaded more evenly, and therefore can grow more evenly with less distortion, which creates better posture. So we may not be able to fix conformation, but we can often drastically improve the amount of uneven force your horse has to deal

Toed out conformation

with, and in turn, increase the odds of your horse staying sounder longer. Isn't that what we're all looking for?

Quick Takeaways

- Conformation predicts hoof distortion and eventual long-term wear and tear damage on bones, joints, and soft tissue.
- Managing hoof distortion through regularly scheduled hoof care will reduce damage done by poor conformation.
- Shoes may be necessary to prevent uneven wear in a horse with poor conformation.

32 ARTHRITIS AND FRACTURES

If you're lucky enough to have had a horse you care about for a long time, the fact is that time and activity take a toll on their bodies, and it's common for an old horse to have some arthritis in his body. Just like with humans, arthritis can tell a story about all the crazy things you did when you were younger, or it can have genetic and conformational causes. Sometimes, it's a combination of causes, like a conformation that puts extra stress on a joint, plus high impact activity.

Arthritis in any part of the horse can affect the hoof, even spinal arthritis! Wherever the arthritis is, your horse is going to change the way that they stand and move to avoid using the painful part of their body, and that changes the way that their hooves are loaded. Some types of arthritis have small effects on the hoof, like most kissing spine cases, while other types of arthritis have huge, noticeable impacts on the hooves.

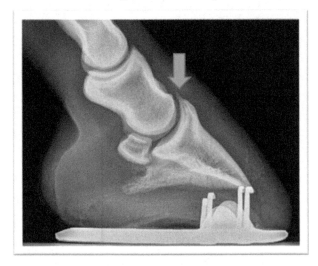

A bone spur on the coffin joint

For instance, if your horse is sporting some coffin joint arthritis, commonly called low ringbone, you may see a physical change in the hoof capsule and a change in the way your horse moves and wears. Usually your horse would make her movements smaller so that the coffin joint isn't going through as wide of a range of motion, and that means that the hoof will be expanding and contracting less. That can lead to a tighter, more contracted hoof. Depending on where the arthritis is in the joint and how developed it is, you might actually see it pushing outward at the front of the hoof capsule near the coronary band. This is where the extensor process is, a small outgrowth of the coffin bone that is the attachment point for the main extensor tendon. If the tendon attachment is affected, x-rays will usually show a lot of new bone growth, or exostosis, and that new bone can actually push the hoof wall out in the center of the toe, making the hoof more triangular in shape.

You might also see some new wear patterns as coffin joint arthritis progress, because reduced joint movement means that your horse is going to be breaking over in whatever direction they find the most comfortable. This is one case where a shoe that allows your horse to break over in any direction they want can be really helpful. Since they have less options for movement in their joint, your farrier will put those options in the shoe instead. That's not to say your horse can't be maintained barefoot. As long as the wear isn't too extreme and your horse still has plenty of protection, you can usually maintain a retired horse barefoot even if they do have arthritis.

High ringbone is the common name for arthritis in the pastern joint, and it's usually easier for a horse to handle than low ringbone. In a healthy horse, the coffin joint has a much bigger range of motion than the pastern joint, so losing the motion of the pastern joint has less negative consequences for the horse. According to a study measuring joint flexion during different gaits, the coffin joint had about a 47 degree range of flexion and extension at the trot, while the pastern joint only had about a 14 degree range[61]. That is still enough motion that the horse will notice it, but the coffin joint is definitely the heavy lifter when it comes to movement.

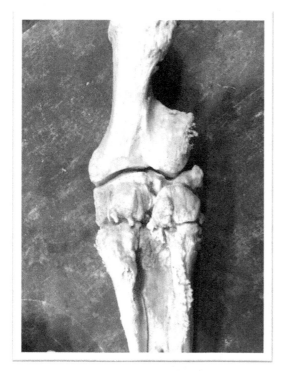

A rear view of a hock with extreme arthritis

Sometimes horses may have their pastern joints surgically fused if they have painful arthritis. This doesn't fix the arthritis, but it does usually make it less painful since the joint doesn't have any more movement. On the other hand, any time that you take away shock absorption in one area (and yes, joint movement does help reduce shock) that force has to go somewhere else. If your horse has a pastern joint fused, you'll want to keep an eye on the coffin and fetlock joints and keep them maintained if necessary.

Another common arthritis that affects the hoof is spavin, or hock arthritis. Horses who have hock arthritis will typically start moving with their hind legs a little closer together than normal, which puts more stress on the outside of the hooves. Hock arthritis most commonly starts on the inside of the hock joints, so bringing her legs in closer moves some of the stress off the inside of the joint and puts more on the outside. You might also see her start to drag her hind feet a little, especially in softer footing like deep sand. Since arthritis makes it harder for her to fully flex and extend her legs, she won't be picking her hooves up as high as she used to.

We see this in the hooves as a squaring off the front of the toe. This isn't a particularly useful compensation, though, because it makes it harder for her to push off as she uses her hind end for propulsion, like we talked about in Chapter 2. Sometimes adding hind shoes can help reduce the amount she wears her toes off, but some horses with spavin can't take the concussion of nailing shoes on, so she may have to be maintained barefoot. If the joint completely fuses, her pain level will probably decrease, and it may be possible to shoe her hind feet again.

So far we've mostly talked about arthritis based on the wear and tear model. However, your horse can also get what is known as septic arthritis, which happens when a joint becomes infected. Even with quick intervention from your vet, damage can happen really quickly in joint infections. Obviously, prevention is the best route here, and if you notice a wound near one of

[61] Clayton, H.M., Sha, D.H., Stick, J.A., Robinson, P. (2007). 3D kinematics of the interphalangeal joints in the forelimb of walking and trotting horses. *Vet Comp Orthop Traumatol;20(1)*: P. 1-7.

your horse's joints, it's a good idea to get your vet out as soon as you can. It can also occur when your horse gets joint injections, so you'll want to follow your vet's directions for any aftercare if you get injections and watch out for any new lameness.

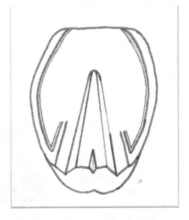

No matter what kind of arthritis you're dealing with, expectations are important. If your horse has arthritis, he won't have the same range of motion that he used to. He might always look short when he moves, and if the arthritis isn't the same between limbs, his movement might be uneven. The arthritis might also affect soft tissue structures in the area, so he may move differently just to avoid pain in the ligaments or tendons around the arthritis. You're looking for comfort and soundness here, not returned range of motion.

Hoof wear from hock arthritis

Some arthritis can also be caused by a fracture that traveled through the joint, and coffin bone fractures are the most likely to affect the hoof. Although coffin bone fractures seem to be extremely common in foals (up to 74% of foals might have non-articular fractures according to one study[62]) they are comparatively few and far between in adult horses.

Thankfully if your horse does get a coffin bone fracture, we aren't shooting horses for

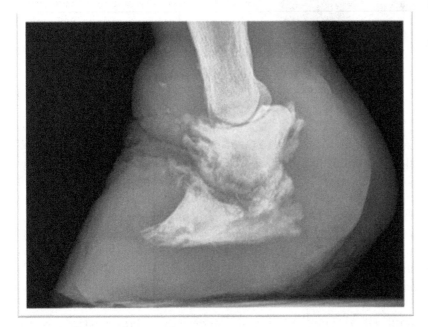

broken bones anymore. There are plenty of tools to help horses heal from coffin bone fractures, and they have a pretty good success rate, depending on the location and type of fracture.

Arthritis from infection can be extreme

[62] Faramarz, B., McMicking, H., Halland, S., Kaneps, A., Dobson, H. (2015). Incidence of palmar process fractures of the distal phalanx and association with front hoof conformation in foals. *Equine Vet J. 47(6):* P. 675-9

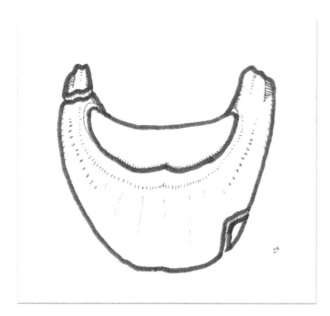

Non-articular fractures do not damage the joint and have a good prognosis

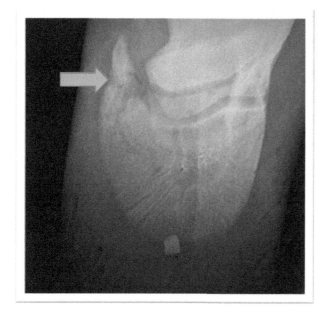

Coffin bone fractures can be divided up into two categories, articular, meaning fractures that run through a joint, and non-articular, fractures that don't affect a joint. Obviously non-articular fractures have better chances of healing with no long-term consequences, while articular fractures carry a higher risk of arthritis down the road, since the joint surface has been damaged. Articular fractures usually are much more painful, too, since there's movement involved.

Either type of fracture will initially be treated the same: just like for humans, we want to immobilize the bone as much as we can. Sometimes casts are used, but they come with their own issues for horses, like the risk of infection since you can't access the bottom of the hoof, and the fact that they wear faster than a shoe. Most fractures will be treated with a shoeing package to limit hoof capsule movement.

Your farrier might use a shoe with extra clips to limit expansion or even a shoe with a metal rim that goes all the way around the outside of the hoof. That will stop the hoof from expanding and contracting, but we also know that the sole flattens and springs back when the hoof is loaded and unloaded too, so a pour-in pad that goes all the way to the ground, or a plate on the bottom of the hoof with a firm packing will help limit the up and down movement of the coffin bone.

It may also be necessary to glue the shoe on instead of nailing, at least for the first shoeing or two. The concussion of nailing is often very painful after a fracture.

Quick immobilization allows the bone to start healing right away before there is much damage done. The last thing you want is for the broken edges of the bone to continue moving and being damaged, because less healthy bone margins require more healing, and more healing means a bigger chance of ending up with some arthritis.

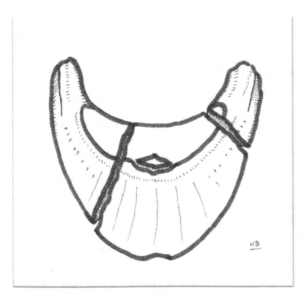

Articular fractures damage the joint and have a more guarded prognosis

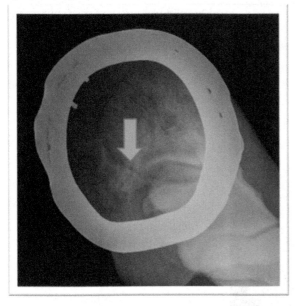

Time heals all wounds and after immobilization, time and rest are your best tools to help your horse recover. Your horse will need stall rest or a very restricted, stall-sized turnout, at least at first. You'll want to make sure you get your vet to recheck your horse with x-rays to confirm that everything is growing back together the way that it should, and you'll definitely want to see a fully repaired bone before your farrier pulls off the special shoeing package. If you did have an articular fracture, you'll want your vet to regularly keep an eye on the joint so that they can treat the beginnings of any arthritis before it gets severe.

Arthritis is mostly managed through veterinary treatment, but farrier care can help reduce some of the negative effects on your horse's hooves. It's a great example of how teamwork really can make a difference in keeping your horse sound, with your vet handling the medical side, your farrier maintaining his hooves, and you making sure his environment and workload are just right. And, of course, your horse reaps the benefits!

Quick Takeaways
• **Arthritis is a painful affliction in horses that can affect any joint in the body and may have a negative impact on even movement and hoof wear.**

- A fractured coffin bone may be treated by restricting hoof capsule movement so that the bone can heal.

A shoe with multiple clips is one way to stabilize a fracture

33 NAVICULAR SYNDROME

Navicular syndrome, navicular disease, palmar foot pain, caudal foot lameness: they're all terms for the same painful problem. Navicular syndrome is the breakdown of one or many of the structures involved in the navicular apparatus, and it is almost always degenerative.

One of the most complicated and confusing things about navicular syndrome is that it affects different horses in different ways. It's very common in Quarter Horses who have tiny upright hooves and also in Thoroughbreds with low, flat hooves, and every type of horse in between. It usually effects horses when they are in their prime, 7-9 years old, but it can also hit young horses, and it's not uncommon in old horses. Some horses have a very slow, almost unnoticeable onset, while others suddenly become very lame. Some horses maintain a decent level of soundness for many years after a diagnosis, while others take a quick spiral downward after the first sign of lameness.

It's actually no surprise that cases labeled as navicular syndrome have such a wide range of symptoms and prognosis though; the term covers injury and damage to a huge range of structures that are all associated with the navicular bone.

Let's start with a quick anatomy review: the navicular bone is a small bone, smaller than your pinky finger in many cases, that fits right behind the coffin bone to increase the surface

The navicular bone

area of the coffin joint, and also provide a leverage point for the deep digital flexor tendon. The navicular bone ends up sandwiched between the coffin bone in front, the short pastern above, and the deep digital flexor tendon wrapping around the back and underneath it.

There are also a couple of smaller ligaments that cradle the navicular bone and hold it in place. The suspensory ligament of the navicular bone (totally different than the suspensory ligament

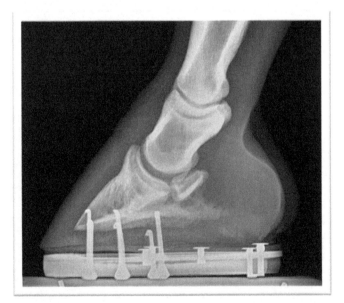

that runs down the back of the cannon bone) attaches on the top and sides of the bone, and then sends branches all the way up to the long pastern bone to suspend the navicular bone.

The impar ligament is another small ligament which attaches the bottom of the navicular bone to the coffin bone, and it hosts small blood vessels which bring about 75% of the blood supply to the navicular bone. It's under plenty of stress since the deep flexor tendon is pulling up on the bone, and the impar ligament has to fight that pull and keep the navicular bone in its place.

The navicular bone is also

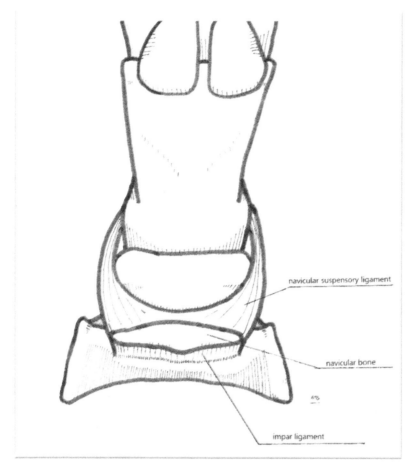

navicular suspensory ligament

navicular bone

impar ligament

equipped with a bursa that fits in between the deep flexor tendon and the bone. It's basically a small, fluid filled sack that helps reduce the amount of friction between the navicular bone and the deep flexor tendon. Picture taking a water balloon and squishing it between your hands. You can push it around and move your hands back and forth, but your hands probably can't even touch each other, much less make friction. That's how the navicular bursa functions when it's functioning properly.

Mother Nature was obviously pretty concerned about the friction that could happen between the powerful deep flexor tendon and the tiny little navicular bone, because there are a lot of special adaptations in this area. The navicular bone has a smooth, slick cartilage covering on the side of the bone that faces the tendon called the flexor surface, and the deep flexor tendon has a smooth, harder section in this area that is meant to glide easily across the bone.

So why does your horse's navicular have all those adaptations to make sure there's no friction between the navicular bone and the deep flexor tendon? The deep flexor tendon is a strong, thick tendon, attached to big muscle bodies higher up in the leg, and it's so strong that when the muscle contracts, it can lift your horse's heels off the ground.

So that's the main anatomy of the navicular region. Each of those adaptive structures plays an important role in keeping the area functioning correctly. If one of those structures fails, all of the other structures have to work harder. Like a group project where one member doesn't do their fair share, each other member of the group is overworked. If another member of the group gets exhausted and quits, it really dumps extra work on the remaining members, until they all want to quit, one by one or en masse.

Research still hasn't been able to pinpoint one key to *all* navicular cases, and that leads us to believe that there are a number of different pathways to navicular syndrome.

For instance, we know that horses can strain their navicular ligaments, just like any other ligaments in the body. But when the ligament isn't allowed to rest and heal after an injury, it can form scar tissue, become less flexible, and more prone to future injury. If the ligament is torn off the bone, even a little bit, the body wants to lock that ligament down and make sure it doesn't move anymore. So what does it do? It builds new bone cells on the attachment point and into the ligament, which can turn into bony spurs. Nobody needs those in their feet.

There are also two very different hoof conformations that are prone to navicular, and they highlight two of the main disease processes really well.

If you're familiar with Quarter Horses, especially some of the halter, cutting, and reining lines, you've probably seen big, bulky horses with dainty, upright hooves. This type of conformation is prone to navicular syndrome, and in all probability it's because of the lack of shock absorption that you get with upright hooves, plus the fact that there is a ton of weight on a very small structure. We know that the hoof flexes open and closed in the heels to absorb shock, and we know that a narrow, tight hoof with a small, high frog doesn't do that very well. If the hoof isn't

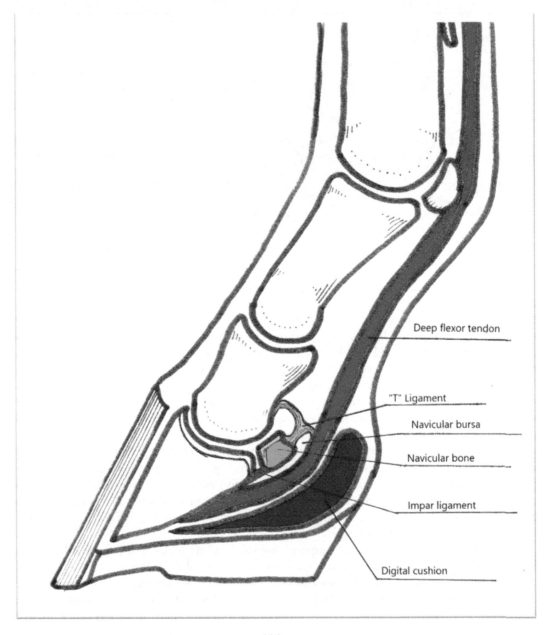

Deep flexor tendon

"T" Ligament

Navicular bursa

Navicular bone

Impar ligament

Digital cushion

helping absorb shock, where does it go? Usually, deeper into the hoof and higher up the leg.

One of the common radiographic signs of navicular syndrome is that the medullary cavity inside the navicular bone becomes denser and sometimes even disappears called loss of cortico-medullary distinction, if you want to get fancy. Since the medullary cavity is important for circulating blood and moving nutrients inside the bone, losing it is dangerous for the health of the navicular bone.

How is concussion connected to a thickened bone? There is a famous principle in anatomy and physiology called Wolff's Law, and it states that bones change shape and strength depending on the forces placed upon them. This is why astronauts who live on the Space Station have to be so careful with their bone health: in zero gravity, bones aren't subjected to the normal stress that they have to deal with on earth, and NASA found that their astronauts lost bone density at a rate of 1-2% per month[63]. The opposite is also true: we develop thicker, stronger bones when we exercise (as long as we are also getting enough bone-strengthening minerals in our diets).

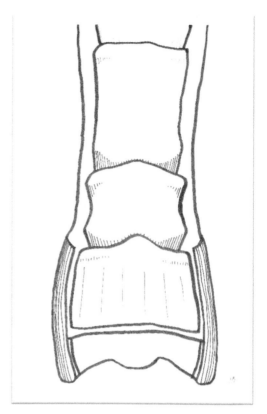

A contracted hoof doesn't absorb shock well

But what if a thicker bone isn't a good thing? When the navicular bone is exposed to more concussion, it might become thicker and denser, but that process can also compress vascular channels and destroy the medullary cavity. Too much of a good thing isn't always better.

Several studies have measured more pressure within navicular bones in horses that are suffering from navicular syndrome than in sound horses[64][65]. It could be that this pressure comes from the remodeling of the navicular bone due to extra concussion, thereby closing off some of the pathways that blood used to be able to move in. Some people suggest that this pressure alone might be enough to cause pain, and that pain could kick off a response in the body that we really don't want. Pressure on the navicular area might also enlarge the channels that naturally occur in the bone. You might hear this called lollipop leisons but the most scientific term is "enlarged synovial invaginations".

When part of your horse's foot hurts, they automatically try to avoid pressure or concussion on that area. For instance, when your horse has an abscess, he'll try hopping on his toe to prevent bearing weight on that hoof. When just part of his foot hurts, like a sore navicular bone, he's

[63] NASA. (2012) *Good Diet, Proper Exercise Help Protect Astronauts' Bones*. Retrieved from https://www.nasa.gov/mission_pages/station/main/bone_study.html

[64] Svalastoga, E., Smith, M. (1983). Navicular disease in the horse. The subchondral bone pressure. *Nord Vet Med. (1):* P. 31-7.

[65] Pleasant, R.S., Baker, G.J., Foreman, J.H., Eurell, J.A., Losonsky, J.M. (1993). Intraosseous pressure and pathologic changes in horses with navicular disease. *Am J Vet Res. 54(1):* P. 7-12.

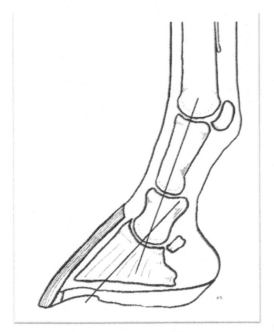

A low angled hoof may increase tension on the deep flexor tendon

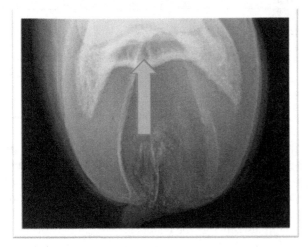

Enlarged synovial invaginations

going to try to avoid that too. In this case, he wants to land toe first if he can, so that all that force doesn't hit his heels, so he tenses up his deep flexor tendon to lift his heels up. Unfortunately, that deep flexor tendon runs right over the navicular bone, so when he tenses it, it adds *more* pressure to his already sore area. It's a negative feedback loop: his heels hurt so he tries to stay off them and accidently makes his heels hurt more, so he makes even more of an effort to avoid them[66].

Extra tension on the deep flexor tendon is also a major factor in the other common form of navicular syndrome. Thoroughbred and some warmblood people will be familiar with this one: low, flat feet with weak heels and toes that only grow straight forward. A lot of the time, this will be accompanied by a broken back hoof-pastern axis (the hoof angle is lower than the pastern angle). Horses with this kind of conformation require a lot more muscular effort to allow their hoof to break over since the toe lever is pretty long (you can review this idea in Chapter 19). Since the navicular bone is meant to act as a fulcrum point for the deep flexor tendon, more tension on the tendon translates to more force on the navicular bone.

Extra force means extra wear and tear, especially on the impar ligament that holds the navicular bone in place, the navicular bursa, and the smooth cartilage on the flexor surface of the navicular bone where the tendon glides over the bone. You can also see damage in the deep flexor tendon itself, which will cause pain during movement. And you know that as soon as one of those structures (the smooth cartilage covering, the navicular bursa, or the smooth tendon surface) isn't doing it's part to get rid of friction, the other two structures are really going to have to ramp it up. Usually we see bursa damage first, then cartilage erosion, and then tendon lesions.

---

[66] Dyson, S.J. (2011). Chapter 30 - Navicular Disease, Editor(s): Ross, M.W., Dyson, S.J., Diagnosis and Management of Lameness in the Horse (Second Edition), P. 324-342. W.B. Saunders, Elsevier, Health Sciences Division 11830 Westline Industrial Drive, St. Louis MO 63146-3313 USA. P. 324-342.

In a worst-case scenario, the cartilage is completely worn away so that the bone underneath is exposed, and that's not nearly smooth enough to have a tendon gliding over it. The tendon fibers can actually start to fray, and the body panics and creates adhesions between the tendon and the bone, trying to lock everything down and prevent movement. This is the kind of damage that your horse really can't recover from.

Okay, so that's the super scary and not-fun-at-all description of what could happen. How would you be able to tell when this is starting to happen, preferably before any huge changes have taken place?

Most people notice their horse acting a little stiff, or not wanting to fully extend their front legs, because a fully extended leg has to land heel

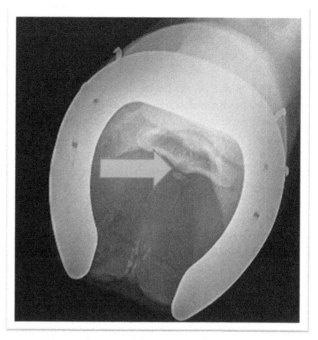

In a worst case scenario, the cartilage and outer layer of the navicular bone have been worn through and the deep flexor tendon has calcified in that area

first. It usually looks like a subtle lameness in one front foot, but when that hoof is blocked it usually shows up in the other front hoof too. It most commonly occurs during a big change in lifestyle, like coming back from being on stall rest, or a big change in turnout or work load. This is probably because the disease process has been very subtly occurring, but a big change in activity puts more stress on the structures involved and could be enough to make it noticeable. It's important to realize that just because you're seeing it now doesn't mean it's new; it's usually been going on for a while but was so low grade that it wasn't really bothering your horse.

Navicular lameness is usually most noticeable on hard surfaces, since landing will send a jolt of concussion through the foot, although if it's an injury to some of the soft tissue structures involved with the navicular, you might see it in soft ground too. Sometimes, your vet or farrier can squeeze on the frog with hoof testers and get a response, indicating that the navicular area underneath the frog is sore. Often, vets will block the back half of the hoof with a palmar nerve block, and if your horse becomes sound it will be a good indicator that the pain is coming from the navicular area, although it won't tell you what structures are affected. Your vet will probably also take x-rays, so that they can see if the cartilage on the navicular bone and the bone itself are healthy. If they are, that's a great thing! It means the damage hasn't progressed that far yet, and you probably have a good chance of making your horse more comfortable. If there are bone changes, it's not necessarily the kiss of death: lots of horses with really scary navicular x-rays feel just fine, while others with perfect x-rays limp around their pasture. Again, this is why navicular syndrome is a tough one to predict.

Usually that will provide enough information for an accurate diagnosis, but if you want to get really specific, you can have an MRI taken to see exactly what structures are affected. You can even have an endoscopy performed on the navicular bursa, where a tiny camera is inserted to see if there are adhesions between the tendon and the bone, how much damage has been done to the cartilage, and how healthy the tendon is.

Care for your horse if she's been diagnosed with navicular disease is mostly going to consist of keeping her on a regular maintenance schedule with both your farrier and your vet. Navicular syndrome is a degenerative condition, so it's important to have the expectation that it will eventually become worse, but we can often slow or even pause the progression with the right care.

Your vet might prescribe medications such as anti-inflammatory pain killers like Bute or Isoxsuprine, an anti-inflammatory vasodilation drug, because a continued pain response is only going to make the issue worse. Remember that we don't want the deep flexor tendon tensing up. Your vet may also be able to inject either the navicular bursa or the coffin joint to help ease some of the pain that comes from friction and tension. In more extreme cases, your vet may suggest nerving, which is the cutting or chemical freezing of the nerve supply for the navicular area. This is a last resort because it comes with a lot of safety concerns since your horse wouldn't have any feeling in the back half of his hoof. If he gets an abscess or steps on a nail, he won't know about it until there is a big infection. Nerved horses also have a higher rate of other injuries in the navicular area, probably because they don't have any pain warning them to take it easy. Even nerving isn't necessarily permanent -- over time the nerve may grow back.

On the less invasive side, your farrier might be able to make a big difference for your horse. But what tactic they take is going to depend on your horse's specific conformation. Conventional wisdom usually says to raise the hoof angle on a horse with navicular disease, but if your horse has upright, tight feet, and concussion is her main problem, raising the angles isn't going to help.

The most important part of the shoeing treatment is to trim the hooves into the best balance possible, on a consistent schedule. It's great to trim the hooves so that there is less tension on the deep flexor tendon by removing extra toe, but your horse will start growing back toward that long toe as soon as your farrier puts his hoof down, so you need to make plans to see your farrier again in six weeks or less. The goal is to *keep* his hooves in balance, instead of swinging back and forth between out of balance with lots of stress and then back to balanced.

What type of shoeing your farrier does will depend on your horse's conformation and how severely she is affected. On low, long hooves that are suffering from too much tension on the deep flexor tendon, your farrier will probably shorten the toe lever and raise the hoof angle. Shortening the toe lever (or breakover distance) reduces the amount of tension needed to lift the heels off the ground, so it reduces peak forces on the navicular bone. This doesn't necessarily mean trimming off a bunch of toe from the bottom of the hoof, though, since as we know from Chapter 3, we definitely want the coffin bone to have some protection and ground clearance. If we can't trim enough off the

A navicular cyst. Drastic angle changes may cause pain with a cyst

bottom of the hoof safely to get the angles we're looking for, we can still shorten the toe lever by trimming the outside of the hoof wall back vertically, setting a shoe back slightly, or applying a rolled or rocker toe shoe.

Raising angle isn't just limited to putting a wedge pad on your horse either. There are some circumstances where that's the best plan, but if your horse has adhesions between her navicular bone and the deep flexor tendon, you don't want to drastically change the angle because that will painfully strain those fibers. However, if your horse mostly works in softer footings or lives in a deeply bedded stall, putting a shoe with a wider heel on your horse can help prevent her heels from sinking into the ground, effectively wedging her up on soft ground but not locking her into a higher angle on hard footing.

If concussion is your main problem, your farrier will still start by balancing your horse's hooves as well as they can. Depending on exactly what structures are injured and how badly, they might use a bar shoe to help protect the back half of the foot or use concussion-reducing tools like pads and soft packings. Reducing the breakover distance can still be helpful on this type of hoof since the deep flexor tendon is still under a lot of stress.

Oddly, this is one of the few hoof problems where rest is not really recommended. Unless your horse has been specifically diagnosed with a soft tissue injury in the navicular area, it's usually better for affected horses to keep moving around. You might have to cut back on intense exercise, but full rest actually makes a lot of navicular horses more lame when they do start going back to work.

Navicular syndrome is a really hard diagnosis to hear, and it is a progressive condition, but it doesn't have to be the end of the road. With good teamwork between you, your farrier, and your vet, your horse can still have many years of comfortable, functional life ahead of him.

Quick Takeaways

- **Navicular syndrome is a catch-all term to describe damage to any of the structures in the navicular region.**
- **Common symptoms include pain in the back half of the hoof, pain when the heel hits the ground, lack of extension, or stiffness, most commonly in one or both front limbs.**
- **Treatment will vary depending on what type of stress is being delt with, but both vet and farrier work will need to be a part of the solution.**

34 LAMINITIS

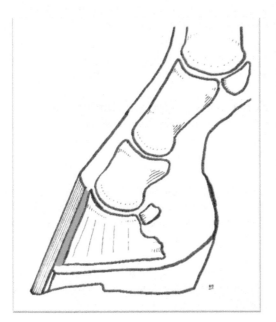

In a healthy hoof, the coffin bone and hoof wall are parallel, and the lamina is tightly connected

Okay, it's the chapter nobody wants to have to read. Nobody likes to hear the L word, but finding out why laminitis happens and how we can prevent it could save your horse's life. So read on and educate yourself!

Laminitis is scary, and if you're not concerned about it, you probably haven't seen it first hand. In a study of 216 horses and ponies with laminitis, a full 20% of the patients had to be euthanized within a year, and 19 of the horses in that group survived less than a week after diagnosis[67]. Once horses have had their first bout of laminitis, they have a higher risk of having it again. A 2019 study of 276 horses and ponies who suffered from endocrinopathic laminitis, which we'll talk about in a second, found that within two years, 34% had suffered another laminitic incident[68]. Obviously, laminitis is no laughing matter.

So we know that laminitis is really bad, but what is it exactly? If you remember back to Chapter 2, the coffin bone is suspended inside the hoof capsule thanks to the sensitive and insensitive lamina. The sensitive lamina grow off of the coffin bone and interlock with the insensitive lamina, which are on the inside of the hoof wall. The lamina hold up the entire weight of your horse, and protect the coffin bone from trauma.

But since the hoof wall is constantly growing, and it's attached to the coffin bone which stays in the same spot, your horse has to have a way to allow the laminar connection to briefly let go, ratchet down a few cells, and reattach. This process is constantly going on at a very low level, thanks to specialized enzymes called matrix metalloproteinases or MMPs. MMPs are constantly circulating in your horse's bloodstream, and they have the power to break the connections between the cells in the sensitive lamina and the cells in the insensitive lamina. Once they do, the insensitive lamina shifts down a couple of cells and reattaches. It's an ingenious and delicate method of allowing the hoof wall to grow past the stationary coffin bone, while still staying securely attached.

[67] Cripps, P.J., Eustace, R.A. (1999). Factors involved in the prognosis of equine laminitis in the UK. *Equine Vet J. 31(5):* P. 433-42.
[68] de Laat, M.A., Reiche, D.B., Sillence, M.N., McGree, J.M. (2019). Incidence and risk factors for recurrence of endocrinopathic laminitis in horses. *J Vet Intern Med; 33(3):* P. 1473-1482

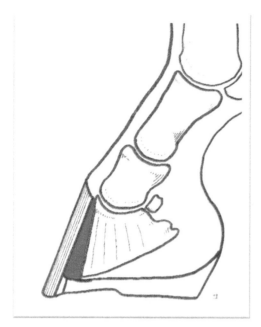

In laminitis, the laminar bond is broken down and the coffin bone may rotate away from the hoof wall

Laminitis is literally inflammation of the lamina. *Itis* means inflammation, so tendonitis is inflammation of a tendon, and laminitis is inflammation of the lamina. That might not sound so bad, except that like an abscess, any swelling inside the hoof capsule means a lot of pressure and pain. Plus, when the sensitive lamina are inflamed, there is a lot of extra blood flow which can bring more MMPs to the area. This means more of the connections between the coffin bone and the hoof wall are being broken, which can lead to destabilization of the coffin bone. Because of the weight of the horse and the pull of the deep flexor tendon, the front part of the bone tears away from the wall and the tip of the bone points downward. In its most extreme form, all of the lamina can break loose at once and the coffin bone can sink straight down in the hoof capsule.

There are four possible results of laminitis. You can have inflammation with no pain and no coffin bone rotation, inflammation with pain and no rotation, inflammation with pain and coffin bone rotation, and inflammation with pain and coffin bone sinking. Unfortunately, even if a case starts mildly, it can easily spiral downward if the cause isn't removed.

If the coffin bone rotates, it can tear the blood vessels that feed the coriums of the hoof, which will change how the hoof wall and sole grow, and how fast. Since the blood supply to the front of the coronary band is usually compressed during rotation, we often see slow growth in the toe with a disproportionate amount of heel growth since the back half of the coronary band is still doing okay. The rotated coffin bone often damages the circumflex artery that supplies the front part of the solar corium, so you can expect to see less sole growth too. If the circumflex artery has been damaged,

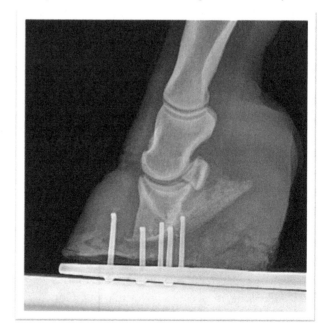

Severe laminitis with rotation and sinking. The coffin bone has also remodeled.

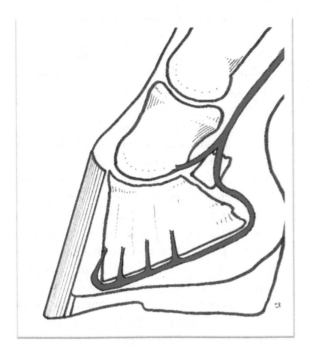

There are many blood vessels wrapping around the coffin bone that may be crushed during rotation

you may see frequent bruising in the toe area of the sole, which might be accompanied by abscessing. In long-term chronic laminitis we also commonly see damage to the coffin bone itself, since it frequently ends up bearing weight on the bottom of the bone instead of being suspended by the lamina. It's also hard for the coffin bone to grow good connection back to the hoof wall, since the wall is constantly being leveraged forward and the bone is being pulled away from it by gravity and by the deep flexor tendon.

But for the hoof to return to a functioning state, and your horse to return to soundness, we need the coffin bone to be stable inside the hoof capsule and tightly secured to the hoof wall. The best way to do that? Remove the original cause of the inflammation, which will hopefully lower the MMP activity and allow new connections to form, and trim and/or shoe the hoof to reduce hoof wall leverage and protect the coffin bone. We'll get into shoeing later, but what could cause this kind of inflammation? It's really important to identify and remove the cause of inflammation, because that is the source of the problem, and it will continue to do damage as long as it's allowed to. Therapeutic shoeing without removing the cause is like building sandcastles while the tide is coming in. You need to get above the water line if you want your work to last, otherwise those waves just keep coming and wiping out your progress.

There are a ton of different causes of laminitis, but they fall into a few big categories.

- Mechanical Laminitis: This is rarely the *only* cause of a laminitic incident but in combination with one of the other methods it can make your prognosis worse. Mechanical laminitis usually looks like long, neglected hooves that put a lot of leverage on the lamina, but it can also be a case like "road founder" where a horse is worked heavily on hard footing and the concussion is enough to inflame the lamina. The upside to mechanical laminitis is that it is easy to remove the cause of the

Chronic bruising and abscessing in the sole is a sign of the circumflex artery being damaged

202

inflammation, either by having a trim done to remove all that leverage, or by allowing your horse to rest if the cause was concussion related. However, mechanical laminitis usually comes into play when your horse was teetering on the edge of getting laminitis from a different source, and the mechanical issue is the straw that breaks the camel's back.

- Ischemic Laminitis: This one functions a little differently than most of the other causes we see, but it's still important to understand it. We mostly see this type of laminitis in horses who have had a severe injury. Ischemia is when the blood supply is disrupted, so nutrients aren't getting to the sensitive lamina, and waste isn't being removed. Since all sensitive tissues need nutrients to survive, if the sensitive lamina aren't being fed, they can essentially start dying and all the connections give way. Uncommonly, you can see this type of laminitis if the arteries that supply the lamina are severed, or if your horse has a traumatic foot or leg injury. It can also be caused by leg wraps or bandages applied too tightly. More commonly, ischemic laminitis shows up when your horse has a painful injury in one hoof which makes them non-weight bearing. If your horse isn't bearing weight on one hoof, he's got to be constantly bearing weight on the opposite leg if he's standing up. Since horses need movement to pump blood back up their legs, a horse that is constantly bearing weight on one hoof ends up with stagnant circulation and no new blood bringing nutrients and all the cellular waste stuck in the hoof. If your horse has a painful injury to one hoof, you, your vet, and your farrier will want to keep tabs on the health of the opposite hoof as well. Don't ignore the "good hoof," because you really need it to stay healthy. If you can, encourage your horse to lay down instead of constantly bearing weight on his hooves by providing a deeply bedded stall with water and food on the ground.

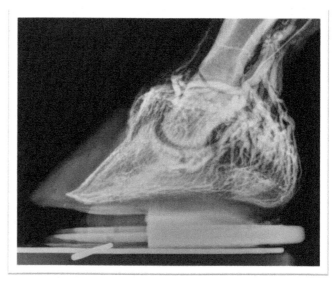

Constant blood flow is necessary for the health of the hoof

- Metabolic Laminitis: Currently thought to be the most common cause of laminitis[69], metabolic laminitis covers all kinds of problems like Cushing's Disease, insulin dysregulation, and obesity. This type of laminitis is a lot like Type 1 diabetes in humans, where the body isn't producing enough insulin to regulate the blood sugar.

---

[69] Karikoski, N.P., Horn, I., McGowan, T.W., McGowan, C.M. (2011). The prevalence of endocrinopathic laminitis among horses presented for laminitis at a first-opinion/referral equine hospital. *Domestic Animal Endocrinology, Volume 41, Issue 3*. P. 111-117.

Normally, your body (and your horse's body) needs insulin to allow certain types of tissue to uptake sugars from the blood, and the pancreas produces more or less insulin depending on the amount of sugars you are eating. Insulin resistance is when tissue becomes less insulin sensitive, so the body has to produce more insulin to keep up. Just like in humans with diabetes, insulin resistance in horses does affect circulation, usually by constricting blood vessels, and the lamina don't seem to get enough glucose to have a strong connection. This can be a really slow weakening of the laminar connection, and you might not notice any pain or inflammation while it's happening, but it is slowly setting your horse up for failure. If you want a hoof symptom to check for, look at the white line. If your horse's white line is widened, you might have lamina that are starting to remodel thanks to metabolic changes. Body wise, obesity is one of the main signs that this could be happening to your horse, since fat pockets are a major sign that your horse isn't processing sugars correctly. Plus, fat pockets produce enzymes that turn naturally occurring cortisone into cortisol, which decreases insulin sensitivity as well. Since cortisol is created by the body when your horse is stressed, a small stressful incident like being separated from friends or stress from extreme weather could kick off an obese horse into laminitis, even if they've never had it before. Corticosteroids, including some joint injections, temporarily block insulin sensitivity on their own, but if your horse already has too much cortisol rolling around in her system, adding corticosteroids can push everything over the edge. If this sounds like your horse, the bad news is that she's at a very high risk for laminitis. The good news is, insulin dysregulation usually improves and even goes away if you can get her to a healthy body weight. Talk to your vet or an equine nutritionist right away to come up with a weight loss plan for your horse, *before* she gets laminitis.

- Enzymatic/ infectious laminitis: Remember those MMPs we talked about earlier? They are always being released on a low level, but there are some things that can cause a huge overdose of MMPs in the lamina. For instance, infections like retained placenta or colitis can release endotoxins into the blood that activate high levels of MMPs. Endotoxins can also enter the blood stream if a horse is exposed to black walnut shavings, eats a toxic plant, or is bitten by a poisonous spider or snake. Even the classic carbohydrate overload laminitis (you know, the one where a horse breaks into the feed room and eats his way through a month's worth of grain) is related to endotoxins. Eating so many carbs all at once drastically changes the pH in your horse's gut, which actually allows bacteria from the gut to absorb through the walls of the hindgut and enter the blood stream. Pasture related laminitis can be a combination of enzymatic laminitis and metabolic laminitis, which makes it extra challenging. This type of laminitis tends to be fast acting and sometimes severe, but the good part is that it's often easier and quicker to remove the inciting cause than if you're dealing with an obesity problem. So if you can get the initial event under control, you have a good chance of success.

Remember, your horse might be able to put up with one of the triggers we talked about above, but if you add a second one, it might be more than he can handle. As far as prevention goes, get rid of as many triggers as you can, as soon as you can. The biggest risk factor is obesity, so if your horse is overweight or has a hard, cresty neck, start a diet as soon as possible. It's also a good idea to talk to your vet about your horse's weight, for two reasons. One, they may be able to prescribe medications to help your horse safely lose weight, and they can help you formulate a weight loss program that won't stress your horse. Remember, stressful situations increase cortisol in the blood stream and increase insulin resistance. Secondly, it's easy to have an unrealistic view of our own pets. In first world countries, horses are frequently overweight, and it can skew our perspective of what a healthy bodyweight looks like. In a study performed on 290 horses and ponies in Saskatoon, 28.6% of the horses they saw were classified as either obese or overweight[70]. Similarly, among 792 horses and ponies in Great Britain, 31.2% were reported as obese[71]. Even more disturbing? A study performed on 229 horses and ponies in Australia, researchers found 24.5% of the population at Pony Club rallies were obese, with higher percentages in pony breeds. But this study also asked horse owners to rate their horse's body weight, and it showed that horse owners consistently and significantly underestimated their horse's weight problems. So getting an outside opinion, especially a trained opinion like your vet's is a good idea.

Managing your horse's body weight is simple in theory, but sometimes tough to put into practice. We all know how to lose weight, right? Eat less, exercise more. But cutting food drastically can be tough on horses who are meant to be grazing animals with multiple small meals a day. So eating less, for your horse, could mean eating less high sugar, high calorie feeds and treats, and switching to getting calories from stemmy hay instead, so that they still have something in their stomachs. It can also mean avoiding fresh grass, and either wearing a grazing muzzle to slow their grass intake, or doing turnout in a dry lot with no grass instead.

Of course, exercising frequently will help your horse lose the pounds too. Obviously, more exercise means burning more calories, but exercise can also help lower your horse's *need* for insulin, since muscle tissue can actually burn blood sugar directly without using insulin during exercise. On the other hand, if your horse suddenly goes from being active to being stall bound, remember that food needs to be reduced accordingly.

Maintaining a healthy body weight is the top thing you can do to prevent laminitis in your horse. But you'll also want to pay attention to your horse's hooves for any early warning signs. For instance, you want her hooves to grow evenly, and if there are any growth rings on her hooves, you don't want to see a bigger distance between the growth rings in her heels than the rings at her toe. This means that there's more blood flow in her heels than in her toes, and while it's not a sure-fire sign of laminitis, it is one of the changes you could see with laminitis. You could also see a stretched white line, especially in the toe. Even if that isn't a sign of laminitis in your horse's case, it shows a weaker laminar connection that won't be able to resist a laminitic event as effectively.

Early intervention is key to preventing more damage, so how can you quickly recognize a laminitic attack when it happens? Watch out for what looks like stiffness in the front end, with a shuffling gate. It can be hard to know where stiffness is coming from, so if you're seeing it, it's time to check her hooves. You should check for higher temperatures and strong pulses at the back of the fetlock, which will tell you that her feet are experiencing inflammation. The stiffness you're seeing is actually a pain response and her trying to keep the weight off her toes.

---

[70] Kosolofski, H.R., Gow, S.P., Robinson, K.A. (2017). Prevalence of obesity in the equine population of Saskatoon and surrounding area. *Can Vet J. 58(9):* P. 967-970.

[71] Robin, C.A., Ireland, J.L., Wylie, C.E., Collins, S.N., Verheyen, K.L., Newton, J.R. (2015). Prevalence of and risk factors for equine obesity in Great Britain based on owner-reported body condition scores. *Equine Vet J; 47(2):* P. 196-201.

Usually, her toe area will hurt worse since it's under the most stress and leverage. If you see your horse leaning backward with her legs out in front of her, she is probably trying to get the weight off of her toes and on to her heels instead. This means that she's really sore, and you'll want to get a vet out right away.

Of course, if you notice any of the hoof changes that we've talked about, such as growth rings that are wider at the heels than the toe or stretched white lines, you'll want to talk to your farrier. They should be able to tell you if it looks like active laminitis, signs of a past case, or best-case scenario, something completely unrelated.

So what should you do if you see signs that look like laminitis? Call your vet immediately. As we talked about in the beginning of this chapter, laminitis is very serious, and you're going to want to get your team working together to help your horse as soon as you can.

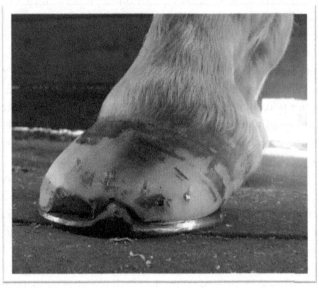

Wider growth rings in the heel than in the toe can be a danger sign

Once you've made that phone call, look around for possible laminitis triggers. Most commonly, fresh green grass, especially in the spring when your horse hasn't seen grass for a while or the fall, when grass is very rich, can overload your horse's metabolic system and kick off laminitis. If that's the case, the first thing you want to do is get your horse out of the field so he isn't eating any more. On the other hand, if your horse has an infection like colitis, you and your vet will need to treat the infection as quickly as possible.

If you're lucky enough to know ahead of time that your horse has had a dangerous incident like gorging on grain, you can start icing your horse's hooves right away. The most effective, proven method of preventing laminitis or reducing its effects is continuously icing the affected limb or limbs[72]. The point of this is to reduce circulation of MMPs or endotoxins to the lamina, so it needs to be constant for at least 48 hours or longer if you can't remove the inciting cause. Freezing and thawing won't help because blood will rush back into the leg as soon as it starts to warm.

Once you have removed the inciting cause of the laminitis, your next step will be first aid for your horse's hooves. Your goal is going to be taking the weight off of

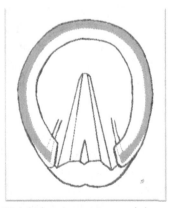

Weight bearing on a normal shoe is focused on the wall, stressing the lamina

[72] Stokes, S.M., Belknap, J.K., Engiles, J.B., Stefanovski, D., Bertin, F.R., Medina-Torres, C.E., Horn, R., van Eps, A.W. (2019). Continuous digital hypothermia prevents lamellar failure in the euglycaemic hyperinsulinaemic clamp model of equine laminitis. *Equine Vet J 51(5):* P. 658-664.

your horse's hoof walls and transferring it onto the frog and the back half of the sole, while cushioning and protecting the hoof.

If you have a stall that you can put your horse, make sure it's deeply bedded so your horse can lay down as much as he wants. Getting the weight off his hooves will help. Deep, soft bedding can also help transfer weight onto his frogs and soles instead of just the hoof wall. A soft sand stall, or turnout on soft sand can help a lot too.

You can also use rigid foamboard insulation as an emergency hoof boot. We're talking about the thick, Styrofoam-like sheets of insulation that you can get at your local hardware store. It's soft enough to cushion the hoof, but firm enough to help transfer load. You can trace your horse's

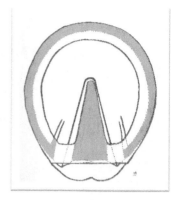

For laminitic horses, sharing weight onto the frog reduces stress on the wall

hoof onto the foamboard and cut it out with a utility knife. Duct tape it onto the bottom of your horse's hoof during the laminitic attack. Within a few days, it will flatten out and stop working so well, so you'll have to change it out every so often.

If your horse is barefoot, you can also use hoof boots with frog support and soft cushioning for the front half of the hoof, like Softride boots. These can be a really effective first aid method since you can easily remove them to check on your horse's hoof condition.

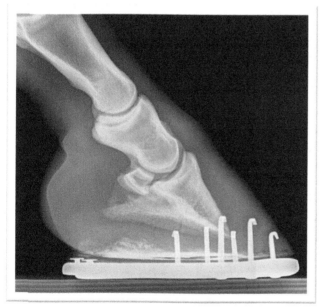

Radiographs show whether the coffin bone has rotated

When your vet arrives, they will probably do some diagnostics, starting with watching your horse walk. They'll also probably use hoof testers to see where your horse is sore, how bad the pain is, and they may take x-rays of the hooves to make sure that there hasn't been any rotation of the coffin bone or tearing and stretching of the lamina. It is also helpful to have a picture showing the health and location of the coffin bone and the health of the hoof capsule at the beginning of the laminitic incident, so that you can compare down the road. These radiographs will also be invaluable to your farrier when it comes time to trim or shoe your horse.

Your vet may also prescribe a nonsteroidal anti-inflammatory to reduce some of the pain and inflammation your horse is experiencing, but it can also be dangerous to make a horse with laminitis feel too comfortable. Although nobody wants to see a horse suffering unnecessarily, pain is a useful warning sign for your horse, telling her that something is wrong and she needs to take it easy. If she feels great, she'll be moving around and putting all the normal stresses on

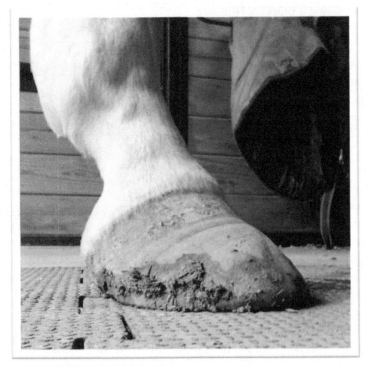

Excessive length and distortion needs to be managed

her hooves. So, unfortunately, although extreme pain isn't healthy, your vet may not want to mask all of her pain.

You'll also want to get your farrier out as soon as possible. If your horse is extremely lame, they may recommend some form of hoof protection, like we talked about above ,while you wait for the initial attack to pass, since your horse could be in too much pain to stand on one hoof while the other is being worked on.

It's still important to get your farrier on board as soon as possible, because they're going to need to actively and regularly manage your horse's hooves throughout the crisis. Of course, if your horse's hooves are long or distorted and there's a lot of stress on the lamina, you're going to want to get a good balanced trim as soon as possible. Even if her hooves are in good shape right now, your farrier can take some preventative steps right away to keep them that way.

As we talked about earlier, your farrier will want to trim and shoe in a way that will keep leverage off of the hoof wall, protect the front half of your horse's hoof where the coffin bone could be rotating, and transfer load off of the hoof wall and onto the frog and the back half of your horse's hooves. They will also be managing any distorted growth that could happen if the blood supply to the hoof is disrupted, so it's important that they see your horse on a regular schedule, so things don't get too far out of whack. During an active laminitic incident, your horse may even need to be seen every three weeks or so.

If your horse is wearing regular, open heeled shoes with no pads, your farrier may pull them during the early stages of laminitis. Most traditional shoes put the

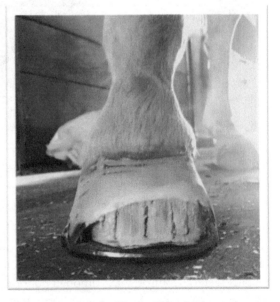

You may see stretched lamina if the toe has to be dressed back

majority of the weight bearing on the hoof wall, so removing them can help share the load. Your farrier might also use a frog support pad, pour in pad, or heartbar to accomplish load sharing as well.

You need your farrier and your vet to be communicating directly with each other. Managing a case of laminitis is a group effort and you need everyone to be working together. Your vet will need to manage any medications, in many cases help remove the cause of the laminitis, and use diagnostics like x-rays to provide information for your farrier to work from. Your farrier will need to trim and shoe your horse's hooves carefully, to help prevent further damage and distortion. And you will have to use the information that they give you to manage your horse's diet and environment, and make sure that no new laminitis triggers are introduced.

It's going to be a long road, because your horse will always be more susceptible to laminitis in the future. Your love for your horse will have to be expressed less by sugary treats and pasture time and more by careful, thoughtful management. You will have to be the grown up and make sure that your laminitic horse isn't chowing down on lush grass, even though he really wants to. You might feel mean or harsh at times, but remember, as much as your horse loves pasture time, it's not worth risking a laminitic attack. The pain that a horse goes through during laminitis is agonizing and constant, but

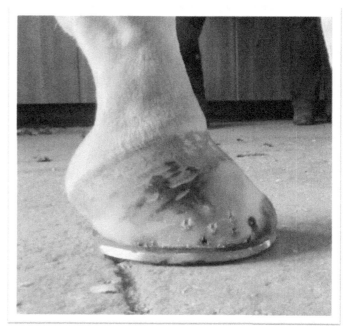

During active rotation, the lamina may show bruising from damaged blood vessels

your horse doesn't remember that when he's thinking about getting into the sweet feed bag. You need to remember it for him and make sure that he's making the best choices for long term health and soundness, not sacrificing his future soundness for a quick treat today. I'd love to lie to you and say that it's going to be easy, that you won't have any setbacks, or that this isn't life and death for your horse, but that wouldn't be doing you or your horse any favors. Laminitis is like a diagnosis of diabetes; it's not a death sentence, but it is going to take hard work, lifestyle changes, and smart thinking to stay healthy long term. Surviving laminitis and even becoming sound again is possible, but you need to commit to managing your horse's health condition for the long haul.

Hopefully this chapter has given you the tools to recognize laminitis early, react quickly, and even prevent it by avoiding common triggers. Laminitis is a classic case of an ounce of prevention being worth a pound of cure, so take care of triggers now and avoid a world of heartache and hurt.

Quick Takeaways

- Laminitis is extremely serious, and prevention is far preferable to treatment.
- Common symptoms of acute laminitis include severe pain, most often in the toe region especially on the front hooves, heat, raised pulses, and unwillingness to walk.
- If your horse is suffering a laminitic attack, you should call your vet immediately and remove any possible triggers.
- Obesity is one of the most common causes of laminitis in first world countries.
- Farrier care will involve removing leverage on the hoof wall, transferring load onto healthy structures, and protecting the sole, as well as managing any imbalance or distortion.

Part 6

First Aid And The Healthy Horse

35 VITAL SIGNS, TAKING PULSES, AND BODY SCORING

If you've ever been concerned about your horse's hoof health and tried to take your horse's pulse, you might have suddenly realized that you don't know what a normal pulse should feel like. Is that pulse rapid or bounding? We need to be able to know what normal looks like if we want to be able to recognize changes and recognize them quickly.

You'll want to familiarize yourself with the numbers, but you'll also want to practice observing them in your own horse *before* an emergency happens. Every horse will have slightly different vital signs (hopefully within the range of normal) just like you probably have a slightly different heart rate or blood pressure than your family members.

If you're confident assessing your horse's vital signs, you will be able to quickly tell if your horse is experiencing stress or is going into shock. You can react quickly if something does go wrong for your horse, instead of having to wait until your horse shows more extreme symptoms.

Even though respiratory rates, temperatures, and capillary refill times don't have a direct effect on your horse's hooves, they can be good indicators of your horse's overall condition, and can indicate problems that can affect the hooves, like an infection, or even pain and stress from a hoof condition, such as rapid breathing in a horse experiencing acute laminitis.

The average healthy range for respiration is between 6 and 20 breaths per minute when your horse is at rest. Of course, if your horse is excited, like if you have her in her stall and she's worried that all her friends are outside without her, she'll probably be breathing faster, so you want her to be as calm as possible. You'll be able to see her inhale and exhale by standing near her shoulder and looking toward her hindquarters, so that her barrel is silhouetted, or you can feel it by putting your hand on her ribcage. An inhale and exhale counts as one breath, so grab your watch or more likely, open the alarm clock on your phone and flip to the stopwatch, and count her breaths for one minute. Horses tend to breathe a little slower than us, since the average human respiratory rate is about 14-16 breaths per minute, so don't worry if it seems like she's not breathing very quickly. Your biggest concern will be if she is breathing more rapidly than the normal range, or if her breathing is labored. If you're monitoring her vital signs because you're concerned about something, you'll want to write down the number of breaths you measured in one minute, as well as the time and date that the measurement was taken. If you have to call your vet out, you can give them some data to start with so that they can tell if your horse's condition has changed since you took the measurements.

Next, you can check to make sure your horse is hydrated. These tests are quick and easy and could provide vital clues about your horse's health. First, try the skin test. Gently pinch the skin on your horse's neck between your thumb and forefinger, then let it go. The skin should smooth out within one second. If it stays peaked up and only slowly goes back to normal, your horse is dehydrated, and you'll want to provide fluids immediately. If he's had access to water, make sure that it is clean and free of debris, and check the temperature. In winter, horses are less likely to drink very cold water (brain freeze anyone?) so adding some warm water might help. You can also add some salt and electrolytes to your horse's diet if he struggles with drinking enough water.

If your horse is cooperative, you can also check his capillary refill time, another important indicator of good hydration. For this one, you'll gently lift his upper lip and firmly press your thumb against his gum for two seconds. When you remove your thumb, you should see a white mark, but within two seconds the gum should have returned to a pink color, showing that his capillaries have refilled.

Taking your horse's temperature is also an important part of checking her vital signs, if not the most glamorous part of the process. Horses' temperatures are taken with a rectal thermometer, and the average temperature should be between 99-101.5 °F. Before you get to the fun part where you convince a thousand-pound animal to let you stick something in her rectum, you're going to need to do a little setup. First, make sure that you have a thermometer with a small hole or loop where you can tie a string. You can use baling twine for this or whatever you have on hand, just make sure that you have a good length of string firmly attached to the thermometer. As you've probably guessed, this is so that the thermometer doesn't get sucked inside your horse (and so you can pull it out if it does -- gently please!). If you're concerned about this happening, you can also clip a clothespin perpendicular to the thermometer to act as a stop, but you should still have a string attached in case anything goes wrong with the clothespin. Nobody needs foreign objects getting lost up there.

Once you've secured the string to the thermometer, grab a tube of petroleum jelly (this is a good thing to keep with the thermometer in your barn first aid kit) and make sure it's body warm. Nobody wants a cold surprise, so get it warm between your hands before generously applying it to the thermometer. Then, standing to the side of your horse's hindquarters, carefully insert the thermometer following the manufacturer's instructions. Once the time specified on the instructions is complete, gently pull it out and record your findings. If her temperature is over 102, you should call your vet right away.

You'll also want to know how to check for heat and pulses in your horse's legs, since this can be an indicator of abscesses, laminitis, and even bruising. Pulses are easiest to take right at the level of the fetlock, since the main artery supplying the foot runs right over the bones at the joint. You'll want to cup your thumb and forefinger firmly behind the fetlock joint and feel for a small bundle made up of a vein, nerve, and the artery we're looking for, just under the skin. This may take some experience, especially if it's winter and your horse has a thick hair coat, but with practice you should be able to find it consistently.

Once you've found the right spot, you'll get out your phone or watch again and count each pulse you feel for thirty seconds, then double it. You're looking for a pulse rate between 30-40 beats per minute, so 15-20 beats in thirty seconds. Of course, this will vary a little depending on how fit your horse is, if he's excited, or if he's been

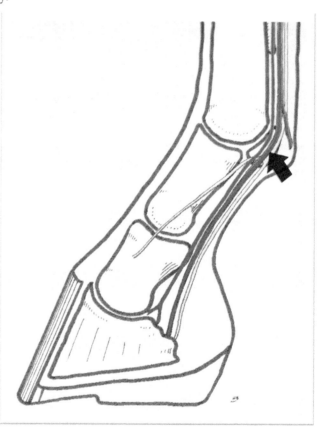

The neurovascular bundle runs over the sesamoid bones in the fetlock

running around. You'll want to take his pulse after he's had a chance to calm down a little so that his heart has returned to its resting rate. Rapid pulses can be a sign of inflammation or stress, but you're also checking for how powerful the pulse is. If your horse has inflammation in his hooves, the pulse becomes stronger, sometimes described as a "bounding pulse". This is more of a feel thing than a numbers game, so make sure you check your horse's pulse relatively regularly so that you know what his normal pulse feels like.

Finding heat in the hooves is also done by feel, so it's not an exact science. What you're looking for is a raised hoof temperature indicating inflammation, or one hoof being warmer than the others. Keep in mind, there are a number of possible explanations for a warm hoof, like exercising or standing in the sun, so if the hoof feels hot, you'll want to wait a few minutes and check again. Just like feeling a human's forehead for a fever, use the back of your hand for more accurate results.

Once you've gone through this checklist of vital signs, you should have a pretty good idea of how your

Use your thumb and forefinger to check the pulse

horse is feeling. If anything is out of the normal range, call your vet and let them know what you observed, as well as any other symptoms, like whether your horse is alert or listless, or if she's reluctant to move. This can give your vet important clues as to the severity of your horse's condition, and even what they might be dealing with before they arrive.

Another major sign of your horse's health is his weight. We've already talked in Chapter 34 about the link between obesity and laminitis, but obesity also has risks for your horse's health in general. Of course, like humans, the heart of the obese horse has to work harder, and every part of the body is under more stress since it's carrying extra weight. But obesity is also linked to chronic low-grade inflammation[73], which is damaging to almost every tissue in your horse, especially to joints and the lamina. And of course, being underweight isn't good for your horse either, since they won't have the right nutritional building blocks or the energy available to grow healthy hooves.

So how can you tell if your horse is

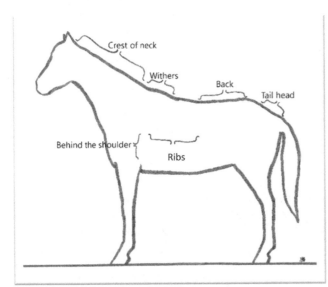

Henneke body condition scoring is based on these points of the body

[73] Pearson, W., Wood, K., Stanley, S., MacNicol, J. (2018). Exploring relationships between body condition score, body fat, activity level and inflammatory biomarkers. *J Anim Physiol Anim Nutr (Berl);102(4):* P. 1062-1068.

overweight, underweight, or just right? Most of us don't have access to horse-sized scales, weight tapes are notoriously inaccurate, and how would you even know what an ideal body weight was for your horse? They come in all shapes and sizes, and a 16-hand thoroughbred will have a different healthy body weight than a 16-hand Friesian, much less a Welsh pony or a Dutch Warmblood.

Luckily for all of us, there's something called the Henneke Body Condition Scoring system, which looks at key areas of your individual horse to help you categorize your horse's weight. Once you get the hang of it, it's pretty straightforward, and it doesn't require any equipment besides your eyes and your hands. It mostly looks at six easy to find regions; the crest of the neck, the withers, behind the shoulder, over the ribs, along the back, and the tailhead region. From there, you'll simply see which description matches the condition of those areas and, voila, you have an idea of your horse's condition!

The Henneke system helps you rank your horse from 1 to 9, with 1 being extremely emaciated and 9 being extremely fat. Don't ask me why it doesn't go up to 10, but let's just say we don't want to see the horse that rates ten on this scale. 1-3 are considered underweight, 4-6 are normal, and 7-9 are overweight. The following descriptions of each grade are based on that scale, which gives detailed, easy to follow explanations[74].

Poor condition

1. **Poor:** Horse is extremely emaciated. Spine, ribs, hipbones, and tailhead project prominently. Skeletal structure of the withers, shoulders, and neck are very noticeable. No fatty tissues can be felt.

2. **Very Thin:** Horse is emaciated. Slight fat covering over spine. Backbone, ribs, tailhead, and hipbones are still obvious. Withers, shoulders, and neck structures are discernable.

3. **Thin:** Fat built up about halfway on spinous processes. Slight fat layer can be felt over ribs, but the ribs easily seen. The tailhead is noticeable, but individual vertebrae cannot be discerned. The hipbones, withers, shoulders, and neck structures are still faintly discernable.

4. **Moderately Thin:** Slight ridge can be felt along back. Faint outline of ribs visible. Fat can be felt around tailhead. Hip bones not easily discernable. Withers, neck, and shoulders not obviously thin.

5. **Moderate:** Back is level. Ribs can be easily felt, but are not visually distinguishable. Fat around tailhead beginning to feel spongy. Withers are rounded at the spine and shoulders and neck blend smoothly into the body.

6. **Moderately Fleshy:** May have a light crease down the back. Fat around the tailhead is soft. Fat over the ribs begins to feels spongy. Fat beginning to be deposited along the sides of the withers, behind the shoulder, and in the crest of the neck.

7. **Fleshy:** May have a crease down the back. Individual ribs can be felt, but noticeable fat deposited over the ribs. Fat around tailhead is soft. Fat is being deposited along the

[74]Henneke, D.R., Potter, G.D., Kreider, J.L. and Yeates, B.F. (1983). Relationship between condition score, physical measurements and body fat percentage in mares. *Equine Veterinary Journal, 15:* P. 371-372

withers, behind the shoulders, and in the crest of the neck.

8. **Fat:** Crease down the back is noticeable. Ribs are hard to feel. Fat around tailhead prominent. Area along withers and behind shoulders filled in flush with fat. Prominent crest of neck. Fat may be deposited along the inner buttocks.

9. **Extremely Fat:** Heavy crease down back. Fat patches appear over rib area, with bulging fat over tailhead, withers, neck, and behind shoulders. Crest of neck is very prominent. Fat along inner buttocks may rub together. Flank is flush with the barrel of the body.

What did you find out? If your horse fell between 4-6, you're probably in good shape. You might have a little bit of finetuning to do, but you're within healthy limits. If your horse landed between 1-3, you're probably already trying to get some weight on her. If she's not eating much, or she's eating and still losing weight, call your vet right away. You could be dealing with something as simple as a parasitic infection, or maybe your horse needs some dental help. Of course, as horses age they can slip into these categories, especially if they were hard keepers to start with, but even

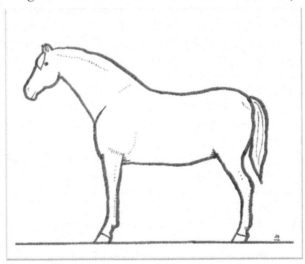

Extremely fat

then, your vet might be able to offer helpful suggestions that you haven't tried yet.

As a farrier who works on a lot of very loved horses, the most frequent weight issue I see isn't lack of nutrition though. I see a lot of overweight horses every day, and it's a concerning trend for all the health issues we've already discussed. Since a lot of us are tempted to show our love to our animals through feeding and treats, overfeeding can be a difficult and painful habit to break.

Remember, though, your bond with your horse goes way deeper than food. You're not just a walking treat dispenser; you are teammates who have built a two-way, trusting relationship. So trust him that he'll still love spending time with you, even if you don't have a pocket full of snacks for him. Trust that he isn't just in it for the grain, and that he actually likes being around you, the grooming time, the activities that you do together.

If your horse is overweight, for her health, you need to help her get back to a good body weight, and that means reassessing the type and quantity of feed, extra treats that she gets (these do add up, like sneaking cookies on a diet), and how much exercise she gets. This is a great time to get your vet or even an equine nutritionist on board to make a game plan that you can both follow. Your horse's hooves, joints, and heart will thank you!

Quick Takeaways
- **Practice observing your horse's vital signs so that you will be able to easily recognize anything out of the ordinary in case of emergency.**
- **Body scoring is an important method for maintaining a healthy body weight for your horse.**

Vital Signs Checklist

Respiration rate:
6-20 breaths per minute

Capillary refill time:
2 seconds

Pulse rate:
30-40 beats per minute

Temperature:
99- 101.5

36 SUDDEN AND SEVERE – FIRST AID FOR THE SURPRISE LAMENESS

In this chapter, we'll be talking about first aid for lameness that don't have an obvious external cause, but makes your horse limp like he broke his leg. We'll be covering first aid for the more obvious kind of injuries like puncture wounds and hot nails in the next chapter, so feel free to flip over there if you're looking at something like that.

Let's get down to business. Your horse was fine yesterday and now he's a sad, limping horse who needs your help. You're there for him, but what's your first move? How do you know what you're dealing with?

We'll start with the most common cause of lameness in otherwise sound horses: an abscess. If you've read Chapter 27 already, you know what an abscess is and how they can be caused. If you skipped ahead to get here, don't worry, I've got you covered with the basics here. You can always go back and learn more once you've got things under control.

Quick recap: An abscess is a bacterial infection inside the hoof capsule that creates pus and painful pressure inside the hoof capsule. The best way to treat an abscess is to get the pressure and pus out of there, and then to keep it clean so that it can heal.

What symptoms should you look for? Sudden onset, rapidly worsening lameness in one hoof. It may fluctuate slightly, particularly if the abscess drains and then seals up again, but it will generally tend to worsen until it drains. Your horse will have an obvious limp on the affected hoof and may even completely avoid bearing weight on it if possible. Heat and an increased pulse are likely. In extreme cases, you may be able to elicit a reaction by pressing with your fingers on the affected hoof.

If that sounds like your horse, what should you do? Your goal is to drain the abscess, and the fastest way to do that is to have your farrier or vet open up a drainage track in the bottom of the hoof. Your first move should be to call up your farrier and vet and see when either one of them could get there to help. In the meantime, you'll want to start soaking the hoof. If you're very lucky, the abscess track will only be sealed up with dirt and manure, and soaking can loosen that and allow drainage to occur. Otherwise, soaking will soften the hoof and make it easier for the abscess to blow out. For tips on soaking, check out Chapter 40. You can also use a poultice pad such as Animalintex to attempt to draw the abscess out, but you should avoid using sticky, dark colored poultices, since these will make it difficult for your farrier or vet to see any dark lines or spots that could indicate the abscess location.

You'll also want to avoid giving your horse any pain meds unless your vet tells you to. Pain meds can mask the location of the abscess and make it harder to open.

There's no reason to restrict turnout for your horse unless they go out in a muddy area, which can pack dirt and bacteria into any drainage track and reseal an abscess. In fact, movement can actually add just enough pressure to the abscess to make it blow. Of course, your horse is in pain, so you won't want to be lunging them or forcing them to move more than they want to.

Once your farrier or vet has opened the abscess, you will want to follow their advice, very likely to soak the hoof several more times over the next few days to make sure that all the bacteria and debris are out of the hoof. This is a great time to use a nice warm Epsom salts soak. You'll also probably want to keep the hoof wrapped for a few days, especially if your horse is messy in his stall or is going outside.

If your horse isn't quite that lame, but is definitely off, she could have bruised her hoof. This looks a little different from an abscess lameness, and it usually isn't nearly as severe.

The symptoms that will clue you in to a bruise are noticeable lameness, especially on hard ground, that doesn't get significantly worse over time. An abscess escalates quickly, but a bruise will stay at about the same pain level until it starts to subside. This shouldn't be limping-like-her-leg-is-broken lame, more like off-but-not-crippled lame. You might find heat or an increased pulse, too.

Although horses can always do crazy things to themselves and bruised their hooves for evidently no reason, usually you can track a bruise back to an activity. Maybe she was stomping a lot on hard ground, like if she was tied on concrete and the flies were really bad. Maybe you had an extra strenuous ride on less-than-ideal footing, or she pulled a shoe halfway through your six-mile trail ride and she had to go barefoot the rest of the ride. Or she could have bruised her hoof kicking her stall wall because a new horse moved in next to her and she needed to let him know who's boss.

Of course, you won't be able to immediately see a bruise on the outside of the hoof, since the bruising is on the inside and there's a good 3/8-inch barrier around it. But over time the blood from the broken capillaries will slowly stain the horn and give you an idea what's going on. Your farrier might also find the bruising the next time they trim her hooves, or even a few trim cycles later, depending on how slowly she grows.

Just like when *you* get a bruise, there's not much you can do besides wait it out. If your horse is pretty lame, you can talk to your vet about using a non-steroidal anti-inflammatory like Bute to help her feel better, but mostly, you'll want to help give her hooves a break. If her hooves are hot, you can cold hose or ice them, and you'll want to give her some time off from work. If you know what caused the bruising, see if you can change up her situation to keep her from hurting herself again.

You'll want to help her avoid super bacteria-laden situations like standing in muddy water, because a bruise is a highly nourishing food source for abscess-causing bacteria. You want that bruise to heel up without any problems, not to develop into an abscess.

If she's bruising her feet a lot, you might want to think about adding shoes with pads to help protect her hooves from concussion. This will also help if she's bruising her feet because she doesn't have a thick enough sole to protect her internal sensitive structures, since the pad will act like an artificial sole.

Another sudden lameness that might look similar to bad bruising or an abscess is laminitis. Although nobody wants to consider it as the reason for their horse's sudden lameness, early intervention is important so you'll want to check for the signs. Best case scenario, the symptoms don't fit and you can rest easier knowing your horse doesn't have laminitis. But if the symptoms do add up, you can get your horse the help he needs right away. We've talked in depth about laminitis in Chapter 34, so you can look back there for the details, but we're going to cover the essential first aid steps here.

Just like an abscess or a bad hoof bruise, heat in the hooves and rapid, bounding pulses are common symptoms during an acute

A classic laminitic stance

laminitis attack. However, unlike most abscesses, laminitis almost always occurs in either both front hooves or in all four hooves at the same time, unless your horse has a non-weight bearing injury in the opposite limb. Look back to the chapter on laminitis for more details on that one. In contrast, most of the time if your horse gets an abscess, he'll only have one at a time.

Also, laminitis is usually the most painful in the toe of the hoof, and you may see your horse rocking backward or even leaning his butt on a wall to take some of the weight off his hooves. He could also be laying down a lot, which is the best thing he can do to make his hooves less painful. If he is laying down, don't try to get him up. Putting weight on his feet right now will only do more damage.

In a study done on 93 diagnosed laminitis cases in the UK, two of the most common symptoms were stiffness and difficulty turning[75]. Since it usually affects both front hooves, you can expect him to be sore turning in both directions. Another common sign is shifting weight from foot to foot.

Interestingly, that study also recorded whether the laminitis cases were owner-suspected (in other words, if the owner recognized the symptoms and called the vet out for a suspected laminitis case) or veterinarian reported (i.e., the vet was called out for un-recognized symptoms and found that it was laminitis). Of the 93 horses in the study, 51 were owner-suspected cases, and every single one was confirmed as laminitis by the attending vet. This means that if you have good reason to suspect laminitis, go with your gut and call your vet. You could be saving valuable time for your horse.

Owners were also more likely to recognize the signs if they had seen laminitis before. Of course, this makes sense since you're much more confident the second time you see something, and it shows that horse owners are doing a good job of being vigilant if they know what they're looking for.

But what about the other 42 horses in the study? Their owners, mostly people who hadn't seen laminitis before, saw that something was off about their horse but didn't know what it was. The most commonly suspected problems reported by those owners were undefined hoof pain or abscesses, colic, and stiffness. Good news though, we get to learn from their mistakes. If you suspect any of those problems, look at the symptom list for laminitis and see if anything raises a red flag. It could save your horse a lot of pain; one well-intentioned owner who suspected colic reportedly walked her horse throughout the night, which only damaged already inflamed hooves.

So let's say that some of this stuff is sounding eerily familiar. Although it's scary to know your horse might be suffering from a painful and dangerous condition, you're going to save your freak-out for later because you've got work to do. You can totally freak out when you're done.

The first thing on your roster after assessing your horse's symptoms is to call your vet. You're going to need their medical expertise, to help you possibly remove the cause of the laminitis and definitely to manage the pain and inflammation and help you come up with a personalized treatment plan for your horse. Once you've gotten them on the phone, explain the symptoms that you've seen, your horse's overall condition and demeanor (is he anxious, calm, or looking depressed?) and your horse's vitals if you've had a chance to check them. This will help your vet know how severe things are, and how your horse is handling it.

Secondly, you'll also want to get in touch with your farrier and let them know what is going on. They may want to be present when the vet is assessing your horse, in case there's anything they can do to help. And they'll definitely be part of your horse's long term recovery plan, so it's important to keep them up to date.

Your next item of business is making sure that whatever kicked off the laminitis isn't still

---

[75]Pollard, D., Wylie, C.E., Verheyen, K.L.P, Newton, J.R. (2017). Assessment of horse owners' ability to recognise equine laminitis: A cross-sectional study of 93 veterinary diagnosed cases in Great Britain. *Equine Vet J. 49(6):* P. 759-766.

affecting your horse. Check back to Chapter 34 for a more extensive description of possible causes, but if your horse is out in a grassy field, you're going to want to get him out of it. Check to make sure there's no possible way he got into your grain storage and look for anything toxic that he could have ingested. If you've changed shavings in your stall recently, make sure that they came from a reputable source and don't contain black walnut, which is known to cause laminitis in horses. If the laminitis has been caused by an infection, your vet will be able to help you take care of that when they arrive. In the meantime, try to think of any recent changes in environment, management, diet, or activity that could be a factor.

Once you've made sure to get any laminitis triggers away from your horse, you're going to do some hoof first aid to transfer some of the load off of his hoof walls and onto his frog and the sole in the back half of his hoof. You can start by making sure that he's in a clean, deeply bedded stall. The bedding can cushion his hooves and transfer some load, and a nice comfy stall encourages him to lie down and get off his feet, which is the best thing he can do right now.

If you have cushioned hoof boots like a Softride boot, especially one with a frog support like Softride's laminitic insert, go ahead and put those on. If your horse is prone to laminitis, a pair of good boots are definitely a useful investment. If you don't have any, don't worry, you can make some pretty good emergency boots with a quick trip to your local hardware store. Rigid foamboard insulation, which looks like a thick sheet of Styrofoam, makes a great supportive pad for the bottom of your horse's hooves. You can easily cut it with a utility knife, so set your horse's hoof on a square of insulation and trace it. Then you'll cut it out and make a duct tape wrap to secure it to the hoof. Boom, instant custom hoof boot! Of course, this is a temporary solution since they will eventually flatten and squash down, but a sheet of insulation will definitely have you covered until your vet gets out. The insulation boot will usually last for about two days, but of course that will vary by horse, so check it once a day.

You can also ice your horse's hooves, which can temporarily reduce inflammation. If you are in a position to continuously ice your horse's hooves for at least 72 hours, you could actually significantly reduce the amount of damage done in a laminitic attack, but the icing does need to be continuous, meaning no waiting for the ice water to melt before you change it, and no taking breaks[76]. The ice water also needs to come up to mid-cannon bone for it to cool enough of the blood vessels to work. This is a huge time commitment, but it is currently one of the most promising laminitis treatments available[77].

Once your vet and farrier arrive, they will be able to perform more diagnostics to find out exactly what's going on, and they'll come up with a plan to help your horse. Make sure that when they're discussing options, you ask any questions you have, especially if they use a term you haven't heard before. You want to make sure you understand what's going on so that you can make the best possible decisions for your horse. Don't be embarrassed to ask questions or ask for an explanation: after all, he's your horse. You deserve to have all the information before you make any treatment decisions.

Good job -- first aid is over. You did it. You got your horse through the initial onset and kept him as comfortable as possible until your vet and farrier could get there. Once the team has come up with a treatment plan, the long-term care starts, but you've got the scariest part out of the

---

[76]van Eps, A.W., Pollitt, C.C. (2004). Equine laminitis: cryotherapy reduces the severity of the acute lesion. *Equine Vet J. 36(3):* P. 255-60.

[77] van Eps, A.W. (2010). Therapeutic hypothermia (cryotherapy) to prevent and treat acute laminitis. *Vet Clin North Am Equine Pract. 26(1):* P. 125-33.

way. From this point forward, you have your vet and farrier as backup.

Quick Takeaways
- Common abscess symptoms include severe hoof lameness worsening over time, heat, a raised pulse, and sometimes swelling in the affected limb. It typically occurs in only one limb at a time.
- Common hoof bruise symptoms include noticeable lameness, heat, slightly raised pulses, sometimes in multiple hooves at once. It can often be traced back to severe or repeated concussion.
- Common laminitis symptoms include severe lameness especially in the toe area, usually on both front hooves or sometimes all four hooves, with heat and bounding pulses. The horse is usually reluctant to move and may rock back to take weight off the front hooves, or in severe cases the horse may lay down.

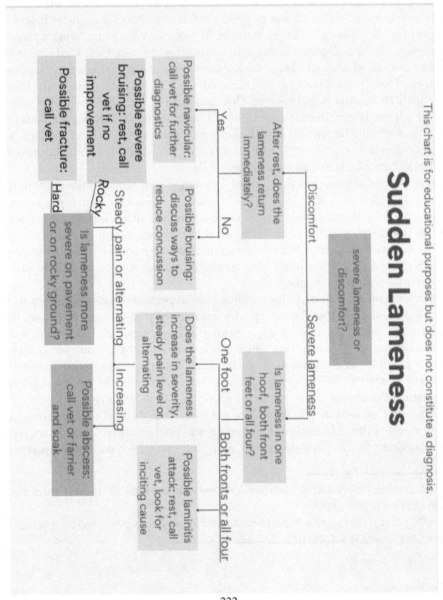

37 CUTS, WOUNDS, AND FOREIGN OBJECTS

In the last chapter, we covered what to do if your horse has a hoof lameness without an obvious cause, but what if your horse injures her hoof? Since we know horses can be rather accident prone, let's talk about what you should do if your horse comes in with a cut or with something stuck in her hoof. We'll also cover hot nails and trimming related lameness in this chapter.

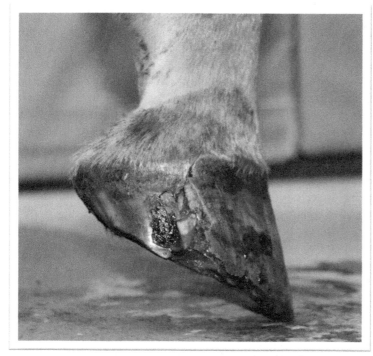

Bleeding hoof wounds require immediate attention

The most obvious problem is when you bring your horse in and there is blood coming from her coronary band or hoof. Maybe she managed to step on herself and caught her coronary band and the top of her hoof wall, or she could have put her hoof through a fence, gate, or into a hole. Some horses even manage to hurt themselves by kicking through a fence board and then jerking their hoof back through the sharp, splintered wood. Some wounds will only involve the soft tissue above the hoof, while others will tear or fracture the hoof wall too.

The first aid steps are the same though, whether or not the hoof capsule is involved. Like all wounds, your first move is going to be to stop the bleeding. You'll do this by applying direct pressure to the injure area. You can use a towel or any other clean fabric that's around, but if you have access to gauze (a good thing to keep in your equine first aid kit) that can be really helpful. You'll want to avoid using paper towels, cotton, wool, or other things that can disintegrate and leave debris in the wound, although if that's your only choice to stop the bleeding, you'll just have to go for it.

If you're by yourself and your horse isn't being too cooperative, it might be hard to put direct pressure on the wound, so your best bet will be to pack some gauze in the wound and wrap it tightly. Then you'll want to keep your horse as calm and still as possible, whether that means holding her, putting her in a clean stall, or even setting up a hay bag to keep her occupied. She needs to hold still long enough to get the bleeding to stop, which might vary depending on how severe the wound is. Arterial bleeding can also be harder to stop than bleeding than veins, since arteries are pressurized. You can tell which kind of bleeding you're dealing with because arterial bleeding is bright red and spurts with the rhythm of her heartbeat, while blood from a vein is duller in color and bleeds more continuously but shouldn't be squirting out.

If the bleeding is severe, give your vet a call right away, especially if you're having trouble getting it stopped or it is from an artery. Your horse may need stitches, and your vet will be able to help you get the bleeding under control, find out what structures are damaged, and prevent infection.

Once the bleeding is stopped, carefully remove your pressure wrap, since cutting off circulation for too long is dangerous for your horse. If the bleeding is significantly slowed or stopped even with the wrap removed, try to clean the wound, especially if your vet won't be able to get out right away. A lot of hoof wounds can get really dirty before we find them since they're close to the ground and therefore close to dirt, manure, and debris. Plus they can already have junk in them from the initial injury, like wood slivers from a broken board, or hair and dirt from the outside of the wound.

If you have access to clean water and a hose, gently rinse the area. You don't want to be power washing it with your sprayer, though, since it's really sensitive and you don't want to push anything farther into the wound. Likewise, you'll want to avoid rubbing or scrubbing the wound since it's easy to damage the tissue and push debris into the wound. If you don't have access to water, gently blot the wound instead. If you can see any foreign objects in the wound that aren't coming out with rinsing, wait for your vet to arrive instead of trying to get them out yourself.

If your horse is calm and cooperative, gently and carefully clip the hair away around the edges of the wound. It's easier to sanitize bare skin than to get every bit of bacteria that might be hiding in the hair.

If you've gotten to this step and your vet isn't there yet, go ahead and bandage the wound to protect it and keep the bleeding under control. Ask your vet if they recommend antiseptic ointment or if they would prefer you to just cover the wound until they see it. If they want you to use ointment, put some on a clean gauze pad, absorptive fabric, or a manufactured wound dressing and then apply it directly to the wound. Otherwise, you'll just apply the same material without the ointment. Wrap it in place with a light, thin, cotton or elastic wrap.

Next, you'll apply a thicker bandage to help absorb fluids and stabilize the wound. This would be where you'd use your sheet or roll cotton. Then you'll top it with vet wrap to hold it in place and protect it.

Then you'll just be focused on keeping your horse calm and comfortable until your vet arrives. They will probably re-clean the wound using sedation so that they can be thorough and make sure there's no more debris in the wound. They'll also be able to closely observe the wound so they can tell what structures are affected and what kind of treatment might be necessary.

Especially if the wound was dirty when you found it, they'll probably put your horse on antibiotics to keep any infection under control. They may also check your horse's tetanus vaccination records.

If the coronary band or

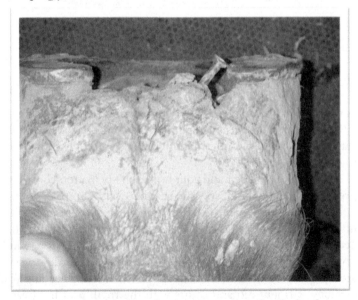

Lameness may be caused by a foreign object puncturing the hoof

224

hoof wall was damaged, you'll want to contact your farrier, too. They won't be able to work on the hoof until your vet has the wound stabilized, but your farrier will be an important part of managing the damaged hoof and the new growth that could be coming from an injured coronary band.

What if your horse is out in the field and when you go out to grab him, he's limping like crazy and doesn't want to put one hoof down? You pick up his hoof, hopefully out in the field instead of making him walk in on it, and you find a nail or a piece of wire or wood stuck in his sole or frog.

Your first instinct is going to be to pull it out, but hold on! You don't know how long the object is, or what structures it might be sticking into inside the hoof. And once you pull it out, your vet won't be able to tell either. But if they can get out right away to take x-rays, you'll have a picture showing exactly what structures are

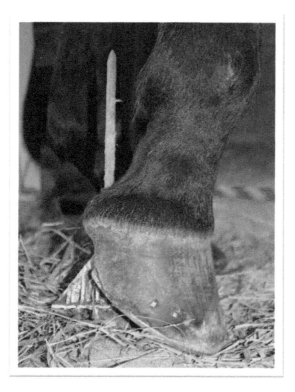

Horses can be accident prone and injure themselves in creative ways

affected.

First, you're going to call your vet right away and let them know what's going on. If it's going to be a few hours before they can get there, you're going to need to protect your horse from any more damage in the meantime, since any step could push the object deeper.

There are a couple of ways you may be able to stop the nail from going in any farther. If you have thick Styrofoam or foam board insulation, you can cut out a hoof shaped section, and then cut out the area with the foreign object so that it's not touching the ground. Then duct tape it onto the hoof securely. This is a very temporary solution since the foam will crush down eventually, so check it hourly to make sure that the nail is still not touching the ground.

If you're really crafty, you may be able to cut wooden blocks to duct tape to the heels of the hoof to wedge it up

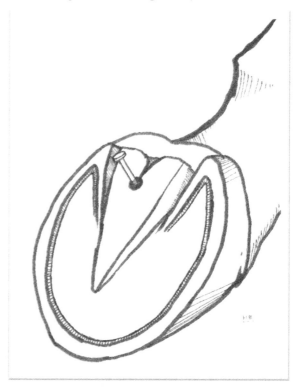

Before you remove a nail, mark the nail and the puncture wound clearly

off the ground. Of course, your blocks need to not be touching the injured area.

You may also be able to create a big, puffy wrap with a towel folded up and wrapped around the bottom of the hoof, but the point of this is to basically make it hard to bear weight on that hoof so that he stays off it as much as possible.

If your vet can't come out for a while, they may recommend that you pull the object yourself. If this is the case, you're going to want to document everything you can before you pull it out.

Taking a picture of the nail with a ruler can help your vet know how far the nail penetrated

- Take pictures from multiple angles with the hoof lifted up. Try to get at least one looking straight at the bottom of the hoof and at least one from the side. If you can, try to get one from the toe or heel so that the vet can see if the object goes in straight or if it's angled.

- Get a Sharpie marker and heavily mark the area around the nail. Especially with a frog wound, the horn is sometimes flexible enough to close up after the object is removed, so it's important to mark the spot so your vet can find it when they arrive.

- Use your Sharpie and draw a clear line on the object right where it goes into the hoof. That way, when you pull it out, you and your vet will be able to see exactly how far it went in.

Ask your vet if they would like you to flush the hole with an antiseptic after you pull it out. You can do this with a plastic tipped syringe, but you do not want to put anything into the hoof without your vet's permission. If they suspect that a joint or bursa might be affected, they might not want any harsh antiseptics in the area.

Then you can carefully pull the object, making sure to keep it angled in the direction that it entered the foot so you don't cause any more damage. Depending on how far in the object goes, you might be able to pull it with your fingers or you

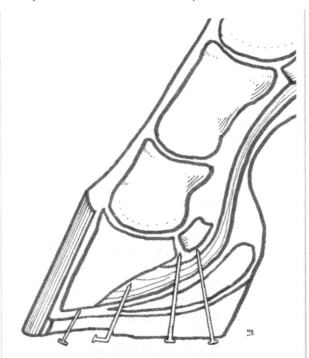

The angle of entry will determine what structures may be affected

226

might have to use a pair of pliers. Go slow and easy and be ready for your horse to try to pull his hoof away, since it may be very painful. Once you've got it out, put the object somewhere safe where it won't get thrown away, so that you can show it to your vet when they arrive.

Your vet may have to debride more tissue from the area if they suspect that there is still debris in the wound, like splinters if you pulled a piece of wood out of the hoof, and they will probably flush the wound to make sure that there's no bacteria or debris in there to cause an infection.

A puncture wound may need to be soaked and cleaned like an abscess

From that point, they'll make a plan based on where the object went and what structures were injured. They might ask you to bandage the hoof until it has a chance to heal for a while, or they may request that your farrier make a shoe for your horse with a removable treatment plate to protect the wound. Your vet will probably also put your horse on some antibiotics and check when his last tetanus shot was.

What if the issue isn't a nail that your horse stepped on, but when your horse was shod last, one of the nails wasn't good? Even the best farrier can occasionally drive a bad nail, since the white line is such a small target. Remember, nails are supposed to be driven into the white line and then outward, only going through insensitive tissue. But if the nail is accidently driven through the sole or doesn't come out soon enough, it can get too close to sensitive internal structures, usually the solar corium or the sensitive lamina. If your horse has really thin walls or a lot of distortion in her hooves, she could be more at risk for a bad nail than the average horse.

The biggest indicator of a bad nail, also known as a hot nail, is the timing after a shoeing. If the nail is actually in sensitive tissue, your horse will be immediately lame and the lameness will get worse fast. If the nail is only close to sensitive tissue and not actually in it, it will start to irritate and pinch over time, especially if you work your horse. This can take a little bit longer, but you're still looking at a pretty short time frame, most commonly within two or three days of the shoeing, and it will get worse consistently over time. In other words, if you're looking at a lameness more than a week after your horse was shod, and it isn't getting worse, you're almost certainly *not* looking at a bad nail.

You might also feel some warmth in the hoof and a raised pulse. In fact, sometimes the heat will even be localized around the nail that is causing the problem. All that inflammation can sometimes develop into an abscess if the nail isn't removed quickly, so you'll want quickly to get in touch with your farrier or vet.

Your farrier will usually be your first phone call for a suspected bad nail. If they did make a mistake (they are human, after all) they will want to get out and fix it as soon as they can. They will use hoof testers to make sure that the lameness is related to one of the nails.

Depending on how long your horse has been sore and how severe the lameness is, they may only pull the offending nail, or they might pull off the whole shoe to make it easier to soak. Often when they pull the nail, your horse might flinch, which is a good indication that was the painful nail. There may even be some drainage if an abscess has started to form.

Like any abscess or injury, you want to make sure that the hole is nice and clean. Usually, your farrier will recommend soaking the hoof a few times to make sure that any abscessing is cleared up. If they pulled the whole shoe, they will usually leave it off for a few days to give you time to soak it and make sure all the inflammation has gone down before they re-attach the shoe.

The good news is that if a bad nail is caught early and removed, lameness is usually quickly resolved with no long-term damage. Even the scariest-looking bad nail that actually bleeds when it's driven in rarely causes a major issue. In fact, since your farrier can see that it was a bad nail right away, nails that bleed when driven are pulled out right away and often don't cause more than momentary pain for your horse.

Another shoeing problem you might run into, especially if your horse has thin soles, flat feet, or had a ton of hoof

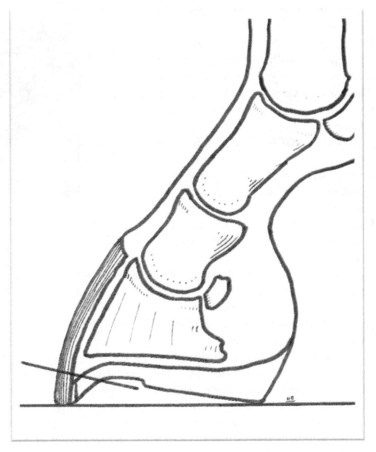

A hoof with a deeply cupped sole may have a deceptively thin sole and easily be trimmed too short

growth or distortion, is being trimmed too short. Some hooves are deceiving and make your farrier think they can safely take more hoof than what your horse actually has to offer. You might be looking at this if your horse became sore immediately after a trim or shoeing and the soreness gets better over time as the hoof grows itself more protection.

If this does happen, you can call your farrier and they may be able to add pads or shoes to protect your horse's hooves until they have a chance to grow. You can also use hoof boots or wrap his hooves to help get him over the hump. Unless the trim was grossly short, give your farrier a chance to fix their mistake. Remember that farriers don't come with x-ray eyes, so they are trimming off of external landmarks on your horse's hooves, and that can be misleading. Of course, if it is a repeated occurrence and your farrier doesn't try to change up their game plan, you might need to look for someone else, because your horse shouldn't be consistently lame after a trimming.

While we're here, let's talk a bit about myths. I can't tell you how many times I've heard people say that you shouldn't ride your horse after he gets shod because he'll be sore. There are few very specific circumstances where your horse might be sore after a shoeing, like if he has a very severe pathology and standing on three hooves for a while makes him sore, or if he has arthritis and flexing his legs for shoeing makes him sore. Otherwise, your horse being sore should *never* be a regular occurrence after shoeing. If it is, tell your farrier right away! They will want to rethink their shoeing or trimming plan to prevent lameness, and they may ask you for foot x-rays so they can see if there's an issue they weren't aware of in your horse's hooves. Please don't assume that lameness after shoeing is normal unless you have a diagnosed issue that is irritated by flexing or weight bearing.

If your horse's hooves did get trimmed too short, you're just trying to protect them long enough for him to grow some more hoof. So you won't want him to be turned out without anything on the bottom of his hooves, or else he'll just be wearing away hoof that he doesn't have. If he needs to go out, he needs to be wearing boots, shoes, or even have his hooves wrapped.

In all these scenarios, I've been telling you to call your vet or farrier. How do you know who you should call first for each problem? Read on to the next chapter to find out.

Quick Takeaways
- **If your horse has a hoof wound, the first priority is stopping the bleeding. Then assess the severity of the wound and call your vet if necessary.**
- **Any time that a joint, tendon, ligament, or bone are involved in a wound, you should immediately call your vet.**
- **Foreign objects should not be removed from the hoof without vet approval.**
- **Bad nails become obvious very quickly, usually within a day or two, and become worse until the nail is removed.**
- **Your horse should not consistently be lame after trimming or shoeing.**

38 VETS, FARRIERS, AND PHONE CALLS

Something has gone wrong with your horse's hooves and you realize you're going to need some help. Who you gonna call? It's not Ghostbusters.

As a general rule, if there's blood involved, you should call your vet first. If the emergency is related to a hoof or shoe problem, your farrier should be your first call. According to most veterinary practice acts, which are the laws that govern the vet industry and what type of services non-vets can offer, farriers are not legally allowed to diagnose pathologies or diseases, prescribe treatments for medical issues, or physically cross the blood barrier. These laws can have gray areas. Your farrier is fully qualified to let you know that your horse has thrush and help you come up with a treatment plan, for instance. If your horse is bleeding, or you need a diagnosis for a lameness, you're going to want your vet to be present. In an ideal world, your vet and farrier can work together to each use their strengths to help your horse, but you don't want to put your farrier in a position where they feel pressured to diagnose a disease or pathology since that puts them in a bad legal position. Your farrier also isn't equipped with diagnostic equipment like x-rays and ultrasounds, so they're working with limited information.

Likewise, your vet probably won't be as comfortable removing shoes or trimming a hoof. Although your vet had to learn about hooves in vet school, they also had to learn about all kinds of different animals and all the systems that go into them, so the amount of hours spent learning hooves is necessarily limited. On the other hand, farriers start out primarily focusing on the hoof and learn less about other structures and systems in the horse. Both vets and farriers gather experience and learn more through continuing ed and working with other professionals but, in general, a well-educated vet will be able to do a lot more with structures above the hoof, and a well-educated farrier will be your best resource for the hoof.

There are situations where you will want both professionals on board from the start. Cases where lameness could indicate a disease or pathology that will need both medical intervention and therapeutic shoeing, like laminitis, navicular, or even a coffin bone fracture, should be treated with both your vet and farrier present and working together. This way, your vet can diagnose the issue, and your farrier can get all the info in real time. Your farrier might also be able to contribute important information, since they are very familiar with what normal looks like for *your* horse. Since they see your horse's hooves every six weeks, they will notice any changes that could be clues to diagnosing the lameness.

Once the issue is diagnosed, your vet and farrier can come up with a plan together. If your horse has a relatively common problem, your vet and farrier will probably each have a preferred treatment, and they may not be the same. Of course, your vet should be making the call on any drugs, surgical interventions, or other treatments on the medical side. But what if your vet prescribes a shoeing plan and your farrier disagrees?

Provided that you are confident in both your vet and your farrier as skilled professionals, this is a really tough position to be in. As the horse owner and chief bill payer it is ultimately up to you whether you should listen to your vet or your farrier when it comes to shoeing. Luckily, it rarely comes down to that. If your vet and farrier are each telling you that your horse needs something different, first, make sure that they are talking directly to each other about the treatment plan, and that all the information is being shared. The vet is hearing what the farrier observed, and the farrier has seen any radiographs that were taken. Most shoeing disagreements come more from misunderstanding or miscommunication than anything else. It's like the old story about the three blind men trying to describe the elephant: if your vet can only feel the elephant's trunk, and your farrier can only feel the elephant's leg, they're going to come up with very different plans.

Ultimately, if your vet has diagnosed a hoof problem, in an ideal world they should inform the farrier of the diagnosis, preferably with as much detail as possible, and let the farrier know what principles they would like to apply to the feet to help that issue. This means, instead of prescribing a specific shoe ("I want a wedged eggbar shoe") they would explain what they want to achieve ("I'd like to move the weight bearing surface of the shoe back under the limb and shorten the breakover distance so the deep flexor tendon isn't under as much stress"). Then the farrier should come up with the specific shoeing protocol that will not only accomplish those goals, but also work for your horse's specific conformation, environment, and activity level. Sometimes the "textbook perfect shoe" doesn't fit your horse's lifestyle, but your farrier might be able to use a different shoe that checks all the same boxes and works for your horse. There are often multiple solutions to a problem, and your farrier can select one that is in their wheelhouse. Of course, once the farrier has come up with a shoeing plan, they'll want to double check with the vet that it's covering all the bases.

What if they still disagree? You're the deciding vote here, so ask each of them to explain what they think needs to be done so that you can logically understand the options. And yes, if someone can't explain it to you or falls back on "because that's how it's done," that should make you question their plan.

You also have the option of requesting a second opinion. This can be touchy, because both vets and farriers take a very personal interest in their horses and might worry that the consulting vet or farrier will try to steal you as a client. And of course, you want to make sure that your second opinion comes from a skilled, experienced professional.

You may also be able to look up articles and studies on the pathology that your horse has been diagnosed with. There are tons of educational articles out there about hooves. Just make sure they come from a reputable source, never someone trying to sell you something, and that the author either has credentials or cites their sources. You want someone who is delivering good, sound information, and can prove it.

One source you should avoid for this kind of decision is internet horse forums or Facebook groups. Although these can be useful sources of information, you really have no idea what, if any, knowledge other posters have. Anyone can say that they are an experienced trainer, vet, or farrier in a forum, but without proof, their advice should be treated very skeptically. You will be much better off talking over the problem with a knowledgeable friend that has experience with that type of pathology than accepting advice from random internet people. No offense, random internet people, but if you don't know them, they could be a mini hoarder who never gets any kind of vet or farrier care for their critters.

To recap: if it's hoof or shoe, call your farrier. If it bleeds, call your vet. If it's lameness in the hoof, you may need to call both. If they disagree, make sure that there is good communication and give and take between them. Then, trust your vet with medical advice and your farrier with hoof and shoe advice. Easy, right?

Quick Takeaways
- **If there is blood or sensitive tissue involved, you should call your vet.**
- **If there is an issue with the shoe or an injury that only affects the hoof, call your farrier.**

39 PULLING SHOES, FIRST AID FOR SHOE LOSS, AND MAKING A HOOF WRAP

If your horse wears shoes, you need to know how to safely pull a shoe, *period*. Horses are accident prone creatures, and they can spring, twist, or bend their shoes as easily as you can pull your sneakers off at the end of a day. Unfortunately, when they do, they can leave the shoe half on, half off, with nails sticking out or with clips stuck into their hooves, and you need to be able to remove the shoe in an emergency. You may also need to pull a shoe if your horse is developing an abscess or has a bad nail.

If you can, ask your farrier to help you pull your horse's shoes at your next appointment. This will give you hands-on practice in a non-emergency situation, and they can show you any specific needs your horse has when it comes to pulling shoes.

Without the right tools, pulling a shoe is a long ordeal complete with sweating and swearing. Luckily, the right tools and a quick lesson in technique make all the difference.

For this project you will need a pair of shoe pull offs, but if you want to make your life easier, grab a pair of crease nail pullers too. Pull offs are used for prying the shoe off, while crease nail pullers fit inside the groove in your horse's shoe and pulls each nail individually. This is a lot easier and you can safely set down the foot at almost any point in the process, which is a big deal when your legs are burning because a thousand-pound horse is leaning on you! Word of warning though -- if your horse wears sliding plates or other plain stamped shoes where the nail hole is punched straight into the shoe, rather than sitting in a groove or fuller, crease nail pullers won't work for you. Pull offs and crease nail pullers are both available at any farrier supply store as well as many feed stores.

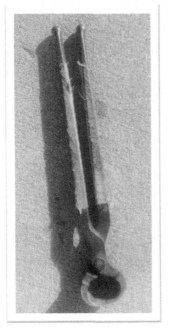

Pull offs

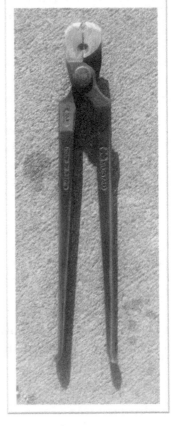

Crease nail pullers

You may also need an old rasp to remove the clinches on the outside of the hoof, especially if your horse has weak hoof walls or the clinches are raised or large. A dull rasp works best for this, so ask your farrier if they have an old one you can keep.

Make sure you have all your supplies and tie your horse in a clear, well lit area, preferably on level ground, just as you would for your farrier. It's hard enough work pulling a shoe without having to watch your feet for trip hazards or not being able to see.

If you can see raised clinches on the outside of your horse's hoof, you'll want to either cut them off or rasp them off so that they don't damage the hoof wall when you pull the nails out. If you're lucky, you might be able to use a pair of wire cutters to snip them off. You can probably cut them off on the ground, but if you're going to rasp them, you will need to stretch your horse's leg forward and hold it on your knee, just like your farrier would.

You'll want to turn sideways so that you can use both legs and lock the hoof in place with one leg under the hoof, and the other keeping the toe from sliding forward. Then use the smoother side of your rasp to lightly file on top of the clinches until they either disappear or thin out.

Next, you're going to pick up your horse's hoof and hold it with your legs the same way that your farrier does, so that you have both hands free to work. Holding with your legs instead of your hands will also keep the stress off your back.

Holding a front foot is easiest. Pick up the hoof as though you were going to pick it out, facing toward the hindquarters. Holding it with the hand that is nearest to the horse which will be your left hand on the left front hoof, right hand on the right front hoof, step your leg that is nearest to the horse forward half a step. Then use your opposite hand to pull your horse's hoof through your legs. Now step your near leg back so that your feet are even with each other, with the hoof between your knees. To hold it securely, place the hoof just above your knees, turn your toes in, and squeeze the insides of your legs. If it sounds complicated, it's really not. Just practice it occasionally when you're picking out your horse's hooves so you're comfortable in case of an emergency.

Holding a hind foot is a little harder to get the hang of, and it's a great leg workout. Again, stand level with your horse's hip, facing backward as though you're going to pick out the hoof. Pick up the hoof with your near hand and lift it up to about knee level. Now the graceful part -- you're going to do a squat, but angling toward your horse's tail. Now set the hoof in your lap, with the front of the

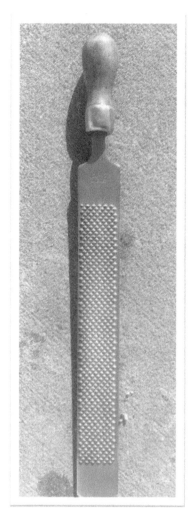

A rasp is helpful for removing clinches

Holding a front foot

233

fetlock resting on the inside of your leg that is nearest to the horse's body and the front of his toe resting on the inside of your farther leg. If this doesn't make sense, take a look at the illustration. You need to be squatting and turned enough to be locking the hoof and fetlock in place, so it doesn't flop down when you try to leverage the shoe off.

Okay, now that you've got the hoof held securely, you've got both hands to pull the shoe off. If you have crease nail pullers, start with the heel nails and dig in under the nail head with the small tips of the crease nail pullers. Once you've got a good grip, squeeze the handles together and lever the tool sharply toward the toe of the shoe. This should pull the nail head up and out of the shoe. The nail may completely clear the shoe, but if it doesn't, grab your pull offs and use them to hold the nail shank as close to the shoe as you can get.

Pulling a hind shoe

Do the same quick lever forward movement and you should have one nail out!

You'll want to switch back and forth between the inside and outside branches of the shoe, working your way toward the toe. The more nails you can get out this way, the easier your next job will be, and the less potential damage you will have to the hoof, especially if the shoe has side or quarter clips.

Once you've pulled all the nails that you can with the crease nail pullers, grab your pull offs and set them so that the jaws of the tool fit between the heel of the shoe and the hoof. Carefully close them so that the jaws are closed between the hoof and the shoe. This might take some force if the shoe isn't loose. Then sharply and firmly rock the handles forward and downward toward the toe of the shoe, aiming for the opposite toe nail. The heel of the shoe should lever up a little off the hoof. If it does, scoot the jaws closer to the toe and repeat. Then switch sides and do the same to the other branch, working your way back and forth toward the toe. If you're doing this with a pair of pull offs, pull each nail out as the head raises out of the shoe, switching back and forth across the shoe. When you've reached the toe, you should have the shoe almost completely off. A few more pulls in the toe from side to side and you have a safely removed shoe.

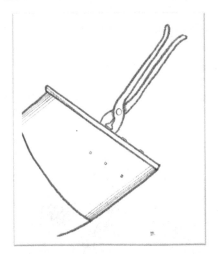

Using crease nail pullers

234

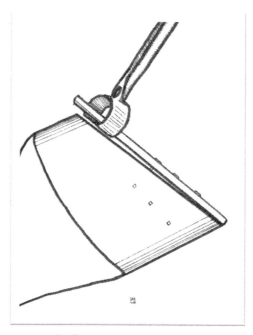

Using pull offs

If you can, pop any remaining nails out of the shoe, throw them away and put the shoe somewhere safe until your farrier can come out to replace it.

So you pulled a shoe, or your horse might have pulled a shoe for you. What can you do to keep the hoof healthy until your farrier can come to reset the shoe?

First of all, there's a myth going around that if your horse pulls a shoe, you should pull of the opposite shoe so that she's "even." This is like saying if you're on a hike and one of your hiking boots breaks, you should ditch the other one and do the rest of the hike barefoot. Why take away protection from one hoof just because the other one is already in a vulnerable state? Let's keep the one that still has a shoe healthy, so your horse has a comfortable foot to walk on.

In fact, our main goal is to protect the hoof that lost the shoe. Hopefully, your farrier can get out before too long to replace the shoe, but if it's going to be a few days, you need to make sure your farrier has a healthy hoof to work with when they come back.

This will depend to some extent on how healthy and strong your horse's hooves are to start with. If he's got super hooves and he only wears shoes for extra traction, he may be just fine for a few days with no protection as long as you skip riding. On the other hand, if your horse has thin hoof walls and flat soles, you're going to need to act fast to protect her hoof. If you're not sure what category your horse falls in to, offer your farrier the options that we're going to talk about below and see what they say.

First, you're going to need to cancel any rides or lessons you had planned with your horse until the shoe is back on. This one is non-negotiable if you want to prevent hoof damage.

You may also need to limit turnout, especially if your horse is very active in turnout or has a hard or rocky turnout area. Now, I understand that you probably can't keep your horse locked in a stall if the farrier can't be there for a week, but if it's only going to be a day or two, please don't turn your horse out unless your farrier says it's okay. Your horse can rip off six months' worth of hoof growth in an hour of turnout if he has weak walls. You may still be able to hand walk your horse or do limited turnout in a small paddock or a sand arena.

If you are planning to allow your horse limited turnout or if he has really crumbly or soft hooves, you can use a protective hoof boot or a wrap to keep his hoof in good shape. If your horse pulls a lot of shoes, it is definitely a good idea to have a boot on hand.

To make a protective hoof wrap, you're going to want some padding like a diaper, sheet cotton, or even several shop towels, vet wrap or a similar elastic tape, duct tape, and scissors.

You're going to start by making your outer duct tape layer. On a flat surface (a plastic binder cover or the back of a clip board works great) stick a strip of duct tape, about 12 inches long for the average sized saddle horse. Add another 12-inch strip, parallel and overlapping half the width of the first strip. Repeat until you have a sheet of duct tape strips, about 12x10. Think close to the size of a normal sheet of paper. Peel it up and cut diagonally in a few inches from each corner, leaving at least 5x5 inches with no cut in the center. Your corner cuts will help you shape your duct tape wrap up and around the hoof later.

Now that you've got the duct tape wrap ready, get your padding. If you're making this wrap to treat an abscess or a puncture wound, this is where you'll be using your poultice pad or medicated gauze. If you're making this wrap to protect your horse's hoof, you'll be using thicker material like a diaper or sheet cotton. Also grab your roll of vet wrap, which is what you'll be using to secure the padding or gauze. With the hoof picked up, place your padding or medicated material on the bottom of the hoof, and hold one end of the vet wrap in place with the hand that's holding the hoof. Start wrapping diagonally from heel to toe, then switch to the other diagonal so that you make an X. Once the X is holding the padding in place, you can circle the roll around the perimeter of the hoof, paying special attention to covering the bottom edge of the hoof wall in the toe, since that's usually the area where a wrap fails. You'll also want to wrap high enough up the wall to make sure that the wrap stays in place, but without constricting any sensitive tissue above the coronary band.

Once you've thoroughly secured the vet wrap, get your duct tape sheet. With the hoof picked up, center the uncut section on the bottom of the hoof and wrap the edges up and around, overlapping at the cut areas. Press it down securely and trim any edges that come up past the coronary band. Again, it's very important that any wrap doesn't constrict circulation in the hoof or put pressure on any sensitive structures. Then make a final loop or two around the hoof with your roll of duct tape to secure any edges that could peel back.

You'll want to check your wrap at least once a day, since horses on abrasive footing or those that like to paw can wear through a wrap pretty quickly. If your horse blows through hoof wraps, try using a tougher tape like Gorilla tape, or using an extra layer of tape in your duct tape sheet.

Good news: you know how to pull a shoe that's been twisted into a dangerous position and how to protect the hoof until your farrier arrives. But what if you had to pull a shoe because of an abscess? In the next chapter, we'll cover good hoof soaking protocols.

Quick Takeaways
- **Make sure you know how to pull a shoe and have the appropriate tools *before* an emergency occurs.**
- **If your horse loses a shoe, ask your farrier if you should wrap the hoof, use a boot, or avoid turnout.**

40 TIPS FOR SOAKING

If your horse has all the red flags for an abscess, you're probably going to give her hoof a soak to help soften the hoof and potentially clean out any little crevices in the hoof that the abscess could drain from. But what should you put in your soak, and what can you do if your horse refuses to stand in a bucket? Don't worry, you've always got options!

Traditionally, Epsom salts have been recommended in the soaking water, sometimes with iodine or betadine mixed in as well. The theory has been that Epsom salts can draw out the abscess, much as it is used to reduce inflammation in sore muscles. However, up to this time, there haven't been any studies proving or disproving this theory.

One thing that we do know about Epsom salts is that, like all salts, they are a drying agent. This is why some people use them in wound care, because the salt reduces the amount of fluid in the inflamed tissue, thereby reducing swelling. That sounds pretty cool, but it's not what we're looking for in an abscess-treating soak. Remember, the fluid and inflammation related to an abscess are sealed up inside your horse's hoof -- that's what's causing all the pain. So applying salt to the outside of the hoof looks pretty doubtful as far as reducing inflammation in the abscess.

But we're also using the soak to try to soften the hoof capsule so that the abscess can break out, so a drying agent isn't exactly what we're looking for.

Epsom salts may not be a great choice when you're trying to get an abscess to burst. On the other hand, when the abscess has popped and you're soaking to clean the abscess pocket out, Epsom salts could be a great option, along with some iodine or betadine to help kill any bacteria that might be left.

You'll definitely want to stay away from adding any harsh chemicals to an abscess soak, no matter what it says on the packaging. Remember that hoof horn can be seriously damaged by soaks in bleach or other chemicals. It's not worth killing bacteria if you cause injury to the hoof doing so.

A simple soak in warm water is a great and safe bet for trying to get an abscess to burst. The water should be warm, but not too hot to leave your finger in comfortably. You'll want to soak for 15-30 minutes, preferably closer to 30.

Despite the social media videos of horses soaking with both front feet in a muck tub full of water, most horses prefer a low container that doesn't make them feel trapped if they try to move a leg. A low-sided, flexible rubber feed pan is a good, hard-to-destroy choice. If you must use a rigid plastic bucket or pan, do a test run before filling it up with water to make sure that it will hold up without cracking.

You'll want the bucket or pan to be filled high enough to completely cover the hoof, so that the hoof is being softened in any area that the abscess may want to blow out, top or bottom. It's also a good idea to have some extra warm water nearby so you can top off the soak if your horse moves around and spills some.

With your horse either held or tied, place her hoof gently into the pan of water. She may try to pick it up because normally she's not supposed to step on things, so be ready to guide her hoof back to the pan. Before long she should figure out that she's supposed to have her hoof in there, but be ready to distract her with a hay net or some grooming if she finds it soothing.

Once your soak is over, wrap her hoof right away with a poultice pad to keep the effects going. The other benefit to wrapping with a pad? You'll be able to see dark colored fluid on the pad if you were successful and the abscess blows. Re-read Chapter 38 for tips on making a sturdy hoof wrap.

You can soak twice a day if you want but you won't want to repeat soaking indefinitely, since it will weaken the hoof capsule. That's fine in the short term to let an abscess break out, but you don't want your horse's hoof waterlogged for long periods of time. This should be considered a temporary measure until your farrier or vet is able to open the abscess for you. Some abscesses may break open without farrier or vet intervention, but if you've been soaking for a few days and it hasn't resolved, it's time to get backup. You should never soak for more than a week without results.

Once the abscess is opened, you'll want to soak one or two more times, this time to help flush out built up pus and bacteria. Again, you'll use warm water and soak for 15-30 minutes, but this time, feel free to add Epsom salts and iodine if you'd like to.

Soaking is a good thing to practice before you need it, although you don't need to practice a full thirty-minute soak. Just practice getting your horse to step in a pan full of water and stand in it for a few minutes. This can be a challenging skill for some horses, and you don't want to be trying to figure it out when he's got a blazing abscess and has just knocked over your soaking pan for the fifth time.

But what if practicing doesn't help, or you didn't get a chance to practice and now your horse needs to be soaked and he's not having any of it? That's where soaking boots and bags come in! Especially if your horse is young or on the nervous, reactive side, he may not have the patience to stand with a hoof in a bucket for half an hour. If that sounds like your horse, don't worry, you can still get the benefits of a soak without the battle.

There are a couple of purpose-made soaking boots available on the market, specifically designed for soaking abscesses. Many of them are reasonably priced and there are a wide variety of sizes and shapes to choose from. You can also purchase soaking bags, which are essentially thick plastic bags that you can secure around your horse's leg.

These types of soaking boots will come with instructions, but typically they are secured to the leg and then you pour warm water in from the top until it's at the height you need it to soak the whole hoof. The soaking works exactly the same as a traditional soak, except your horse can move his leg without disrupting the whole process. Of course, you want to keep him still so that he doesn't break the bag, but you've got a lot more wiggle room.

If you don't want to buy a soaking boot or bag, you can also ask your vet for an IV fluid bag. You'll need a large one, but they are made of really thick plastic, so they work great for a soaking bag. You'll cut off the end with the ports in it and fit it over your horse's leg, then fill with fluid. Grab your trusty duct tape roll and tape the top of the bag so that it fits closely to your horse's leg.

Sometimes, you might need to do an emergency soak without having time to order supplies or go by your local tack store. In that case, you still probably have what you need. Do you have an empty grain bag laying around? Most feeds come in plasticky bags nowadays, and that's what you're looking for. Trim it down so that it comes to just below your horse's knee or hock, and voila, you've made yourself a soaking bag. Again, you'll put it on your horse first, then fill it from the top and duct tape it closed.

I'm sure you already got this, but if your horse is terrified of plastic bags or things that crinkle, for your own safety and hers, please don't tape a bag on her leg. That said, as you can see, you've got a lot of options at your disposal if you need to soak a hoof.

Quick Takeaways

- **Practice soaking options with your horse if they don't enjoy having their hooves in water.**
- **Make sure you have a soaking option that your horse approves of in your first aid kit.**

41 YOUR FIRST AID KIT FOR HOOVES

Look, if you've read this far, you've probably got the general idea when it comes to the first aid activities you should be prepared. But if you don't have the right tools for the job, an already stressful time can become an absolute nightmare. If you know that you're prepared and you have all the tools and supplies you need, you can rest a little easier and feel more confident about handling whatever crazy emergencies your horse throws at you.

So what we're going to look at in this chapter are the items you should have in your barn, or in your trailer if you travel with your horse, to be prepared to treat any hoof emergency. Of course, in addition to this list, you should also have a regular equine first aid kit for general medical emergencies, and a human first aid kit, if there's anyone who needed to hear that.

The most important, absolutely necessary things on the list are going to be in bold. I'm also going to suggest some tools and supplies that can make your life easier, but you don't have to feel like a bad horse owner if you don't keep them handy. You might already have some of this stuff around, especially if you've had horses for a while. It can be helpful to organize all of your hoof items together so that you know right where to look in an emergency. So, ready for your scavenger hunt?

General Care:
- o **Hoof pick**
- o Firm wire brush such as a welder's brush for cleaning the hoof
- o Thrush treatment of choice (if you live in a wet area or your horse is prone to thrush, you should always have this on hand).
- o **Gauze**
- o **Antiseptic Ointment**
- o Wire cutters, if your horse is turned out in an area with wire fencing.
- o **Clearly written emergency number list** including yourself, your vet, and your farrier as well as any medical information that might be necessary in an emergency such as allergies or medications
- o Medium sized syringe with plastic tip for flushing hoof wound or thrushy frog
- o **Clean towel or roll of Shop towels**

Shoe pulling supplies:
- o **Pull offs (the cheapest pair you can find should work just fine)**
- o **Old rasp (ask your farrier if they have an old one available)**
- o Crease nail pullers (well worth the investment if your horse likes to twist shoes frequently)

Hoof protection:
- o Hoof boots
- o **Duct tape**
- o **Diaper, cotton wool, or sheet cotton**
- o **Vet wrap**
- o **Scissors**
- o Poultice pads
- o Rigid foamboard insulation (if your horse has had laminitis in the past or is at risk)

Soaking supplies:
- o **Flexible rubber feed pan, low bucket, soaking boot, or soaking bag**
- o Epsom Salts
- o Iodine

Quick Takeaways

- Make sure that you are ready for any emergency with a well-stocked first aid kit.
- Personalize your first aid kit by preparing supplies specifically for any condition your horse is prone to.

GOING BEYOND THE BOOK

If you've read this far, congratulations! You now know more about horse's hooves than the majority of horse owners, and that's a wonderful thing for your horse's well-being. You've always wanted to do what's best for her, and now you have more tools and resources to make that a reality.

What if you want to know more? Maybe there's a topic we touched on that you'd like more details on, or maybe, like me, when you started learning about hooves, you find out that there's a lot to learn and you want to dig deeper. Well, luckily for you, many of the hoof care resources available to professional farriers and vets are also available to you.

If you want to know more about how your horse's hooves fit into all this, your best, most personalized resource is your farrier. Most farriers are excited to share their knowledge when they see that you are actually interested in learning about hooves, too. Don't be afraid to ask your farrier to show you what they see in your horse's hooves, if there's anything you can do to improve them, or to explain any issues they might see. This is a great way to learn, and to learn specific knowledge about the horses you care about the most.

If you're interested in knowing more and supporting equine hoof care research, farrier education and farrier certification, you can become a Horse Owner Member of the American Farrier's Association. This is an association dedicated to the improvement, education, and certification of farriers, as well as sponsoring relevant hoof care research. As a Horse Owner Member, you will receive the AFA's newsletter which contains educational articles, cases, and news, and you can sign up for Eblasts with more hoof care content. You'll also be able to attend AFA clinics and conventions. You can check it out at americanfarriers.org or on the American Farrier's Association app.

If learning more through books is right up your alley, these are some of my favorite books about the science behind what we do. Many of these books are cited throughout this one.

Adams' Lameness in Horses, Ted S. Stashak - this is a vet textbook, so it covers all kinds of lameness, not just hoof related stuff.

Corrective Farriery, Volumes 1-2, Simon Curtis - a set of farrier textbooks, this collection covers most therapeutic farriery topics.

Diagnosis and Management of Lameness in the Horse, Mike W. Ross and Sue J. Dyson - another excellent vet textbook.

Distal Limb Pocket Guide, Jenny Edwards and Paige Poss - from *Anatomy of the Equine*, this book is mostly photos of partially dissected hooves. If you want to understand anatomy, this book is it.

Equine Podiatry, Andrea Floyd and Richard Mansman - if you want to understand the in-depth science behind farriery, this is a great textbook.

Exploring Laminitis, Jenny Edwards and Paige Poss - this book contains comparative photos of laminitic hooves versus normal, healthy hooves. If you have a horse with laminitis and you want to know what's going on in there, I would highly recommend this little book.

Hoof Distortion, Jenny Edwards and Paige Poss - Another illustrated guide from *Anatomy of the*

Equine, this one showing what happens inside hooves when they flare and crack.

The Hoof of the Horse, Simon Curtis - The ultimate, in-depth guide to the hoof.

The Horse Conformation Handbook, Heather Smith Thomas - a good resource if you're interested in learning conformation.

The Mirage of the Natural Foot, Michael Miller - This small book is based on the Dr. Miller's FWCF thesis, comparing "natural" trimming styles with traditional trims.

Understanding the Horse's Feet, John Stewart - This book is a great resource if you want to learn more about laminitis.

Anatomy of the Equine also offers an online course, loaded with their amazing anatomy images, which will guide you through your horse's hoof anatomy.

I sincerely hope that you've enjoyed learning more about your horse, and about horses' hooves everywhere. I realize that time is your most precious resource, so I appreciate the fact that you've taken the time to read this book and learn more. It shows how important your horse is to you, that you chose to spend some of your precious time reading this book, and I hope that it has been a good investment for yourself and for your horse. Best wishes for all the good times with your horse, and that if troubles come, you'll be prepared for them with the information you learned in this book. You've got this!

Sources cited in this book

American Farriers Journal. (2017) *Tackling Those Nasty Thrush Concerns*. Retrieved from https://www.americanfarriers.com/articles/9218-tackling-thrush-barn-call-charges

Apprich, V., Spergser, J., Rosengarten, R., Hinterhofer, C., Stanek, C. (2010) Scanning electron microscopy and fungal culture of hoof horn from horses suffering from onychomycosis. *Vet Dermatol. 21(4):* P. 335-40.

Arndt, J.L., Pfau, T., Day, P., Pardoe, C., Bolt, D.M., Weller, R. (2013) Forces applied with a hoof tester to cadaver feet vary widely between users. *Vet Rec. 172(7):* P. 182.

Buffa, E.A., Van Den Berg, S.S., Verstraete, F.J., Swart, N.G. (1992) Effect of dietary biotin supplement on equine hoof horn growth rate and hardness. *Equine Vet J. ;24(6):* P. 472-4

Carter, R.A., Treiber, K.H., Geor, R.J., Douglass, L. and Harris, P.A. (2009), Prediction of incipient pasture-associated laminitis from hyperinsulinaemia, hyperleptinaemia and generalised and localised obesity in a cohort of ponies. *Equine Veterinary Journal, 41:* P. 171-178

Clayton, H.M., Sha, D.H., Stick, J.A., Robinson, P. (2007) 3D kinematics of the interphalangeal joints in the forelimb of walking and trotting horses. *Vet Comp Orthop Traumatol;20(1):* P. 1-7.

Cole, S.D., Stefanovski, D., Towl, S., Boyle, A.G. (2019) Factors associated with prolonged treatment days, increased veterinary visits and complications in horses with subsolar abscesses. *Vet Rec.; 184(8):* P. 251.

College of Veterinary Medicine, Perdue University. *Understanding and Treating Scratches in Horses*. Retrieved from https://vet.purdue.edu/vth/large-animal/equine-health-tip-understanding-and-treating-scratches-in-horses.php

Colles, C.M. (1989), The relationship of frog pressure to heel expansion. *Equine Veterinary Journal, 21:* P. 13-16

Crevier-Denoix, N., Audigié, F., Emond, A.L., Dupays, A.G., Pourcelot, P., Desquilbet, L., Chateau, H., Denoix, J.M. (2017) Effect of track surface firmness on the development of musculoskeletal injuries in French Trotters during four months of harness race training. *Am J Vet Res. 78(11):* P. 1293-1304.

Crevier-Denoix, N., Camus, M., Pourcelot, P., Pauchard, M., Falala, S., Ravary-Plumioen, B., Denoix, J., Desquilbet, L. and Chateau, H. (2014), Effect of Speed on Stride Parameters and Limb Loading: Comparison between Forelimb and Hindlimb at Training Trot on a Firm Surface. *Equine Vet Journal, 46:* P. 38-38.

Cripps, P.J., Eustace, R.A. (1999) Factors involved in the prognosis of equine laminitis in the UK. *Equine Vet J. 31(5):* P. 433-42.

Csurhes, S., Paroz, G., and Markula, A., (2009) Feral Horse Risk Assessment. *State of Queensland 2016*. Retrieved from https://www.daf.qld.gov.au/__data/assets/pdf_file/0004/51961/IPA-Feral-Horses-Risk-Assessment.pdf

Curtis, S., (2018), *The Hoof of the Horse*. 59, The Street, Icklingham, Bury St. Edmunds, IP28 6PL, UK, NFC

de Laat, M.A., Reiche, D.B., Sillence, M.N., McGree, J.M. (2019) Incidence and risk factors for recurrence of endocrinopathic laminitis in horses. *J Vet Intern Med; 33(3):* P. 1473-1482

Douglas J.E., Mittal C., Thomason J.J., Jofriet J.C. (1996) The modulus of elasticity of equine hoof wall: implications for the mechanical function of the hoof. *J Exp Biol. Aug;199(Pt 8):* P. 1829-36.

Dyson, S.J. (2011) Chapter 30 - Navicular Disease, Editor(s): Ross, M.W., Dyson, S.J., Diagnosis and Management of Lameness in the Horse (Second Edition), P. 324-342. W.B. Saunders, Elsevier, Health Sciences Division 11830 Westline Industrial Drive, St. Louis MO 63146-3313 USA. P. 324-342.

Faramarz, B., McMicking, H., Halland, S., Kaneps, A., Dobson, H. (2015) Incidence of palmar process fractures of the distal phalanx and association with front hoof conformation in foals. *Equine Vet J. 47(6):* P. 675-9

Freestone, J.F., Beadle, R., Shoemaker, K., Bessin, R.T., Wolfsheimer, K.J. and Church, C. (1992), Improved insulin sensitivity in hyperinsulinaemic ponies through physical conditioning and controlled feed intake. *Equine Veterinary Journal, 24:* 187-190

Geyer, H., Schulze, J. (1994) The long-term influence of biotin supplementation on hoof horn quality in horses. *Schweiz Arch Tierheilkd 136(4):* P.137-49.

Gravlee, F. (2017) *A Guide to Proper Care and Nutrition For the Equine Hoof.* Retrieved from https://www.lifedatalabs.com/docs/Hoof%20Booklet%20US%202017_Web.pdf

Gravlee, J.F., and Gravlee, H.S. *Nutrients that Influence Hoof Health.* Retrieved from https://www.lifedatalabs.com/hoof-and-joint-articles/nutrients-that-influence-hoof-health

Green, S.L., Little, C.B., Baird, J.D., Tremblay, R.R., Smith-Maxie, L.L. (1994) Tetanus in the horse: a review of 20 cases (1970 to 1990). *J Vet Intern Med. 8(2):* P. 128-32.

Grundmann, I.N., Drost, W.T., Zekas, L.J., Belknap, J.K., Garabed, R.B., Weisbrode, S.E., Parks, A.H., Knopp, M.V.,

Maierl, J. (2015) Quantitative assessment of the equine hoof using digital radiography and magnetic resonance imaging. *Equine Vet J. Sep;47(5):* P. 542-7.

Hampson, B.A. and Pollitt, C.C. (November, 2011). *Improving the Foot Health of the Domestic Horse: The Relevance of the Feral Horse Foot Model.* Retrieved from http://horsefx.com.au/wp-content/uploads/2015/07/Pollitt-and-Hamson-Improving-health-of-domestic-horse-hoof.pdf

Hampson, B.A., de Laat, M.A., Mills, P.C., Pollitt, C.C., (2012) Effect of environmental conditions on degree of hoof wall hydration in horses. *Am J Vet Res. 73(3):* P.435-8.

Henneke, D.R., Potter, G.D., Kreider, J.L. and Yeates, B.F. (1983), Relationship between condition score, physical measurements and body fat percentage in mares. *Equine Veterinary Journal, 15:* P. 371-372.

Higuchi, H., Kurumado, H., Mori, M., Degawa, A., Fujisawa, H., Kuwano, A., Nagahata, H. (2009) Effects of ammonia and hydrogen sulfide on physical and biochemical properties of the claw horn of Holstein cows. *Can J Vet Res. ;73(1):* P. 15-20.

Hill, S., (2017) The Relationship Between Superficial Digital Flexor Tendon Lesions and Asymmetric Feet in Equine Forelimbs.

Hiney, K., (May 2017) *Minerals for Horses: Calcium and Phosphorus.* Retrieved from https://extension.okstate.edu/fact-sheets/minerals-for-horses-calcium-and-phosphorus.html

Hinterhofer C., Stanek C., Binder K. (1998) Elastic modulus of equine hoof horn, tested in wall samples, sole samples and frog samples at varying levels of moisture. *Berl Munch Tierarztl Wochenschr; 111(6):* P. 217-21.

Hinterhofer, C., Stanek, C. and Haider, H. (2001), Finite element analysis (FEA) as a model to predict effects of farriery on the equine hoof. *Equine Veterinary Journal, 33*: P. 58-62.

Holzhauer, M., Bremer, R., Santman-Berends, I., Smink, O., Janssens, I., Back, W. (2017) Cross-sectional study of the prevalence of and risk factors for hoof disorders in horses in The Netherlands. *Prev Vet Med. 140*: P. 53-59.

J. R., (June, 2014) *Selenium Levels for Horses.* Retrieved from https://www.horsefeedblog.com/2014/06/selenium-levels-for-horses/

Josseck, H., Zenker, W., Geyer, H. (1995) Hoof horn abnormalities in Lipizzaner horses and the effect of dietary biotin on macroscopic aspects of hoof horn quality. *Equine Vet J.27(3):* P. 175-82.

Karikoski, N.P., Horn, I., McGowan, T.W., McGowan, C.M. (2011) The prevalence of endocrinopathic laminitis among horses presented for laminitis at a first-opinion/referral equine hospital. *Domestic Animal Endocrinology, Volume 41, Issue 3.* P. 111-117.

Kempson S.A., Campbell E.H. (1998) A permeability barrier in the dorsal wall of the equine hoof capsule. *Equine Vet J Suppl. (26):* P. 15-21.

Kosolofski, H.R., Gow, S.P., Robinson, K.A. (2017) Prevalence of obesity in the equine population of Saskatoon and surrounding area. *Can Vet J. 58(9):* P. 967-970.

Lancaster L.S., Bowker R.M., Mauer W.A.. (2013) Equine hoof wall tubule density and morphology. *J Vet Med Sci. 75(6)*: P. 773-8.

Leśniak K., Williams J., Kuznik K., Douglas P. (2017) Does a 4-6 Week Shoeing Interval Promote Optimal Foot Balance in the Working Equine? *Animals (Basel). Mar 29;7(4):* P. 29

McGreevy, P. & Rogers, L. (2005). Motor and sensory laterality in Thoroughbred horses. *Applied Animal Behaviour Science - APPL ANIM BEHAV SCI. 92.* P. 337-352.

Miller, M. E., (2010) *The Mirage of the Natural Foot.*

Mishra, P.C. and Leach, D.H. (1983), Electron microscopic study of the veins of the dermal lamellae of the equine hoof wall. *Equine Veterinary Journal, 15:* P. 14-21

NASA. (2012) *Good Diet, Proper Exercise Help Protect Astronauts' Bones.* Retrieved from https://www.nasa.gov/mission_pages/station/main/bone_study.html

National Park Service, (2018). *Cape Lookout National Seashore Shackleford Banks Horses 2018 Annual Report.* Retrieved from https://home.nps.gov/calo/learn/management/upload/Annual-Horse-Findings-Report-2018-final.pdf

Oosterlinck, M., Royaux, E., Back, W., Pille, F. (2014) A preliminary study on pressure-plate evaluation of forelimb toe-heel and mediolateral hoof balance on a hard vs. a soft surface in sound ponies at the walk and trot. *Equine Vet J. 46(6):* P. 751-5.

Pearson, W., Wood, K., Stanley, S., MacNicol, J. (2018) Exploring relationships between body condition score, body fat, activity level and inflammatory biomarkers. *J Anim Physiol Anim Nutr (Berl);102(4):* P. 1062-1068.

Peterson, M., Roepstorff, L., DVM, Thomason, J. J., Mahaffey, C., McIlwraith, C.W., (2012) Racing Surfaces: Current progress and future challenges to optimize consistency and performance of track surfaces for fewer horse injuries. Retrieved from http://www.racingsurfaces.org/whitepapers/white_paper_1_20120508.pdf

Petrov, K.K., Dicks, L.M. (2013) Fusobacterium necrophorum, and not Dichelobacter nodosus, is associated with equine hoof thrush. *Vet Microbiol 161(3-4):* P. 350-2.

Pleasant, R.S., Baker, G.J., Foreman, J.H., Eurell, J.A., Losonsky, J.M. (1993) Intraosseous pressure and pathologic changes in horses with navicular disease. *Am J Vet Res. 54(1):* P. 7-12.

Pollard, D., Wylie, C.E., Verheyen, K.L.P, Newton, J.R. (2017) Assessment of horse owners' ability to recognise equine laminitis: A cross-sectional study of 93 veterinary diagnosed cases in Great Britain. *Equine Vet J. 49(6):* P. 759-766.

Reilly, J.D., Collins, S.N., Cope, B.C., Hopegood, L. and Latham, R.J. (1998), Tubule density of the *stratum medium* of horse hoof. *Equine Veterinary Journal, 30:* P. 4-9.

Reilly, J.D., Cottrell, D.F., Martin, R.J., Cuddeford, D.J.(1998) Effect of supplementary dietary biotin on hoof growth and hoof growth rate in ponies: a controlled trial. *Equine Vet J Suppl. (26):51-7.*

Robin, C.A., Ireland, J.L., Wylie, C.E., Collins, S.N., Verheyen, K.L., Newton, J.R. (2015) Prevalence of and risk factors for equine obesity in Great Britain based on owner-reported body condition scores. *Equine Vet J; 47(2):* P. 196-201.

Roepstorff, L., Johnston, C. and Drevemo, S. (2001), *In vivo* and *in vitro* heel expansion in relation to shoeing and frog pressure. *Equine Veterinary Journal, 33:* P. 54-57.

Ross, M.W., Dyson, S.J., (2010) *Diagnosis and Management of Lameness in the Horse.* W.B. Saunders, Elsevier, Health Sciences Division 11830 Westline Industrial Drive, St. Louis MO 63146-3313 USA.

Setterbo, J.J., Fyhrie, P.B., Hubbard, M., Upadhyaya, S.K., Stover, S.M. (2012) Dynamic properties of a dirt and a synthetic equine racetrack surface measured by a track-testing device. *Equine Vet J. 45(1):* P. 25-30.

Steward, J., (2013) Understanding the Horse's Feet, The Stable Block, Crowood Lane, Ramsbury, Wiltshire, SN8 2HR. Crowood Press.

Stokes, S.M., Belknap, J.K., Engiles, J.B., Stefanovski, D., Bertin, F.R., Medina-Torres, C.E., Horn, R., van Eps, A.W. (2019) Continuous digital hypothermia prevents lamellar failure in the euglycaemic hyperinsulinaemic clamp model of equine laminitis. *Equine Vet J 51(5):* P. 658-664.

Svalastoga, E., Smith, M. (1983) Navicular disease in the horse. The subchondral bone pressure. *Nord Vet Med. (1):* P. 31-7.

Thomason J.J., Peterson M.L. (2008) Biomechanical and mechanical investigations of the hoof-track interface in racing horses. *Vet Clin North Am Equine Pract. Apr;24(1)*: P. 53-77.

Thomason, J.J., Peterson, M.L., (2008) Biomechanical and Mechanical Investigations of the Hoof-Track Interface in Racing Horses. *Veterinary Clinics of North America: Equine Practice, Volume 24, Issue 1*, P. 53-77.

van Eps, A.W. (2010) Therapeutic hypothermia (cryotherapy) to prevent and treat acute laminitis. *Vet Clin North Am Equine Pract. 26(1):* P. 125-33.

van Eps, A.W., Pollitt, C.C. (2004) Equine laminitis: cryotherapy reduces the severity of the acute lesion. *Equine Vet J. 36(3):* P. 255-60.

van Galen, G., Saegerman, C., Rijckaert, J., Amory, H., Armengou, L., Bezdekova, B., Durie, I., Findshøj, D. R., Fouché, N., Haley, L., Hewetson, M., van den Hoven, R., Kendall, A., Malalana, F., Muller Cavalleri, J., Picavet, T., Roscher, K., Verwilghen, D., Wehrli Eser, M., Westermann, C., Mair, T. (2017) Retrospective evaluation of 155 adult equids and 21 foals with tetanus in Western, Northern, and Central Europe (2000-2014). Part 1: Description of history and clinical evolution. *J Vet Emerg Crit Care (San Antonio);27(6)*: P. 684-696.

Vick M.M., Adams A.A., Murphy B.A., Sessions D.R., Horohov D.W., Cook R.F., Shelton B.J., Fitzgerald B.P. (2007) Relationships among inflammatory cytokines, obesity, and insulin sensitivity in the horse. *J Anim Sci. May;85(5):* P. 1144-55.

Wahyuni, S., Widodo, S.E., Retnowati, R. (2016). The Relationship of Interpersonal Communication, Working Motivation and Transformational Leadership to Teachers' Job Satisfaction *Post Graduate Program, Universitas Pakuan Bogor, Indonesia International Journal of Managerial Studies and Research (IJMSR) Volume 4, Issue 8, August* P. 89-93

Wegst, U.G.K. and Ashby, M.F. (2004) The mechanical efficiency of natural materials. *Philos Mag 84*, P. 2167-2181

Williams, C.A. (2004) *The Basics of Equine Nutrition.* Retrieved from https://esc.rutgers.edu/fact_sheet/the-basics-of-equine-nutrition/

Yarnell, K., Le Bon, M., Turton, N., Savova, M., McGlennon, A. and Forsythe, S. (2017), Reducing exposure to pathogens in the horse: a preliminary study into the survival of bacteria on a range of equine bedding types. *J Appl Microbiol, 122*: P. 23-29.

If you enjoyed this book, please take a moment to give it a rating or review on Amazon. This helps other horse owners just like you find it and know that it is worth their time. You can also recommend it to your friends in the horse world. I wrote this book to try to get hoof care knowledge into the hands of horse owners so that you can make informed, confident decisions about your horse's hooves, and your ratings, reviews, and recommendations help me do just that. So thank you for helping share the knowledge!

Although I am a trained Certified Journeyman Farrier, that doesn't make me your farrier, and therefore I cannot offer specific advice, diagnoses, or treatment plans for your horse. The information provided in this book is designed to provide helpful information on the subjects discussed. This book is not meant to be used, nor should it be used, to diagnose or treat any medical condition. For diagnosis or treatment of any medical problem or hoof issue, consult with your own veterinarian and farrier since they know your horse and her specific environment, activity level, condition, and medical history. Although I have done my best to provide accurate information, there is no one right answer for every horse. The publisher and author are not liable for any damages or negative consequences from any treatment, action, application or preparation to any equine after reading or following the information in this book. References are provided for informational purposes only and do not constitute endorsement of any websites or other sources.

ABOUT THE AUTHOR

Heather Beauchemin is a Certified Journeyman Farrier with a Therapeutic Endorsement from the American Farrier's Association. She lives and works in northern Illinois.

Made in the USA
Columbia, SC
27 August 2023

22159217R00148